Organizational and Racial Conflict in Maximum-Security Prisons

Organizational and Racial Conflict in Maximum-Security Prisons

James G. Fox
State University College
at Buffalo

LexingtonBooks
D.C. Heath and Company
Lexington, Massachusetts
Toronto

Library of Congress Cataloging in Publication Data

Fox, James G. (James Gordon), 1939–
   Organizational and racial conflict in maximum-security prisons.

   Includes index.
   1. Prisons and race relations–United States–Case studies. 2. Prison administration–United States–Case studies. 3. Correctional personnel–United States–Case studies. 4. Prisoners–United States–Case studies. 5. Social conflict–Case studies. I. Title.
HV9471.F64   365'.33   81-47710
ISBN 0-669-04727-9   AACR2

Prepared under Grant Number 78-NI-AX-0033 from the National Institute of Justice, U.S. Department of Justice. Points of view or opinions stated in this document are those of the author and do not necessarily represent the official position or policies of the U.S. Department of Justice. Both the publisher and the author acknowledge and hereby grant to the U.S. government a royalty-free, irrevocable, world-wide, nonexclusive license to reproduce, perform, and otherwise use the work for government purposes, but not for commercial purposes such as sale.

Published simultaneously in Canada

Printed in the United States of America

International Standard Book Number: 0-669-04727-9

Library of Congress Catalog Card Number: 81-47710

Contents

Tables   vii

Foreword   *C. Ronald Huff*   ix

Acknowledgments   xi

Introduction   xiii

Chapter 1   **Prisons at the Crossroads**   1

The Roots of the Crisis   2
The Nature of Coercive Organizations   4
The Need for Organizational Change   8

Chapter 2   **Prison Management: The View from the Top**   13

Contemporary Prison Management   13
Managerial Effectiveness   14
Managing Organizational Goals   14
The Target of Our Inquiry   15
Descriptive and Demographic Characteristics   16
Attitudes toward Organizational Change   18
Varieties of Prison Management   23

Chapter 3   **Prison Guards: The Front Line in the Workplace**   29

The Guard Role   29
Guard Stress and Frustration   31
Race Relations and Racial Conflict   33
Conceptual and Methodological Framework   36
Descriptive and Demographic Characteristics   37
Occupational Concerns of the Front Line   41

Chapter 4   **Maximum-Security Prisoners: A Community
in Conflict**   83

Early Theoretical Views   83
Contemporary Views   84
Women in Confinement   87
Conceptual and Methodological Framework   87
Prisoner Demographic Characteristics   89
Prisoner Social Values   96

Chapter 5   **Prisoner Organizations: United We Stand,**
                   Divided We Fall   135

                   The Evolution of a Pluralist Prisoner Community   135
                   Management Reaction   137
                   Conceptual and Methodological Framework   139
                   Characteristics of Organizational Members   141
                   Types of Prisoner Organizations   141
                   Regulation and Control   153

Chapter 6   **Where from Here: Conflict or Consensus?**   157

                   Summary of Major Findings and Implications
                       for Change   158
                   Consensus and Collaborative Intervention   164

Appendix A   **A Note on Methods**   167

Appendix B   **Item and Scale Correlations**   171

                   Index   185

                   About the Author   193

Tables

2-1	Correctional Manager Demographic Characteristics and Social Background	17
2-2	Mean Values of Organizational Change Items	20
2-3	Distribution of Dichotomized Organizational Change Scale Scores	21
2-4	Observed Prison-Management Intervention Styles	25
3-1	Distribution of Correctional Officer Samples at Five Research Sites	37
3-2	Demographic and Background Characteristics of Correctional Officers at Five Maximum-Security Prisons	38
3-3	Power Scores Rank Ordered by Item Means	43
3-4	Control Scores Rank Ordered by Item Means	48
3-5	Safety Scores Rank Ordered by Item Means	52
3-6	Communications and Support Scores Rank Ordered by Item Means	56
3-7	Resistance to Change Scores Rank Ordered by Item Means	62
3-8	Racism-Sexism Scores Rank Ordered by Item Means	67
3-9	Summary of Correctional Officer Occupational Concern Scale Scores	76
4-1	Distribution of Prisoner Samples at Five Research Sites	89
4-2	Prisoner Demographic and Social Background Characteristics	90
4-3	Prisonization Scores Rank Ordered by Item Means	98
4-4	Distribution of Aggregated Prisonization Scores	103
4-5	Radicalism Scores Rank Ordered by Item Means	105
4-6	Distribution of Aggregated Radicalism Scores	108
4-7	Collective-Action Scores Rank Ordered by Item Means	110

4-8   Distribution of Aggregated Collective-Action Scores   112

4-9   Racism-Sexism Scores Rank Ordered by Item Means   115

4-10   Distribution of Aggregated Racism-Sexism Scores   121

4-11   Criminalization Scores Rank Ordered by Item Means   124

4-12   Distribution of Aggregated Criminalization Scores   125

4-13   Summary of Prisoner Social Values Scale Scores   126

5-1   Self-Reported Memberships by Organization and Site   142

5-2   Distribution of Formal Organization Memberships   143

Foreword

Research on American prisons during the past decade has departed in significant respects from traditional lines of inquiry. The social conflict of the 1960s, which included challenges to every social institution in our society, had fully penetrated the walls of our prisons by 1970, ushering in a decade of intense conflict. Increasingly politicized prisoners involved themselves in organized protests and insurrections, challenged the constitutionality of prison conditions and practices, and rejected traditional explanations of crime and rationales for incarceration.

But the conflict was not confined to inmate grievances and ideology. There was conflict among inmate groups, especially along racial and ethnic lines; conflict between increasingly powerful guard's unions and their perceived adversaries; expanded inmate power and administrative regulation; and conflict between treatment and custody staff—the latter group newly armed with academic research challenging the efficacy of treatment. Prison administrators and managers complained that court decisions on prisoners' rights, coupled with the militancy of guards' unions, had severely restricted the degrees of freedom available to them and had created an avalanche of paperwork and regulation. It is hardly surprising, therefore, that researchers increasingly adopted theoretical models based on the conflict paradigm, rather than the traditional functionalist explanations.

The research reported in this book represents a valuable contribution to the "new sociology of the prison" that has been emerging (although it might be argued that it should be called "the sociology of the new prison" instead). Very complex issues are addressed in a sophisticated, yet highly readable manner. All three spheres of the prison organization—management, staff, and prisoners— are analyzed as they interact with each other in this organizational context. This holistic approach to the prison as a social organization introduces a much more appropriate level of analysis for correctional decision makers and academics alike.

This penetrating study encompasses such issues as racism, sexism, inmate radicalism, the female correctional officer, guard-inmate relations, make-believe families among female inmates, and the nature and composition of formal inmate organizations. The analyses are logically developed, empirically based, and laden with important implications. All of this is made even more impressive because of challenges that had to be overcome in collecting these data in five maximum-security prisons. Having had the opportunity to serve as a research consultant on this project, I was aware of these challenges and the highly innovative, dedicated manner in which the research plan was carried out. Given the sensitive nature of this project and ample opportunity for failure, the high quality of this book is indeed a tribute to the intellectual and interpersonal skills of its author.

C. Ronald Huff
Associate Professor and Director
Program for the Study of Crime and Delinquency
Ohio State University

Acknowledgments

It is impossible to give adequate recognition to all of those who made this research possible. I am deeply indebted to the American Justice Institute project staff and professional colleagues for the many long hours they spent in frustrating and seemingly unrewarding tasks. I am also grateful to C. Ronald Huff for providing valuable guidance and assistance during the early stages of the project and for his strong encouragement during the many long months of field work. His commitment to quality research and insight into the complexity of the project are deeply appreciated. Special thanks must also be extended to Larry Greenfeld, the project moniter at the National Institute of Justice, for his patience, understanding, and determination to see the project accomplish its mission. My most sincere and special appreciation is extended to R.M. Montilla, who since suffered a fatal coronary stroke, for the opportunity to play a major role in this project and for his understanding during the most stressful moments of the field research. Finally, this research could not have been possible without the strong cooperation shown by hundreds of prisoners who gave us their trust, and countless correctional officers and managers who shared their personal experiences and insights into maximum-security corrections without reservation. The facilities cooperating in this research, listed in order of data collection, were: the Correctional Training Facility: Central and South (Soledad) and the California State Prison (Folsom), California Department of Corrections, May-July 1978; Minnesota State Prison (Stillwater), Minnesota Department of Corrections, October-November 1978; Correctional Facility for Women (Bedford Hills), New York State Department of Correctional Services, November-December 1978; New Jersey State Prison (Rahway), New Jersey Department of Corrections, November 1978-January 1979, Oregon State Penitentiary (OSP), Oregon Department of Human Resources, Corrections Division, March-April 1979.

Introduction

Numerous sociological studies of the prison have directed their attention disproportionately at the social structure of the prisoner community without considering the effect of the larger organization or the influences of other organizational members. Our ambition in conducting the research described in this book was to shed new light on complex relationships at all levels of the maximum-security-prison organization.

We focused our attention on three organizational ranks: prison management (executive and security), correctional officers, and prisoners. Our research interests included an assessment of the relative power and influence of these three ranks within the prison organization, the nature and scope of intraorganizational conflict, and the factors underlying the growth and development of formal prisoner organizations. To assess the relative influences and contributions of prisoners, we focused on prisoner values and attitudes, memberships in formal organizations, and the extent of prisoner involvement in routine management decisions. The focus on correctional officers centered on their perception of their own role within the organization and on specific job-related concerns. Unlike the approach to prisoners and correctional officers, the assessment of prison management was "soft," and remained free of predetermined or standardized management constructs and performance indicators. However, in an attempt to strengthen the assessment, we developed objective measures of prison management's responsiveness to two different organizational change perspectives. Overall, we attempted to capitalize on the strengths of both quantitative and qualitative approaches. Our methods included the use of open-ended interviews, systematic and general observations of prison operations, and multidimensional scales built into questionnaires administered to randomly and systematically selected samples. Whenever possible, we utilized more than one measure, observer, or interviewer to ensure that our data accurately reflected the views of all organizational members and objectively described the organizational dynamics of each of the five prisons.

We approached our research tasks with a principal focus on the nature and scope of organizational and racial conflict. Recognizing that conflict is firmly embedded in the foundation of maximum-security prisons, we directed special attention to the organizational dynamics underlying structural and situational conflict. Of particular interest were the combined effects of extraorganizational influences on the management of internal order and control.

Like most multisite field studies, the selection of research sites involved working out a compromise between the interests of the project and the concerns of prison administrators. These concerns typically revolved around the allocation of organizational resources, the potential for disruptions of institutional routine, and the likelihood of stimulating hostility from participants. Our selection of five state maximum-security prisons was intended to overcome the weaknesses of a single-site study, as well as to provide the opportunity to assess the relationships between management policies (and organizational structures) and the dynamics of prisoner communities across five very different prisons. The problems of selecting five ideal or typical maximum-security prisons quickly became apparent. The inclusion of sites such as Stateville, Pontiac, Jackson, Santa Fe, or Attica would have given representation to prisons facing serious problems. However, at some point our concern for gaining entrée took precedence over the need to include at least one very unstable site. In the end, we selected the most cooperative and supportive prisons, which provided a good basis for comparison and illustrated the diversity in prison-management problems and policies.

The findings presented in this book illustrate the attitudes, values, concerns, and frustrations held by different elements of the organizational structure of five maximum-security prisons. Somewhat surprisingly, we found more similarities than differences among sites—although we expected similar findings from similar sites. The degree of similarity in both the nature and magnitude of the conflict we observed provides convincing evidence that the numerous problems stemming from organizational and racial conflict in maximum-security prisons are among the most pressing issues facing corrections in the 1980s.

1

Prisons at the Crossroads

Maximum-security-prison management is facing one of the most profound and potentially disruptive periods of the past two decades. The nature of this crisis is rooted in historical and contemporary events and encompasses nearly everyone within the prison-organizational structure. It is a crisis that involves external and internal influences, many of which lie outside of management's ability to effectively control or alter the situation. Among these influences are changing public attitudes toward the lawbreaker, a backlash to hard-won prisoner's rights, union militancy of prison guards, and the channeling of prisoner needs and interests into formal prisoner organizations.

In the midst of escalating internal conflict within large maximum-security prisons, lay members of society continue to push for longer, mandatory, and determinate sentences, costly prison construction projects, and a general decline in the quality of prison life for prisoners and staff alike. Motivated largely by fear of urban street crime and violence, citizens are demanding more stringent crime control measures from law enforcement and legislators.[1] In spite of over two hundred years of demonstrated failure, American citizens cling to their belief that greater use of imprisonment is a solution to the growing crime problem.

Perhaps the greatest distinction between contemporary crime-control trends and our earlier reliance on incarceration is the conspicious abandonment of our social obligation to provide prisoners with basic economic survival skills. Rehabilitation, and all its widely contested benefits and liabilities, has been laid to rest as another example of failure by social and political liberalism. Contemporary conservative Americans continue to believe that our archaic penal system offers both deterrence and protection against predatory street crime. Increasingly, *criminal justice* is becoming operationally defined as swift and certain punishment, which in turn translates to lengthy periods of confinement in state maximum-security prisons. As a result of this contemporary trend, the nation's state prison populations have soared to a record midyear total of 349,118 prisoners in 1981, and the overall rate of incarceration has climbed from 98 to 147 per 100,000 general population during the period from 1969 to June 1981.[2]

Prison management and staff have little choice but to accommodate these trends and continue their primary mission—order, security, and control. With job stress steadily increasing, prison management and custodial staff have tightened their grip on prisoner activity and evoked new bureaucratic social controls intended to undermine prisoner opposition and solidarity. Prisoner adaptations have not gone unnoticed. Many recent scholars have argued that the new convict openly defies authority and stands ready to defend intrusions into his shrinking personal space.[3] While many experienced prisoners may have evolved a more rigid posture toward prison survival, there are numerous prisoners who live day-to-day and cope with conflict within the prisoner community by seeking refuge in one of many ameliorative segments of the prison organizational structure.[4] Furthermore, racial stratification and racial conflict have intensified to the point where three separate (but interrelated) social systems appear to have evolved within the prisoner community, each with a slightly different normative code governing adaptation to confinement.[5] Black, white, and Hispanic prisoners in many state prisons have forged specialized collective adaptations, based heavily on racial and ethnic solidarity and common needs and interests.[6] While some form of cooperative relations remain out of necessity, the prisoner social system has become increasingly competitive. Under these conditions, cohesion is more apt to be situational rather than normative, and *black time* and *white time* are recognized as an unavoidable reality of maximum-security imprisonment.

The Roots of the Crisis

The present conflict in American prisons cannot be fully understood by focusing only on internal stresses, impacts, and organizational dynamics. Nor can it be described tautologically as some political leaders and prison administrators have recently done, pointing to overcrowding as the source of mounting internal conflict. Such an analysis has mistakenly prompted prison-expansion proposals at the federal executive level and has triggered massive construction bond issues in at least two states.[7] In each instance, the emphasis has been on accomodating the will of the general public who want more convicted felons sent to prison for longer periods of time.

Clearly, overcrowding is a major concern. Not only for prison management, but for line staff and prisoners who traditionally experience the brunt of the tension, frustration, and explosive reactions that often result from overcrowded conditions and limited resources. However, a closer examination of the over-crowding issue reveals a pattern much more concerning than mere numerical increases. That pattern is a disproportionate use of imprisonment for blacks who have been incarcerated nationally at a rate far surpassing the rate for whites. According to Scott Christianson, the white incarceration rate increased slightly from 46.3 to 65.1 per 100,000 between 1973 and 1979, whereas the incarceration rate for blacks jumped from 368 to 544.1 per 100,000 for the same period.[8]

These rates alone do not accurately represent the scope of the problem. Using the representation of black males rather than the general state population as a base, Christianson found alarming evidence of the disproportionate number of black males in state prisons. For example, when the rate was calculated in this manner, the data reveal that the incarceration rate for black males in 1978 was over 2000 per 100,000 in four states, and over 1000 per 100,000 in thirty other states.[9]

This shocking disparity between black and white incarceration rates is indicative of similar patterns and trends of racial injustice throughout society. Racial imbalances in the outcomes of discretionary judgments have been widely documented in the criminal-justice literature and will not be developed here.[10] However, it is important that incarceration rates are examined in light of other social indicators of black standing within our society. One indicator which has historically revealed black economic disadvantage has been the unemployment rates. Only recently the U.S. Department of Labor announced that unemployment among black youth had reached an all-time national record, and economic forecasters see this trend increasing steadily during the present decade. Chronic unemployment among urban blacks lies at the foundation of many crime problems in our cities. Feelings of powerlessness and resentment contribute to the openly hostile black perspective of white society and the criminal-justice system.

Douglas Glasgow has shown that structural factors, such as chronic unemployment, the legacy of racism, and maintenance by social welfare institutions entrap many urban blacks into a permanent underclass.[11] He argues that feelings of anger, and the black perception of white economic and political power, foster rejection of the basic goals and values underlying law enforcement and social justice:

> [A]s intense as the anger is concerning law enforcement and other institutions controlled by the broader society, these ghetto youth maintain an envy toward the effectiveness and pervasiveness of this persecuting machinery. There is little doubt that they are angry at the world of "whitey," the world that surrounds them in seeming luxury and plenty and denies them by putting them in the "trick bag" of ghetto living. In their minds, poverty, unemployment, and the constellation of deprivation in which they are caught is the result not of chance but of deliberate disqualification, deceit, racism, and the use of power by the "man." It is this perception that arouses an almost envious deference to white power, its organization, its ability to fulfill its purpose, and its magnitude.[12]

Unless structural racism is uprooted from the foundation of American society, there is little doubt that the criminal-justice system, especially the police and prisons, will be increasingly expected to carry the burden of our failures to evolve enforceable standards of racial equality and social justice. At some point in the not too distant future, that expectation may not be realized without a return to the use of force, violence, and bloodshed that characterized the Civil Rights Movement, prison riots in Santa Fe, Pontiac, and Attica, and the period of racial violence at Soledad, San Quentin, and Folsom.

Violent reactions to racial inequality may once again become a social reality as violence is rapidly becoming an integral part of black youth's experience in our nation's cities. In some American cities, violent death (*homicide*) has increased to the level where it has surpassed accidents as the leading cause of death among black males. For example, a recent study indicates that the homicide victimization rate for black males (and all other racial minorities) in Cleveland and surrounding Cuyahoga County rose from 39.2 to 135.7 per 100,000 between the periods from 1958 to 1962 and 1969 to 1974.[13] In contrast, the white male homicide victimization rate for the same period rose a mere 2.6 to 10.5 per 100,000.[14] Furthermore, the homicide rate for all nonwhite males between the ages of fifteen and nineteen years increased by 283 percent during the seventeen-year study period to an alarming rate of 132.3 per 100,000.[15] If we were to compute these rates using black youth representation in the population as the base, they would increase at least tenfold.

To the extent that black males are socialized in environments where violence and conflict are commonplace, coupled with the increased rate of incarceration for blacks, we can expect an increase in prison violence and hostility. However, unlike much of the street violence, blacks are likely to turn much of their outrage, anger, and frustration toward white guards and prisoners (who frequently serve as a handy scapegoat for black revenge).[16]

The Nature of Coercive Organizations

Our research grew out of a conceptual model based on Etzioni's perspectives on compliance relationships in complex organizations.[17] Etzioni views each organizational rank (higher to lower) as having its own compliance structure. According to Etzioni, a focus on the lower participants (prisoners) is essential because "(first) their compliance is more problematic than that of higher participants, and second because organizations can be most fruitfully distinguished from each other at this level."[18] Etzioni has also argued that most studies of complex organizations and bureaucracies have tended to

> include only persons who are a part of a formal hierarchy; priests, but not parishioners; stewarts, but not union members; guards, but not inmates; nurses, but not patients. We treat organizations as collectivities of which the lower participants are an important segment. To exclude them from the analysis would be like studying colonial structures without the natives, stratification without the lower class, or a political regime without the citizens or voters.[19]

A maximum-security prison is not a typical organization. It has special features that are not found in most social organizations. It is necessary, therefore, to consider the characteristics that distinguish the prison from other types of organizations. Etzioni classified complex organization into three major types: coercive, utilitarian, and normative. Prisons, like other institutions that restrict the individual freedom of its participants, are seen as coercive organizations:

[C]oercive organizations are organizations in which coercion is the major means of control over lower participants and high alienation characterized the orientation of most lower participants to the organization.

Force is the major means of control applied in these organizations to assure fulfillment of the major organizational task: keeping inmates in. Obviously, should the restraints on movement be lifted, hardly any inmate would stay inside. The accomplishment of all other tasks depends on the effective performance of this custodial task. The second major task of these organizations, keeping the inmates disciplined, is also attained through the potential or actual use of force, although here differences among various types of organizations are greater.[20]

Control (and its numerous applications) is the foundation of maximum-security prisons, whether it is used directly, in the case of physical restraint, or indirectly, in the case of inducements and punishments. As subsequent chapters illustrate, most organizational and racial conflict is related to the exercise of control (and social-control strategies). In our view, the emphasis on achieving control goals not only fosters alienation and conflict among prisoners but also among line custodial workers who share the lowest organizational strata with the prisoner community.

Etzioni's characterization of coercive organizations provided a reasonably good tool for examining internal conflict in maximum-security settings, but it offered few guidelines with which to assess differential applications of control (or force) over the various racial and ethnic groups within the prisoner community.

Sources of Conflict

Prison management is confronted with several dilemmas that severely limit the scope and nature of meaningful organizational change. First, the long-term effects of structural racism in free society has created a situation where racial conflict and violence are commonplace in the prison organization. The social and organizational dynamics of racism cannot be easily overcome, particularly in a coercive setting. For example, prison guards (typically a predominantly white custodial staff) represent not only the coercive power of the prison organization, but they also symbolize white authority over black members of the prisoner community. Frequently, custodial staff manipulate racial conflict among prisoners to the advantage of organizational control interests. This divide-and-conquer strategy is one of the major sources of black prisoner hostility. Until guards are willing to replace these control tactics with more positive approaches, there can be little reduction in racial conflict. In addition, black prisoner solidarity has increased in response to a reduction in support from community groups who provided substantial assistance during the late 1960s and early 1970s. Consequently, whites who earlier had controlled many prison resources, now find themselves in strong competition with blacks and other racial and ethnic groups for limited organizational resources, opportunities for empowerment, and jobs or assignments that serve as a sanctuary from situational violence.

Second, the greater number of prisoners entering the prison has strained already overburdened resources. Under conditions of overcrowding, effective use of innovative or flexible management strategies is highly unlikely. Most prison wardens and superintendents tend to rely on coercive methods to insure order and maintain control during periods of organizational conflict and stress. Consequently, overcrowding not only limits space, but it influences the nature of management intervention and organizational priorities as well. Prison management usually has no control over the number and type of prisoners received. During periods of overcrowding, it is not uncommon for management to receive new arrivals without having available bedspace.

Third, custodial staff have presented an additional source of internal (and external) conflict. Correctional officer unions have demanded more management support for control-oriented policies and procedures, more influence in selection of top correctional management, and more recognition for their work-related problems. Many of the concessions made to union demands have resulted in a reduction in organizational resources previously committed to prisoner programs and activities.[21] While there have been only a handful of work stoppages or slowdowns, management is frequently required to balance custodial personnel interests against prisoner needs. Prison guards, at nearly every site included in this study, asserted that prisoners wielded "too much power," were "rarely punished for rule violations," and revealed "little respect" for their authority. Whereas individual guards have little influence on management decisions regarding these issues, the union has become a strong voice for correctional officer concerns.

Fourth, the prisoner social structure has undergone substantial change during the past decade. In addition to the formation of racial subgroups within the larger prisoner community, a wide range of formal prisoner organizations have emerged, reflecting specialized prisoner needs and interests. Prisoner social organization has traditionally been viewed as an informal, rather than formal, aspect of the prison organization.[22] Only recently have scholars examined the nature and impacts of formal organizational structures within the prison setting.[23]

Many prisoner organizations represent the formalization of informal social structures within the prisoner community. Generally, these groups pursue activities seen as being compatible with prison organization goals. Increased specialization of prisoner interests has spawned bureaucratic procedures for gaining official recognition and sponsorship, and stimulated competition among prisoners for limited resources and legitimate opportunities within the prison. Some of these formal organizational structures have usurped traditional prisoner collective power and influence in the prison. Others have provided a legitimate means of strengthening racial and ethnic ties. Regardless of their motives or goals, these formal organizations have emerged as a new source of prisoner power and influence within the prison organization.

Quite often conflict between management decisions authorizing formal prisoner organizational activity and correctional officer interest in maintaining direct control over prisoners inadvertently divides the prison organization into three competitive camps: executive management (coordination); correctional officers (security); and prisoners (program activity). Conflict between these three organizational ranks is inherent in their different roles and interests. The relative lack of involvement by prisoners and guards in organizational decisions tends to promote specialized interests and adaptations to preserve the integrity of existing organizational roles. Involvement in decisions considered essential to organizational goals, under current management approaches, remains solely in the hands of representatives of higher management. Prisoners and guards are rarely seen as participants who management involves in organizational decisions. Instead, they are more often seen as members of the organization who management controls and regulates according to current organizational needs. In this regard, both formal prisoner organizations and guard unions serve as potential vehicles for providing input into specialized management decisions. However, without a formal management policy supportive of shared decision making or collaborative management, these formal organizational structures tend to promote nearly as many organizational problems as they are intended to solve. Effective participative roles would have to emerge from a more comprehensive collaborative scheme extending opportunities for meaningful involvement to custodial personnel and prisoners alike.

Sources of Consensus

Not all relations between organizational ranks can be characterized as emerging from structural conflict. Many daily prison activities performed by members of the prison organization represent substantial cooperation and consensus. For example, without prisoner labor, the production of prison goods and services would come to a standstill. The vast majority of daily tasks are performed willingly, in exchange for remunerative considerations and/or fulfillment of specialized needs. Most prisoners, like members of free society, prefer to be engaged in some form of meaningful activity. While there has been significant changes in the prisoner community, several former prison officials have asserted that they could achieve full employment in the prison if they had the resources to develop useful and productive tasks.[24]

Prisoner participation has rarely been the central problem in the coordination of work in the prison organization. Rather, many (if not most) prison managers find it to be desirable to maintain social control leverage by limiting the number of desirable jobs and reassigning those prisoners who fail to comply with prison rules governing job behavior. One approach capitalizing on prisoner involvement would be to make a greater number of desirable tasks available to a greater number of prisoners and to discard policies prescribing less desirable work as retribution for undesirable conduct. Another would be to extend greater autonomy and self-determination to prisoners seeking and performing productive tasks. Several progressive prison systems have had successful experiences in allowing prisoners to develop and market computer software programs as a small business. Similar endeavors were found during our study, largely under the auspices of not-for-profit corporate structures serving a small number of prisoners.[25] Hence, failing serious security concerns, management and prisoners tend to agree on the desirability of productive activity. The precise level of cooperation, needless to say, would be determined by a host of organizational dynamics and considerations.

Another area of general agreement among organizational ranks is stability and predictability within the prisoner community. Most prisoners, particularly those serving lengthy sentences, expect stable and predictable responses in their contacts with others, not only among members of the prisoner community but also in their relations with representatives of the prison organization. Prisoners and guards cannot easily cope with random or situational outbursts of hostility, aggression, or violence. Most maximum-security prisoners accept violence as being a part of prison life, but only insomuch as violence remains a predictable outcome of interpersonal conflicts or disputes.[26]

Line custodial staff also share a strong need for predictability and stability in the prison environment. Without stable relations with prisoners, their personal safety may be jeopardized and maintenance of security and discipline may become extremely difficult. On the broader scale, guards and prisoners each have an important stake in maintaining stable and cooperative relations within the organizational structure of the prison.

The Need for Organizational Change

There is little debate among prison administrators on the need for change in maximum-security prisons—the only radical proposal is keeping prisons in their present state of turmoil. Most serious discussion centers on what changes and how they are to be carried out.

Many organizational change proposals have been based on the need for expansion, such as construction of small (400-bed) maximum-security facilities and renovation of existing space to improve both control capability and delivery of human services. There has been little discussion of developing initiatives aimed at improving race relations, extending greater line-staff and prisoner involvement in policy or operations level decisions, or plans for limited prisoner self-determination, and a complete absence of methods of reducing prison populations such as facilitating the removal of first-time and nonserious offenders and expansion of community-based corrections. While these interventions have been considered by some prison administrators to offer positive value and utility,[27] recent management emphasis has centered specifically on population management and control. Severe overcrowding and a strong indication that more prisoners are on the way has tempered proactive management and stifled organizational development and planning. Prison management has, for the greater part, returned to policies limited to control goals. The image of professional corrections that slowly emerged during the 1970s, for all intents and purposes, has been submerged under pressures of overcrowding and racial conflict.

To insure bureaucratic survival, prison management is going to have to develop the means of pursuing organizational change and development goals simultaneously with population-control goals. Unless management can effectively respond to mounting organizational pressures and racial conflict, an increasing number of prisoners and staff will experience needless suffering and hardship. However, organizational change cannot be accomplished merely by deciding to do it (although that is an important first step). Careful analysis of the salient concerns, interests, needs, and attitudes and values held by all members of the prison organization must be made before any change initiatives can be fully successful.

Notes

1. The current trend toward greater use of mandatory and determinate sentencing reflects a growing emphasis on crime control and a concomitant decline in societal willingness to view crime as an inevitable by-product of social and economic injustice. Consequently, during the past four years, thirty-seven states have enacted mandatory sentencing statutes (without considering the impact on prison populations) and another fifteen have passed some form of determinate sentencing legislation.

2. Bureau of Justice Statistics, *Bulletin: Prisoners at Midyear 1981* (Washington, D.C.: U.S. Department of Justice, September 1981), pp. 1-3.

3. John Irwin, *Prisons in Turmoil* (Boston: Little, Brown, and Company, 1980).

4. Hans Toch, *Living in Prison: The Ecology of Survival* (New York: The Free Press, 1977).

5. Leo Carroll, *Hacks, Blacks, and Cons: Race Relations in a Maximum Security Prison* (Lexington, Mass.: Lexington Books, D.C. Heath, 1974); James Jacobs, "Race Relations and the Prisoner Subculture," *Crime and Justice: An Annual Review of Research, Vol. 1,* edited by Norval Morris and Michael Tonry (Chicago: The University of Chicago Press, 1979).

6. Carroll, *Hacks, Blacks, and Cons;* Irwin, *Prisons in Turmoil.*

7. New York and Ohio are each seeking voter approval of large construction programs through bond issues. In New York, $350 million of the $500 million bond issue was earmarked for new construction of three 512-bed prisons

and expansion of existing facilities to bring bedspace to 4,078 additional male prisoners.

8. Scott Christianson, "Our Black Prisons," *Crime and Delinquency* 27 (July 1981):365.

9. Ibid., p. 368.

10. See: Scott Christianson and David Parray, *Black Crime: An Annotated Bibliography,* Education Project Monograph (Albany, New York: Graduate School of Criminal Justice, SUNY, March 1980); Robert Staples, "White Racism, Black Crime, and American Justice: An Application of the Colonial Model to Explain Crime and Race," *Phylon* (March 1975):14-22; Bernice Just, "Bail and Pre-Trial Detention in the District of Columbia: An Empirical Analysis," *Howard Law Journal* 17 (1973):844-857; Stevens Clarke and Gary Koch, "The Influence of Income and Other Factors on Whether Criminal Defendants Go to Prison," *Law and Society Review* (Fall 1976):57-92; Leo Carroll and Margaret Mondrick, "Racial Bias in the Decision to Grant Parole," *Law and Society Review* (Fall 1976):93-107.

11. Douglas G. Glasgow, *The Black Underclass: Poverty, Unemployment, and Entrapment of Ghetto Youth* (New York: Vintage Books, 1981).

12. Ibid., p. 103.

13. Normal Rushforth, Amasa Ford, Charles Hirsch, Nancy Rushforth, and Lester Adelson, "Violent Death in a Metropolitan County," in *Perspectives on Crime Victims,* edited by Burt Galaway and Joe Hudson (St. Louis: C.V. Mosby Company, 1981), p. 119. For an additional view of this trend see: Warren Brookes, "Crime: Economic Scourge of the Ghetto," in *Perspectives on Crime Victims,* edited by Burt Galaway and Joe Hudson (St. Louis: C.V. Mosby Company, 1981), pp. 92-97.

14. Rushforth, et al., p. 199.

15. Ibid., p. 120.

16. See: A. Cohen, G. Cole, and R. Baily, eds., *Prison Violence* (Lexington, Mass.: Lexington Books, D.C. Heath, 1976); Anthony Scacco, *Rape in Prison* (Springfield, Ill.: Charles C. Thomas, 1975); John J. Gibbs, "Violence in Prison: Its Extent, Nature and Consequences," in *Critical Issues in Corrections: Problems, Trends, and Prospects,* edited by Roy Roberg and Vincent Webb (St. Paul: West Publishing Company, 1981): Irwin, *Prisons in Turmoil,* Carrol, *Hacks, Blacks, and Cons.*

17. Amitai Etzioni, *A Comparative Analysis of Complex Organizations,* 2d. ed. (New York: The Free Press, 1975).

18. Ibid., p. 22.

19. Ibid., p. 20.

20. Ibid., p. 27.

21. John Wayne, Jr., *Prison Employee Unionism: The Impact on Correctional Administration* (Sacramento, Calif.: The American Justice Institute, 1977); Scott Christianson, "Corrections Law Developments—How Unions Affect

Prison Administration," *Criminal Law Bulletin* 15 (May-June 1979):238-247; J. Jacobs and N. Crotty, *Guard Unions and the Future of Prisons,* Institute of Public Employment, Cornell University, Monograph no. 9 (Ithaca, N.Y.: New York State School of Industrial and Labor Relations, 1978).

22. Donald Clemmer, *The Prison Community* (New York: Holt, Rinehart and Winston, 1940); Gresham Sykes, *The Society of Captives* (Princeton: Princeton University Press, 1958); John Irwin, *The Felon* (Englewood Cliffs, N.J.: Prentice-Hall, 1970).

23. Ronald Berkman, *Opening the Gates: The Rise of the Prisoners Movement* (Lexington, Mass.: Lexington Books, D.C. Heath, 1979); C. Ron Huff, "Unionization Behind the Walls," *Criminology* 12 (August 1974):175-193.

24. R.M. Montilla, who served as Deputy Director of the District of Columbia Department of Corrections and as a central office staffer under Richard McGee in the California Department of Corrections, argues that he had nearly achieved full employment at Soledad without additional resources. A similar view toward prisoner activity is held by Richard McGee, presently the retired chairman of the board of directors of The American Justice Institute (personal communication).

25. The Lifer's Group at Rahway is organized as a corporation. While prisoners serve as executive officers, the board of directors is made up of distinguished citizens and criminal-justice professionals. During a survey conducted as part of the research project, it was found that twenty-three of the twenty-eight states responding had at least one not-for-profit corporation involving prisoners. See: R.M. Montilla, *Administrative Report: Prisoner Organization Research Project* (Sacramento, Calif.: The American Justice Institute, 1980).

26. For one of the best literary accounts of prison violence and the development of violent reactions to prison conflict, see: Jack Henry Abbott, *In the Belly of the Beast* (New York: Random House, 1981).

27. Minnesota and Oregon have passed Community Corrections Acts which, according to recent prison population data released by the U.S. Department of Justice, have kept maximum-security-prison populations well within the design capacity of their institutions. Minnesota is unique in that its sentencing guidelines take into account existing prison bedspace. For a discussion of the issues raised by prisoner involvement in organizational decisions, see: J.E. Baker, *The Right to Participate: Inmate Involvement in Prison Administration* (Meuchen, N.J.: Scarecrow Press, 1974); Thomas Murton, "Inmate Self-Government," *University of San Francisco Law Review,* 6 (October 1971):87-101; Thomas Murton and Phyllis Jo Baunach, *Shared Decision-Making as a Treatment Technique in Prison Management* (Minneapolis: Murton Foundation for Criminal Justice, 1975).

Prison Management: The View from the Top

Historically, the management of prison business has been centered around the personal goals and powers of the warden and a deputy warden or principle keeper who served as chief disciplinarian and top security officer. Literature describing early prison wardens presents an image of autocratic, sometimes charismatic figures who commanded the obedience and loyalty of rank and file custodians.[1] Until the courts abandoned their hands-off policy, wardens and their deputies held nearly unlimited authority to administer their own system of punishments and rewards.[2]

The early period of American prison history produced several wardens who survived not only partisan politics but managed to gain widespread support for policies of strict discipline and tight security at a time when reform efforts were being initiated in many state prisons. Many wardens had so firmly established their power base, that only a major riot could result in their removal. Among the most famous was Stateville's Joe Regan, who served as warden from 1936 to 1961. His management style and political power symbolized the personal dominance and authoritarian leadership of many early prison wardens.[3]

Contemporary Prison Management

Today, the prison warden or superintendent serves as top executive of a large prison organizational hierarchy. Unlike early wardens, contemporary chief executives must rely heavily on the skill, judgment, and cooperation of numerous middle and lower management staff. In addition, contemporary prison managers face completely different organizational problems and political influences. Most notably, the organizational structure of the prison has become more complex and the prison has been integrated into a sophisticated corrections bureaucracy responsive only to a political leadership. Consequently, prison management is frequently asked to adapt their operations to meet an increasing number of external influences such as central office directives, prisoner population increases, and shifting public opinion. Today, effective prison management must simultaneously address external and internal influences, some of which lie outside the scope of their authority or ability to change. For example, extreme overcrowding in most state prisons, arising from recent changes in sentencing policy and practices, new legislation mandating imprisonment for specific offenses, and a trend toward retributive justice cannot be regulated solely by prison management.

Other external factors that affect management decisions are the importation of new attitudes and expectations of prisoners, the demands of correctional officer unions, and an increasing emphasis on formal guidelines and standards.

Several recent works have addressed the impact of these influences on correctional policy and decision making. Thomas and Peterson, for example, have asserted that contemporary prison management has become more responsive to an external public than to an objective assessment of assigned organizational goals.[4] Others have argued that correctional organization and management have become more directly affected by a wider variety of economic and political influences which have markedly altered the setting of priorities, treatment of prisoners, and the nature of communications with elected political officials.[5] This situation has tended to distract management attention from internal organizational problems and in some states has contributed to a serious imbalance in the powers held by correctional officers and prisoner groups and organizations.

Managerial Effectiveness

Presently, there is little indication that prison management has attempted to develop effective (and lawful) strategies for reducing organizational conflict and turmoil. Some prison officials argue that organizational pressures such as overcrowding, racial violence, and guard union demands have reduced the likelihood of successful organizational change in contemporary maximum-security prisons.[6] To an increasing extent, political and economic considerations inhibit or severely limit the scope of intended change. For example, most wardens or superintendents inherit facilities, staff, and budgets that they played little or no part in planning or developing. In addition, they often have little control over the number or characteristics of prisoners or when they may be released. Consequently, managerial effectiveness is often determined by the degree of freedom and range of options available to managers. Where organizational constraints are tightly drawn, we would expect to observe management policies emphasizing status quo objectives.

Maximum-security-prison management's responsibility extends beyond maintenance of internal order. Other responsibilities include improvement of the quality of life of prisoners (and staff) and the setting of priorities consistent with state-of-the-art prison programming. Executive management, in particular, has a responsibility to chart the course of the organization and to evolve effective and meaningful change goals even when attention is drawn to immediate control issues.

Managing Organizational Goals

The conceptualization of significant organizational goals and the management of change tend to be highly idiosyncratic elements of overall managerial effectiveness. Maximum-security prisons, by definition, have control or restraint goals which must be met before any secondary goals may be operationalized. However, organizational resources may be either appropriately or inappropriately directed toward the achievement of control goals. Achieving control goals and "keeping the lid on" frequently become self-justifying ends and adequate consideration is rarely given to developing measures intended to evaluate the long-term impacts of restrictive policies. Furthermore, limited organizational resources may be committed to a perceived need for control, resulting in a decline in the availability of resources for change strategies. Prison management rarely develops an assessment of a real need for control and, consequently, seeks to reduce its risk of failure by overcommitting resources to control goals and security priorities. In this regard, prison management tends to perpetuate structural conflict among organizational members and increases the likelihood of becoming trapped into reacting to control situations that could otherwise be avoided.

Even well-intended prison executives, who prefer a human-relations approach to organizational problems, find themselves unable to gain strong staff support for change objectives because control goals have traditionally fostered and reinforced inflexible and autocratic responses. When control goals become the primary task of the prison organization and resources are committed to maintain order and security, little attention can be given to the development of human services that directly affect the quality of life of prisoners. Once set into motion, this type of management response breeds conflict between front-line custodial staff and prisoners for access to limited organizational resources.

When top management reacts to problems within the organization, rather than developing a strategy that accomodates the potential impact of these problems, the greater part of the organization's activity, particularly within upper and middle ranks, is likely to become focused on how to gain more power and control over lower members. Reactive management, by definition, also reduces the possibility of gaining positive commitment from lower members. Proactive management, in contrast, has a greater likelihood of fostering the development of meaningful participant involvement in the organization and of promoting greater compatibility in the compliance structure among organizational ranks.[7] If prison management is to achieve more than mandated control goals, it must introduce changes that counterbalance the social, political, and economic influences affecting the organizational structure.

The Target of Our Inquiry

Our research focused on management's intervention into their unique organizational problems and practices. The measurement included objective assessment of management resistance to change, interviews with top, middle, and lower management (functionally divided into executive, security, and program management), and systematic observations of management in action. Attention was primarily focused on executive management, who we saw as being responsible for setting the framework for the other managerial priorities and strategies.

We viewed security management (which varied in importance within the management hierarchy at each of the five prisons studied) as an extension of the security force but with substantial power to affect positive or negative influences within organizational ranks.

A major part of the inquiry relied on systematic and general observations of the internal workings of the prison organization. Most of our observations of *management style* (use of coercive powers, willingness to involve lower organizational participants, and ability to conceptualize the prison organization into a framework for planned change) were tailored to each organizational structure. Since each organization was unique, these observations tended to shift focus to accomodate the specific information needs and interests. While some loss of information may have occurred from this approach, comparability of observations among prisons was at best tenuous even without such methodological specialization. This approach is not uncommon in organizational research.[8]

The interviews with key management personnel and observations at each prison were intended to identify those management strategies and internal constraints unique to each research setting. To assess the level of management support for organizational change, we developed an instrument measuring two different change strategies and priorities. Our structured observations of management were geared toward understanding the relationship between higher and lower organizational members and the sources of structural conflict.

It was difficult to accurately define prison management positions in *pro forma* terms as many members of the organization frequently assumed managerial roles corresponding to situationally defined tasks and needs. Our definition of *prison management,* therefore, was limited to executive management (superintendents and their respective assistant or associate superintendents), security management (chief security managers and their captains and lieutenants), and other middle and lower management personnel who routinely participate in key organizational functions. Consequently, correctional management at each research site consisted of formally defined management personnel who routinely performed significant assignments.

Descriptive and Demographic Characteristics

Table 2-1 provides a brief description of the demographic and background characteristics of the aggregated management sample. As indicated, the average age of correctional managers was forty-four years, with a substantial majority (46 percent) being over the age of forty-five years. In addition, blacks and women comprised a very small proportion of the total sample, 9.6 percent and 7.4 percent, respectively. Nearly all female managers completing the questionnaire were black, leaving black males to account for less than 2 percent of the sample.

Table 2-1
Correctional Manager Demographic Characteristics and
Social Background

	N	*Percent*
Age		
35 and under	9	18.8
36 to 45	17	35.4
46 and over	22	45.8
Total	48	100.0
$\bar{X}$ = 44.1 years		
Race		
White	47	85.5
Black	5	9.1
Response withheld	3	5.4
Total	55	100.0
Sex		
Male	47	92.6
Female	4	7.4
Total	51	100.0
Education		
Less than 12 years	2	3.7
High school	11	20.3
Some college	15	27.8
College graduate	7	13.0
Post-Graduate	19	35.2
Total	54	100.0
$\bar{X}$ = 14.8 years		
Marital Status		
Single	4	7.5
Married	46	86.8
Split family	3	5.7
Total	53	100.0
Employment (career)		
1 year or less	0	0.0
2 to 5 years	7	13.2
6 to 10 years	7	13.2
More than 10 years	39	73.6
Total	53	100.0
$\bar{X}$ = 15.5 years		

Note: $\bar{X}$ = Arithmetic mean.
     N = Number of cases.

Table 2-1 also reveals that managers included in the sample had worked in the field of corrections for a substantial number of years. As shown, nearly 74 percent had been employed in corrections for over ten years, and many of these had remained at the same institution for a larger part or their careers. In sum, the sample reflects a predominantly white, middle-aged, male managerial group that has worked in the field of corrections for a lengthy period of time.

The characteristics of the sample are similar to the adult institution sample obtained during the Joint Commission of Correctional Manpower and Training study of correctional administrators. For example, Nelson and Lovell reported that over 60 percent of their adult institutional management sample were over forty-five years of age and 49 percent had worked in corrections for ten or more years.[9]

Attitudes toward Organizational Change

Prison management, like their counterparts in both private and other public areas, have explicit and implicit responsibility for promoting organizational change compatible with official goals. This responsibility is essential to organizational development and insures that management fulfills organizational roles and obligations beyond that accorded to institutional caretaker.

Organizational change in maximum-security prisons presents a special problem in that the official goals of the organization are most often statutorily defined and the range of options are frequently limited to change strategies that alter only the internal organizational structure. Such restrictions may not entirely inhibit the opportunity for achieving meaningful change. However, they do tend to significantly limit objectives to structural, rather than fundamental change. The most basic ideological issue arising from conceptualizing change in prisons and other coercive organizations raises the question of whether any change can significantly alter the level of alienation and oppression experienced by prisoners and front-line staff. The key factor in deciding whether any intended change will ultimately make a difference in the quality of life of lower organizational members, in our judgment, is *empowerment.*[10] If organizational change results in prisoners and line staff having a substantially greater amount of decision-making power and control over their individual destiny, then the change may be viewed as more than just another organizational band-aid. Conversely, organizational changes that serve to further reduce the status of prisoners and front-line custodians and tend to concentrate power and influence within upper and middle management ranks are nothing more than structural modifications without significant consequence.

To assess the extent to which prison managers rejected (or supported) organizational change, we asked the fifty-five managers included in the sample to respond to fourteen questionnaire items comprising two different organizational change scales. The items represented hypothetical change initiatives familiar to most correctional managers. One scale, *structural change,* reflected changes that have the potential of altering the basic design of the organization, but which have only secondary implications for altering relationships between management and prisoners.

Structural Change Items

S1 Decriminalization of most victimless crimes, such as prostitution, possession of marijuana, and gambling.
S2 Establishment of determinate (fixed) sentences in place of indeterminate sentences.
S3 Elimination of mandatory prison sentences for minor property offenses.
S4 Continuation and extension of the use of pretrial and presentence diversion to treatment programs for all except violent offenses.
S5 Providing the director of Corrections with broad authority to establish and administer institutional work release and furlough programs for all prisoners who have served one-half of their minimum sentences.
S6 Elimination of parole and parole boards.
S7 Establishment of family (conjugal) visiting for all married prisoners, except where a reasonable basis for denial can be shown.

The second scale, *participatory change,* reflected changes that have a more direct effect on prison management and have the potential of altering the extent to which lower members participate in organizational decisions.[11]

Participative Change Items

P1[a] Prisoners in this institution should be given much more say in decisions that affect their lives in confinement.
P2 Establishment of a Corrections Ombudsman who reports to the director of Corrections and who has the authority to reconcile all (staff and prisoner) grievances.
P3 Creation of an organizational framework for prisoner and staff to work together to share more of the decisions which are now made by management and/or staff alone.
P4 Establishment of a Human Relations Council where staff and prisoners can work together to develop plans to eliminate or reduce racism, sexism, and other variations of discrimination in prison operations.
P5 Prisoners should have the right to associate with organizations of their choice and to be represented by them.
P6 Prisoners should have the right to choose their own educational, vocational, and therapeutic programs, and such choices should not be subject to discipline, loss of privileges, transfer, consideration for parole, work release, or furloughs.
P7 Prisoners should have the right to full control over their personal funds and their disbursement.

[a]Polarity of scale was reversed during analysis.

For example, the involvement of prisoners in decisions concerning their role and power within the organization may require management to share powers previously held by a small number of middle or upper management personnel. Each questionnaire item was scored on a one-to-five scale assessing manager's agreement or disagreement to change initiatives. The low end of the continuum was intended to measure the extent of rigidity toward change, while the high end was intended to measure the amount of flexibility.

Hence, we conceptualized management style as falling within two extremes, ranging from managerial *rigidity* to managerial flexibility. The former was seen as being closely associated with an emphasis on expediency and efficiency and stresses the use of coercion to accomplish organizational objectives. In contrast, *flexibility* was seen as being based on principles of self-determination and participation, and stresses the value of mutual and collaborative intervention. Together, these contrasting managerial styles, with their underlying assumptions about human behavior, represent a theoretical continuum that characterizes management's orientation to change. Thus, the model provides a two-dimensional perspective of manager change orientation. We expected to observe a positive relationship between rigidity and structural change orientation and between flexibility and participatory change.

Table 2-2 presents the arithmetic mean and standard deviation for each of the items within each change scale. A mean value between 3.25 and 5.00 may be interpreted as representing strong agreement (flexibility). Similarly, a mean value between 1.00 and 2.75 may be viewed as representing substantial disagreement (rigidity). The aggregate scale scores are also provided to illustrate overall scale differences.

Table 2-2
Mean Values of Organizational Change Items

Structural Change (N = 54)			Participative Change (N = 55)		
Item	$\overline{X}$	*S.D.*	*Item*	$\overline{X}$	*S.D.*
S1	3.51	1.35	P1	2.00	.74
S2	3.49	1.84	P2	3.38	1.16
S3	3.60	1.01	P3	2.49	1.22
S4	3.78	.98	P4	3.16	1.15
S5	3.16	1.03	P5	2.18	1.26
S6	2.45	1.21	P6	2.71	1.30
S7	2.45	1.42	P7	2.11	1.05
Scale $\overline{X}$ = 3.20 S.D. = .57			Scale $\overline{X}$ = 2.58 S.D. = 1.32		

Note: $\overline{X}$ = Arithmetic mean.
        S.D. = Standard deviation of the mean.
        N = Number of cases.

The findings indicate that prison managers reveal rigidity toward organizational change in general; however, they showed less rigidity (or greater flexibility) toward structural than participatory change. According to these results, prison managers, as an aggregate group, did not view participatory change as a desirable goal within the context of their respective organizations.

We expected to observe some differences in change orientation according to the background and demographic characteristics of managers. To assess these differences we examined the relationship between flexibility toward change and several descriptive variables such as age, education, and length of correctional career. To make the data compatible with a crosstabulation model, scores from each of the two change scales were reorganized into high and low flexibility scores. This was accomplished by first computing the total number of items that were scored in the direction of flexibility (four or five on the one-to-five point scale) and then dichotomizing them into two categories: *high flexibility* and *low flexibility*. Table 2-3 illustrates the distribution of scores within these dichotomous categories.

As shown, only 22 percent of the participatory change scores, compared to over 57 percent of the structural change scores, fell into the high flexibility category. Our data indicated that only 14 percent of the correctional managers revealed high flexibility for both structural and participatory change, whereas 36 percent revealed low flexibility in both organizational change scales.

Several interesting findings emerged from the crosstabulation of these scores with selected demographic characteristics. For instance, the majority (72 percent) of those managers who had worked in corrections for less than ten years revealed high flexibility toward structural change; whereas 57 percent of those who had careers extending between ten and fifteen years and 45 percent of those who had been in corrections for more than fifteen years revealed low flexibility. Similarly, 43 percent of those who had worked in corrections for less than ten years revealed high flexibility toward participatory change, compared to only 11 percent of those whose careers extended beyond fifteen years.

Table 2-3
Distribution of Dichotomized Organizational
Change Scale Scores

	Structural Change		Participatory Change	
	N	Percent	N	Percent
Low Flexibility	23	42.6	43	78.2
High Flexibility	31	57.4	12	21.8
Total	54	100.0	55	100.0

Note: N = Number of cases.

These findings suggest that the longer prison managers work in corrections, the more likely that they will reject organizational change. Normally, we may attribute some contribution to this relationship to age, assuming the conventional relationship between age and conservative attitudes. However, this assertion is not supported because no significant or substantial relationship was found between age and flexibility toward either type of organizational change. Hence, length of correctional career appeared to be an independent indicator of receptiveness to organizational change.

Similar findings were revealed between flexibility and education. For example, the data indicated that 64 percent of those managers with twelve or less years of formal education revealed low flexibility toward structural change. In contrast, over 63 percent of those managers with at least some postgraduate education revealed high flexibility toward structural change. Similar findings were revealed for participatory change. That is, 67 percent of those with some postgraduate education had high flexibility and 93 percent of those managers with twelve or less years of education had low flexibility. These findings suggest that education may play a major role in influencing correctional managers' support for organizational change.

As the management sample included a large proportion (47 percent) of security management personnel, it was important to examine the relationships between management position and flexibility to change. The data revealed what many prison scholars may anticipate; namely, security managers tended to reveal much higher resistance to change than either executive or program managers. For example, we found that 96 percent of the security managers revealed low flexibility to participatory change, compared to 60 percent of the executive managers and 60 percent of other key management staff. These findings suggest that security managers strongly reject organizational changes which grant greater participatory powers to prisoners.

While the relatively few black and female managers included in our sample did not permit a statistical comparison with their white (or male) counterparts, the data clearly pointed to a greater acceptance of structural change by blacks and women. However, little or no difference between races or sexes was indicated for their acceptance of participatory change.

These findings raise several important considerations for the potential for organizational change in maximum-security prisons. For instance, if executive management desires to implement changes that may increase the success of existing organizational goals (such as reducing idleness), but which allows prisoner participation in some management decisions, security management may be expected to show substantial resistance. The specific form of such resistance may vary from simple attempts to discount the desirability of the change to a demand that security interests be placed above change objectives. In either instance, executive management will be unable to pursue the intended change without risking the chance of conflict with front-line supervisors, lieutenants, and other ranking security officers who comprise the bulk of lower and middle security management. Without security management cooperation and support, an extension of participatory powers to prisoners may produce additional organizational problems. Hence, conflict among executive and security management may result in that conflict being carried into normal organizational operations.

Varieties of Prison Management

Earlier in this chapter we touched briefly on management style, suggesting that an individual warden's approach to organizational problems tends to establish a precedent of *proactive* or *reactive* management intervention. We also argued that prison-management style frequently reflected the manner in which wardens or superintendents organized and supervised their staff to pursue those objectives essential to the official mission of the prison organization.

While this conceptualization has served to broaden our basic understanding of the influence of top management on middle and lower management ranks, it has not facilitated an analysis of management as a team or collective body. Rather than viewing management style as being personified by the top executive (even though it may be the predominant style), we saw management style as the cooperative effort of those sharing responsibility for the development and outcome of problem-solving initiatives. Consequently, we expanded our information gathering efforts to encompass combined or team responses of management personnel.

Our approach consolidated systematic and general observations of prison operations and structured interviews with key staff within all management ranks. As a result of our observations and interviews, we were able to identify eight organizational problems that were common to all five sites.

Common Organizational Problems Faced by Prison Management

1   Concentration of authority within upper-management ranks.
2   Overemphasis placed on the cultivation of informal information networks to obtain organizational intelligence.
3   Lack of real opportunities for line staff and supervisors to participate in daily organizational decisions.
4   Few management staff meetings to allow lower- and middle-management personnel to provide information and to obtain feedback on earlier organizational decisions.
5   Lack of accessibility to upper management by line staff and prisoners.
6   Lack of line-staff support for female correctional officers' assignment to security posts.

7   Line-staff resistance to innovative management strategies intended to develop greater use of existing resources and manpower.
8   Lack of lower management and line-staff support for expanding opportunities for prisoner self-determination.

Several problems appeared to be unique to a single prison and, therefore, were not included in the analysis. While such departures were of interest, we focused attention on organizational problems that were experienced by all sites so that any relationship between organizational problems and management style could be observed.

Three predominant management styles, restrictive, participative, and innovative, were observed at the five sites. *Restrictive management* followed traditional custody-oriented policies and practices, emphasized loyalty and conformity to organizational norms, used autocratic or power-based methods to insure achievement of goals, were basically unreceptive to change, and had information flow downward from higher members in the form of directives. In contrast, *participative management* was oriented toward shared decision making and collective involvement of other organizational members; appeared to be open to the ideas, interests, needs, and concerns of lower staff; placed less emphasis on custody and control; and appeared willing to grant limited power and autonomy to prisoner organizations and prisoner-initiated programs. Finally, *innovative management* was more frequently open to change and risk-taking in their approach to organizational problems, to have valued human relations (which appeared to be linked to self-motivating staff), and to have staff members who held a positive view of their role within the organization.

Our effort to conceptualize prison-management style was complicated by the extent to which any given management team relied on any particular style of intervention. In an attempt to consider these factors, and provide a meaningful summary analysis, management style was divided into primary and secondary applications. Table 2-4 presents the classification of each of the five sites according to their primary and secondary intervention styles. As indicated, restrictive-management style was the primary style used by Soledad, Oregon, and Bedford Hills management. However, our observations and interviews revealed that all sites except Soledad tended to employ participative-management styles as a secondary management approach. The use of participative approaches, as a primary management style, was limited to Stillwater which tended to employ restrictive styles as a secondary intervention. In a similar vein, Rahway was the only site that tended to use innovative-management styles but, like Stillwater, relied on restrictive styles as a secondary management intervention.

These management styles frequently reflected the organizational structure of the prison. For example, the primary management style at Stillwater (participative) tended to be an extension of unit management. Stillwater's housing areas were organized into different management units governed by a unit director

Table 2-4
Observed Prison-Management Intervention Styles

	Primary	*Secondary*
Restrictive	Soledad Oregon Bedford Hills	Stillwater Rahway
Participative	Stillwater	Oregon Bedford Hills
Innovative	Rahway	

who provided coordination and supervision for all unit functions, including custody, discipline, and social services. Unit management in housing areas, and other functional units within the prison, allowed for a greater amount of inter-action between prisoners and middle management, as well as between the front-line security staff and management. Furthermore, many unit problems or issues could be dealt with on an informal level, allowing the unit manager to determine which issues were appropriately decided by higher management levels. In con-trast, Oregon State Penitentiary (OSP) management tended to follow traditional lines of authority and emphasized strict control and discipline. Consequently, organizational change occurred very slowly and most attempts to establish inno-vative programs and opportunities were overshadowed by control concerns.

The nature of maximum-security prisons may severely limit the type of management-intervention strategies available for most organizational prob-lems. Given the current trend toward retributive justice and swelling prison populations, management may feel that they have little choice but to proceed with some variation of restrictive policies with an emphasis on control. However, our observations of management practices and policies suggest that a reliance on traditional custodial approaches tended to be accompanied by an arbitrary re-jection of the merits of participative management. Prison management, with the exception of Stillwater, which used unit management for most prison opera-tions, and to some extent Rahway, which used a variation of a collaborative model for program activity, appeared to be unwilling to consider the possible advantages (or consequences) of expanded participation roles and opportunities for line staff and prisoners.

There are consequences to this course of action, particularly when the larger organizational goals are centered on control. Thomas and Peterson suggest that

the adoption of a coercive organizational structure as a means by which control can be insured has farreaching consequences for the prison as an organization and for the inmates who are confined within it. Perhaps the most significant of these consequences is that it confronts the in-mates with a variety of alienating and depersonalizing pressures as a broad spectrum of structurally generated problems that must somehow be countered. It so isolates inmates at the bottom of a rigidly stratified organization that many of the reward and punishment contingencies that are effective in shaping attitudes, values, and behavior become far more subject to control by those within the informal structure of the inmate society than by representatives of the formal organization.[12]

In this perspective, to achieve compliance with formal organizational goals, control tends to increase the social distance between the prisoner community and the official world of the prison administration.

Notes

1. See: C. Duffy and J. Jennings, *The San Quentin Story* (Westport, Conn.: Greenwood Press, 1957); G. Erickson, *Regan of Joliet* (New York: Dutton, 1957); and F. Tannenbaum, *Osborne of Sing Sing* (Chapel Hill: University of North Carolina Press, 1933). Also see: James Jacobs, *Stateville: The Penitentiary in Mass Society* (Chicago: The University of Chicago Press, 1977), pp. 15-70.

2. The Sixth Circuit Court of Appeals, in *Coffin* v. *Reichard,* 145 F. 2nd. 443 (1944), ruled that "a person retains all the rights of an ordinary citizen except those which expressly or by necessary implication are taken from him by law." Prisoners' legal challenges, however, have been viewed by the courts as confronting the legitimate aims of the institution to maintain security.

3. Jacobs, *Stateville,* pp. 15-70. Many prison wardens still use Joe Regan as an example of a powerful prison leader. During our interviews with prison management at Oregon (OSP), Superintendent Hoyt Cupp frequently used Regan's leadership style as an illustration of a "strong" warden.

4. C. Thomas and D. Peterson, *Prison Organization and Inmate Subcultures* (Indianapolis: The Bobbs-Merrill Company, 1977), pp. 27-29.

5. See: David Duffee, *Correctional Management: Change and Control in Correctional Organizations* (Englewood Cliffs, N.J.: Prentice-Hall, 1980), pp. 65-69. Also see: Todd Clear and Martin Schwartz, "Corrections as Political Enterprise," in *Critical Issues in Corrections: Problems, Trends and Prospects,* edited by Roy Roberg and Vincent Webb (St. Paul, Minn.: West Publishing Company, 1981), pp. 279-307; and R. Allinson, "Politics of Prison Standards," *Corrections Magazine,* 5(March 1979):54-62.

6. For example, John Conrad, well-known researcher and critic of institutional corrections, has repeatedly argued that overcrowding is one of the greatest impediments to sound correctional practices. During our field studies, state-level corrections administrators, as well as prison wardens and superintendents, consistently stated that overcrowding was their greatest obstacle to organizational development and change. Overcrowding, straining already limited

resources, has stimulated legal challenges in over twenty-eight states. See: *Annual Status Report,* "The Courts and Prisons" (Washington, D.C.: National Prison Project, April 1980).

7. See: Amitai Etzioni, *A Comparative Analysis of Complex Organizations* (New York: Free Press, 1961), pp. 3-21.

8. Selznick, for example, argues that organizations represent a "resultant of complex forces" and, consequently, no single analysis can be used to fully explain all organizations. See: Phillip Selznick, "Foundations of the Theory of Organization," in *A Sociological Reader on Complex Organizations,* 2d. ed. edited by Amitai Etzioni (New York: Holt, Rinehart and Winston, 1969), pp. 19-32.

9. See: E. Nelson and C. Lovell, *Developing Correctional Administrators* (Washington, D.C.: Joint Commission on Correctional Manpower and Training 1969), pp. 23-32.

10. Prisoner empowerment, in our application, also implies a shared responsibility for both desirable and undesirable outcomes of collaborative policy formulation and decision making. Rights without responsibilities would neither further the ability of prisoners to evolve meaningful and acceptable roles within the prison organizational hierarchy nor reduce the resistance of line staff to expanded participatory roles for prisoners. See: J. Regens and W. Hobson, "Inmate Self-Government and Attitude Change—An Assessment of Participation Effects," *Evaluation Quarterly* 2(August 1978):455-479.

11. The item-to-item and item-to-scale correlations for these two change scales are presented in appendix B.

12. Thomas and Petersen, *Prison Organization and Inmate Subcultures,* p. 41. Reprinted with permission.

3

Prison Guards: The Front Line in the Workplace

Correctional officers in maximum-security prisons are the primary agents in maintaining social control and achieving prisoner compliance with official organizational goals. They are most commonly known as guards, hacks, or screws by nearly all members of the prison community.[1] The particular characterization of the front line tends to be influenced by several factors including the nature and scope of their authority, the security policies of prison management, the unique control strategies aimed at preserving order, and the historical development of their role. At Rahway, front-line workers were commonly known as *cops* or *bulls,* terms consistent with their active membership in the New Jersey Police Benevolent Association. In contrast, nearly all front-line custodial positions at Stillwater held the official title of *correctional counselor,* but prisoners continued to use the term *hack* or *screw* to characterize the role and status of security staff within the prison organizational hierarchy. Front-line custodial staff saw their title of correctional counselor as being "more respectable" when meeting members of the free community, but told us that the term guard was more consistent with their major duties within the prison.

The Guard Role

In spite of nearly two decades of deliberate efforts to change the image of front-line security personnel, their role is most frequently characterized as low status (and sometimes brutal) guards who have little responsibility beyond the supervision and surveillance of prisoners.[2] The major prison-guard role in the United States is *custodian,* that is, preventing escapes, enforcing prison discipline, and maintaining social control.[3]

Cressey states that the custodial role often creates a number of basic conflicts and concerns for front-line workers.[4] According to Cressey, guards are put in a position of having to follow official policies, for example, strict conformity to prison rules and procedures, and, at the same time, are expected to exercise good judgment and discretion so that prisoners do not become disgruntled or potentially rebellious.[5]

Prison guards also perform a number of contrasting roles, such as helper during moments of prisoner's personal crisis and as controller during numerous situations that require immediate judgment and use of discretion.[6] These contradictory roles often promote confusion about guard performance expectations and the legitimate use of their authority. Bartollas and Miller state that conflicting sources of information increase the guard's difficulty in understanding the nature of the job. In addition, they argue that while many guards may have genuine interest and concern about the welfare of prisoners, they are often unsure about the proper action to be taken.[7]

Ambiguity of performance expectations surrounding formal and informal guard responsibilities (and obligations) can easily affect organizational goals which, by necessity, combine helping and guarding roles. The front-line worker appears to have a much more diverse role than many earlier descriptions suggested. For example, in a recent study intended to examine the "nature and extent of helping roles played by guards," Johnson reported that only one-fifth of the guards at two New York state prisons combined custodial and human service roles in conducting their duties.[8] In a later phase of this study, Johnson found that program staff made little effort to enlist the assistance of custodial staff as an organizational resource in the delivery of human services.[9] While several program staff members had developed limited cooperative relationships with custodial staff, the relative impact on effective utilization of human-service resources was negligible.[10] In addition, over one-half of those guards who were designated as helping persons indicated that program staff were unresponsive to receiving input from custodial personnel.[11]

Multiplicity of goals and ambiguity of performance expectations are among the primary factors influencing relationships between guards and prisoners. Guards who adhere to *hard line* custody approaches, that is, strict enforcement of prison rules, tend to establish greater social distance between themselves and prisoners.[12] Conversely, guards who support principles of fair treatment and rehabilitation are more likely to evolve closer social relationships with prisoners and view their work as an important part of the network of human-service professions. Frequently, there are consequences attached to the use of one approach over the other, such as being seen as a "hard ass" or "easy mark" by prisoners,[13] or being subjected to ridicule by other guards. Hence, there may be less of a choice of guard roles than may be expected by casual observers.

There are indications that much of the on-the-job behavior of guards is linked to values and attitudes held by fellow workers. Early studies suggested that the informal social network of correctional workers can have a profound affect on job performance.[14] More recent literature indicates that many guards have rigid norms governing their relationships with prisoners and management.[15] For example, Bartollas, Miller, and Dinitz report that custody staff at a maximum-security institution for delinquent boys had an established normative system designed to regulate worker behavior.[16] Among those norms proscribing appropriate conduct for custody workers were: "unless you have been there you don't know what it's like," "the administration will screw you," "don't do more than you get paid for," "don't listen to the social workers," "stay cool, man," and "be loyal to the team."[17] According to Bartollas, Miller, and Dinitz, these norms reflect attitudes and values intended to insulate relatively low-status custody workers from organizational pressure and influence over their work.[18]

Duffee asserts that a "correctional officer subculture" may emerge from conflict between officer's interests (and perceptions), and those held by prison management, and prisoners. While the sociological meaning of *subculture* does not readily describe many of the collective social patterns of the custodial staff, it does capture a part of the growing sense of solidarity among prison guards, particularly around issues concerning their role, status, and relationship with prison management.[19] In Duffee's perspective, guards perceive themselves as being relegated to the same low-status position within the organization without recognition for their efforts, spend much of their idle time identifying dishonesty and hypocrisy in those above them in the organizational structure, and experience high alienation from the middle class.[20]

Role conflict faced by prison guards is not limited to informal work relationships and status within the organizational hierarchy. Frequently, guards discover that few concrete guidelines are available that determine the appropriate course of action in response to prisoner misconduct. As a result, many guards evolve strategies intended to insure smooth-running operations without risking official reprimand for their efforts. This is most likely to emerge in job assignments or posts that require constant contact with prisoners, such as in cell blocks or on work details where the guard's discretion may require overlooking minor infractions to maintain order and stability. However, Lombardo reports a greater likelihood of guards reporting violations of rules in high contact job locations such as the yard, cell block, and shops,[21] although the guard's perception of authority and low social distance tend to influence the formal reporting of rule violation as much as the opportunities provided by the job location.[22]

Guard Stress and Frustration

Many guards view the expansion of prisoner's rights and court-mandated due process (for example, disciplinary hearings) as an erosion of their traditional authority and power. However, acceptable degrees of guard authority tend only to be determined through experience and with the knowledge that official support varies from supervisor to supervisor. Many guards discover that the underuse or overuse of their authority often results in official sanctions imposed by supervisors. They also may discover that the rule violation they reported was not perceived as serious by an institutional disciplinary committee and that the prisoner received only a reprimand for misconduct. These areas of authority and rule enforcement remain ambiguous in spite of a trend toward the establishment of official policies and procedures governing every aspect of prison operations. Guards are faced with the constant reminder that their discretionary judgments are subject to review by management and supervisory staff who, in their view, are not fully cognizant of the aggravating circumstances of the misconduct.

Most guards find it to be nearly impossible to escape the frustration that accompanies less well defined performance expectations and roles. As a result, a substantial number carry high levels of job-related stress into many facets of their personal lives and work assignments. Increased stress influences on-the-job decisions and relationships with peers and prisoners. While such stress has been widely recognized as being a primary factor in determining police performance,[23] little empirical evidence has been gathered in an attempt to determine stress levels or sources among high-security prison guards.

One recent study of sixty-five state and seventy-eight county correctional officers attending the New Jersey Correctional Officer Training Academy,[24] found that the major perceived areas of guard's stress was remarkably similar to that found for police.[25] Cheek and Miller reported that guards saw the lack of clearly defined guidelines for job performance, poor communication of institutional policies, and conflicting orders from supervisors as being among the important sources of job-related stress.[26] Like their police counterparts, New Jersey guards viewed their source of stress as arising more from administrative conditions than from relationships with prisoners, although prisoner violence, such as stabbings, was a common tension-producing problem.

Job satisfaction (or dissatisfaction) appears to play a major role in shaping the quality of guard performance and developing guard compliance with official organization goals. Currently, there is little research or literature that directly addresses guard's perception of their work and the implications of work-related concerns on the performance of the prison organization. The few works that have examined guard work roles have not revealed substantially new knowledge nor have contributed overall to our understanding of the nature of prison work.[27] Typically, guards are cast as an "unhappy lot" suffering from lack of clarity of work roles, fear and boredom,[28] confusion concerning relationships with prisoners, perceived lack of opportunity to provide meaningful input into management decisions, or low self-esteem.[29]

However, some recent research has focused more carefully on the social dynamics affecting job performance and working conditions. Lombardo, for example, interviewed fifty guards at Auburn Correctional Facility in New York, exploring a variety of factors associated with job satisfaction, as well as rule enforcement and handling of prisoner problems.[30] Among the job dissatisfaction themes identified by Lombardo were relationships with inmates (physical danger and mental strain, prisoner behavior toward guards, maintaining impartiality), powerlessness (lack of support, lack of responsibility, lack of effective input), and inconsistency and inadequate communication (inconsistent policies and procedures, inconsistent supervisory direction, inconsistent and inadequate information received from prison administration).[31]

Lombardo found that most guards (54 percent) were concerned with a lack of support from prison management, supervisors, and fellow guards. Another large proportion (50 percent) expressed concern about the physical danger and mental strain stemming from their relationships with prisoners. Other concerns expressed by Auburn guards were very similar to those reported elsewhere in the literature, for example, dissatisfaction with general departmental policy, prison administration's policy toward prisoners, prison administration's policy toward guards, role expectations, supervision, conflict between custodial and program functions, boredom, and the routine nature of their work.[32]

Carroll, who studied a small state prison in an eastern state (ECI), identified substantial anomie among guards who, collectively, experienced difficulty in coping with role conflict, ambiguity of organizational goals, and an absence of written guidelines for use of authority during period of change from traditional custody goals to humanitarian reform.[33] According to Carroll, the "anomic state of the custodians is the result of ambiguous and contradictory role definitions, which in turn are a function of the contradictory goals assigned to the prison and the resultant conflict among top administrators."[34] In addition, ECI guards expressed frustration and resentment stemming from a perceived lack of support from supervisors, a general deterioration of relationships among guards, and a trend toward granting greater privileges and rights to prisoners. At the peak of guard dissatisfaction with the direction set by prison management, Carroll observed the evolution of union militancy as an adaptive response to anomie.[35] This pattern tends to coincide with the general trend toward greater correctional officer union involvement in prison policy and operations.[36]

In more recent analysis of the impact of organizational and social changes on prison guards, Crouch points to three major social changes that have influenced institutional practices and the work experiences of guards: the rise of rehabilitation as an objective of imprisonment; the entry of the federal judiciary into daily prison operations; and changes in the size and composition of prisoner populations.[37] Crouch argues that these three influences have had the affect of making working conditions substantially more difficult and potentially more dangerous for the prison guard.[38] His analysis was based on the premise that the nature of the relations between prisoners and the front line have been fundamentally changed. According to Crouch, this change was based on a shift from paternalistic to competitive relations, which has the impact of altering guard and prisoner status and role, redirecting the motives and focus of prisoner aggression, changing guard perceptions of prisoners, and increasing the importance of the legal and social interests of lower organizational members.[39] The primary factor in the shift from paternalistic to competitive relations, according to Crouch, is greater prisoner empowerment, which stems from a decreased dependence of prisoners on the front-line staff to respond to personal and social needs.[40]

Race Relations and Racial Conflict

The greatly expanded prison organizational bureaucracy that has evolved around the delivery of specialized human services, for example, legal assistance, educational, vocational, therapeutic, and religious programs, and outside-based volunteer programs, has directed prisoner needs and interests toward civilian and professional staff attention and away from the scope of authority of front-line custodial staff. Such a fundamental change in relations between guards and prisoners is most profound for black, Hispanic, Native American, and other racial minority prisoners who frequently view front-line staff as "gatekeepers" having racist motives and values behind their discretionary judgments. In this regard, the emergence of a black ideological perspective during the 1960s,[41] placing an emphasis on economic, social, and political justice, has tended to alter the nature of race relations between guards and prisoners as well as among members of the prisoner community. For instance, what may have previously been merely routine enforcement of a particular prison rule now may be interpreted by racial minorities as an act representing racial prejudice and hatred. The increased rates of incarceration of blacks and other racial minorities, along with severe overcrowding, has placed a greater burden on predominently white, rural guards to perform their assigned duties in an unbiased and nondiscriminatory manner.[42]

This statement should not be construed as suggesting that the problem of race relations in prison may be lessened with a strategy as simplistic as nondiscriminatory treatment. The factors associated with racial conflict and racial stratification are multidimensional and are extremely complex. We cannot expect even the best trained and well-intended prison guards to counteract the affects of institutionalized racism throughout the criminal-justice system. However, knowledge of the social dynamics and impacts of race relations in prison settings may be useful in guiding our understanding of racial conflict, and possibly serve to stimulate the development of more effective race relations in the prison. Observations of recent prison researchers, including myself, suggest that substantial effort will be required to foster guard understanding and awareness of cultural and social differences among members of different racial groups.[43] The prison setting, with a social climate charged with uncertainty, coercion, and intimidation, tends to encourage aggressive (or defensive) responses rather than mutual understanding.

Frequently, guards unwittingly perpetuate the potentially destructive cycle of racial polarization with their actions toward prisoners. On other occastions, they may employ traditional divide-and-conquer strategies where one racial group is pitted against another in an attempt to increase the front line's social control over the larger prisoner community. One common reaction of many guards faced with a situation or pattern of racial conflict is to fall back on demonstrated custodial or control strategies, such as strict enforcement of prison rules or more intensive supervision of prisoner groups. Lombardo indicates that guards tend to react most strongly to prisoners whose "attitude and behavior" threaten the "social order" of the prison.[44] In addition, Auburn guards frequently provoked prisoners who were known to react strongly to verbal antagonism, thus manipulating the situation into a more serious rule violation such as "showing disrespect to an employee."[45] While Lombardo did not address racial differences in his study, the likelihood of black or other racial minority prisoners reacting to guard provocations may be higher than among whites.[46]

This is consistent with a trend toward less social distance between white prisoners and guards, particularly in prisons where white prisoners are the minority. *Social distance,* used most frequently in the prison literature to describe the dynamics surrounding guard authority and rule enforcement, is one indicator of the extent to which prisoners and guards seek common objectives and make modifications in roles and behavior structured by their respective normative system.[47] Adjustments made by guards to gain greater control and minimize their difficulty in personal contacts with prisoners has been conceptualized as "corruption of authority," where guards may grant illicit favors in exchange for more cooperative relations with prisoners.[48] However, closer social relations initiated by prisoners tends to place the prisoner in a more vulnerable position, particularly when it may involve conduct proscribed by the inmate code. On the one hand, the prisoner may risk rejection by the prisoner community, as well as the possibility of severe sanctions. On the other hand, the prisoner is placed in a situation where guards can manipulate the situation to gain access to information not previously shared. When racial conflict (or violence) is added to this dilemma, the dynamics become much more complex.

White prisoners may be motivated to develop closer ties with guards in anticipation of a need for support and protection. At prisons where racial violence is a common reminder of racial conflict and tension, unorganized white prisoners may view the front line as their only readily available opportunity for safety.[49] The steadily increasing numbers of white prisoners seeking protective custody partially illustrates the impacts of racial conflict on the prisoner community.[50]

The concern for personal safety is not limited to whites. Violent conflict between organized racial gangs in states such as California and Illinois, and greater competition among prisoners for limited goods and services (spurred both by overcrowding and changes within the prisoner normative system), tend to put pressure on a greater number of prisoners. There is a belief among some prison scholars that what may have been a stable prisoner community, content with manipulating goods and services, has been divided by contrasting racial attitudes, minorities seeking new status and racial identify, and competition with other racial groups for power, distribution systems, and limited access to counterband goods.[51] The overall impact of such changes in the nature and structure of the prisoner community on the front line is not clearly understood. However, what remains clear is that greater work-related stress, collective (union) efforts to influence prison policy, and changes in social relations between guards and prisoners has tended to coincide with basic changes in the size, composition, and nature of the prisoner community.

Conceptual and Methodological Framework

Our interest in prison guards focused on their relationship with members of the prisoner community, supervisors, and top management. However, we saw these relationships as being influenced by both the nature and extent of guard power and influence within the prison organizational hierarchy and the nature of their work-related concerns. In our judgment, guard work-related concerns may directly influence the operation of prisoner activities and programs and indirectly affect the outcome and direction of organizational goals. We also assumed that the specific concerns of guards would vary according to the unique organizational dynamics of each research site, the extent to which guards had positive or negative experiences with prisoners, and the degree to which they perceived themselves as being supported by supervisors and top management. Each of these possible influences were in turn seen as stemming from the direct involvement of the custodial work force in organizational decisions affecting those policies and procedures most related to the guard's work.

Guard work-related concerns were central to the analysis of their relations with prisoners, particularly with formally organized prisoner groups within the prisoner community. We assumed that most guards would be unwilling to support the empowerment of prisoners (individually or through organizations), including the extension of greater decision-making ability, when they perceived their own position within the prison organizational structure as serving low-status "guarding" and "order maintenance" functions without an opportunity to provide meaningful input into policy and procedure development.

Like the assessment of prison management presented in chapter 2, the study of prison guards was guided by knowledge and insight gained during the three-month pilot study at Soledad (CTF-Central).[52] Open-ended interviews and informal conversations with over thirty guards, as well as records inspection and structured field observations, allowed us to identify six major themes characterizing their work-related concerns. These themes subsequently were developed into thirty questionnaire items and given to a sample of front-line custodial staff at the pilot-study site. Hence, the research instruments used in the five maximum-security sites were shaped by Soledad guards' view of their work and their relations with supervisors, management, and members of the prisoner community. The specific research methods, such as sampling techniques, item analysis, and interview strategies, are discussed in appendix A.

We obtained questionnaire and interview responses and systematic observations at each research site to provide a fuller and richer picture of the guard's work world. While guards' relationships in the home and the community may have a bearing on their work-related concerns, we did not attempt to study these areas. Neither did we explore, systematically, the motives behind their selection of prison work. Other research has examined these issues and the limited resources of this study demanded that they be used to describe the guard's role and relationship with the three principle elements of the prison organizational structure.

As indicated in table 3-1, we obtained an aggregate questionnaire sample of 381, and 104 completed interviews from the five sites included in the study. While there are some variations in the percentage of populations sampled, the combined questionnaire and interview responses portray guard's job-related concerns and perspectives of their role within their respective prison settings.

Descriptive and Demographic Characteristics

Table 3-2 illustrates the demographic characteristics and employment backgrounds for each of the five samples included in the study. This provides a description of each sample and illustrates differences among guards at the five maximum-security prisons studied. With the exception of Rahway, the samples generally reflect the characteristics of their respective institutional custodial staff.[53]

The data pertaining to age present an interesting contrast among research sites. For example, compared to all other sites, a substantial proportion of Bedford Hills guards were over fifty years of age. The data reveal that over 23 percent of the Bedford Hills guards, compared to 18 percent of the Folsom guards, 13 percent of the OSP guards, and only 5 percent of the Stillwater guards were over the age of fifty. In addition, a substantial proportion (40 percent) of the Bedford Hills guards were between the age of thirty-one and forty, which would tend to contribute to their slightly higher median age (38.2 years). It should be noted, however, that Bedford Hills guards were more unwilling to report their age than any other sample. That is, nearly 18 percent of the Bedford Hills guards, compared to only 9 percent of the Folsom guards and 4 percent of the OSP guards, did not include age with their responses to the questionnaire. Consequently, it was not known whether most of these 18 percent were in lower age categories, which would tend to make the Bedford Hills age range similar to other guard samples.

Observations and personal contacts during the field research at Bedford Hills suggest that female guards in women's corrections represent a more stable work

Table 3-1
Distribution of Correctional Officer Samples at Five Research Sites

Site	Defined Population	Questionnaire Sample	Percentage of Population Sampled	Interview Sample
California	195	43	22.1	10
Minnesota	190	55	28.9	32
New York	156	57	36.5	32
New Jersey	200	28	14.0	15
Oregon	206	198	96.1	15
Total	947	381	40.2	104

Table 3-2
Demographic and Background Characteristics of Correctional Officers at Five Maximum-Security Prisons

	Folsom		Stillwater		Rahway		OSP		Bedford Hills	
	N	Percent	N	Percent	N	Percent	N	Percent	N	Percent
Age										
Under 31 years	9	23.1	21	38.9	16	57.1	66	34.7	10	21.3
31 to 40 years	14	35.9	16	29.6	8	28.6	56	29.5	19	40.4
41 to 50 years	9	23.1	14	25.9	4	14.3	43	22.6	7	14.9
Over 50 years	7	17.9	3	5.6	0	0.0	25	13.2	11	23.4
Total	39	100.0	54	100.0	28	100.0	190	100.0	47	100.0
Median age	32.0 years		31.5 years		29.5 years		34.8 years		38.2 years	
Race										
White	36	87.8	46	86.8	23	82.1	178	93.2	8	15.4
Black	2	4.9	4	7.5	3	10.7	1	.5	36	69.2
Hispanic	1	2.4	1	1.9	2	7.1	7	3.7	2	3.8
Others	2	4.9	2	3.8	0	0.0	5	2.6	6	11.5
Total	41	100.0	53	100.0	28	99.9	191	100.0	52	99.9
Sex										
Male	43	100.0	48	88.9	28	100.0	190	97.9	3	5.3
Female	0	0.0	6	11.1	0	0.0	4	2.1	54	97.7
Total	43	100.0	54	100.0	28	100.0	194	100.0	57	100.0
Education										
Under 13 years	5	11.6	14	25.9	11	39.3	64	33.2	23	40.4
13 to 14 years	25	58.1	27	50.0	11	39.3	76	39.4	22	38.6
15 to 16 years	12	27.9	11	20.4	6	21.4	44	22.8	12	21.0
Over 16 years	1	2.3	2	3.7	0	0.0	9	4.6	0	0.0
Total	43	99.9	54	100.0	28	100.0	195	100.0	57	100.0
Median education	13.9 years		13.4 years		12.9 years		13.6 years		13.3 years	

	N	%	N	%	N	%	N	%	N	%
Job Classification										
Trainee	2	5.4	9	17.0	1	3.7	21	12.2	7	13.5
Junior officer	12	32.4	24	45.3	11	40.7	60	34.9	16	30.8
Senior officer	20	54.1	12	22.6	14	51.9	67	38.9	28	53.8
Sergeant	3	8.1	8	15.1	1	3.7	24	13.9	1	1.9
Total	37	100.0	53	100.0	27	100.0	172	99.9	52	100.0
Length of Correctional Career										
Under 2 years	3	7.3	13	24.0	5	17.9	17	8.9	13	24.5
2 to 5 years	10	24.4	31	57.4	17	60.7	85	44.5	8	15.1
6 to 10 years	17	41.5	4	7.5	4	14.3	50	26.2	9	17.0
Over 10 years	11	26.8	6	11.1	2	7.1	39	20.4	23	43.4
Total	41	100.0	54	100.0	28	100.0	191	100.0	53	100.0
Median employment	7.7 years		2.7 years		3.0 years		5.1 years		9.4 years	
Time at this Institution										
Under 2 years	8	18.6	16	29.6	6	21.4	35	18.2	17	30.9
2 to 5 years	9	20.9	32	59.3	16	57.1	85	44.2	18	32.7
6 to 10 years	17	39.5	2	3.7	4	14.3	36	18.8	4	7.3
Over 10 years	9	20.9	4	7.4	2	7.2	36	18.8	16	29.1
Total	43	99.9	54	100.0	28	100.0	192	100.0	55	100.0
Median employment	6.9 years		2.3 years		2.8 years		3.9 years		2.6 years	

Note: *N* = Number of cases.

force. Furthermore, we were told by a number of the Bedford Hills interviewees that front-line experience at men's prisons was more likely to enhance their careers in corrections than assignments solely in women's institutions. Consequently, many younger guards entering the field did not choose Bedford Hills as their first preferred work location.[54] The extent of employment stability among Bedford Hills guards is illustrated by data presented in table 3-2. Over 43 percent of the Bedford Hills guards had worked in corrections for over ten years, with a substantial proportion (29 percent) having worked at the same facility during that same period. The Folsom and Oregon guards represented the only male samples that reflected a similar pattern of employment. However, neither sample reflects the proportion of long-term employees of Bedford Hills. Conversely, the Stillwater and Rahway samples represented correctional security units with a high rate of employee turnover. Table 3-2 reveals that only 11 percent of the Stillwater guards and 21 percent of the Rahway guards were employed at their respective institutions for five or more years, suggesting that many male guards at these facilities either left the field or obtained positions in other correctional facilities.

The racial characteristics presented in table 3-2 point to a white majority at each of the five maximum-security prisons. According to departmental statistics for each state represented in the study, white male guards historically constituted the majority of the maximum-security work force. Some researchers and writers have pointed to the rural location of most maximum-security prisons and their corresponding lack of appeal to most urban black families.[55] Others point to the lack of social and cultural support shown by members of the predominately white security force.[56] Regardless of the reasons, until very recently blacks have not been well represented among front-line custodial staff in state prisons.

Bedford Hills, New York State's only high-security prison for women, is an exception to this pattern. Blacks and other racial minorities comprise nearly 85 percent of the front-line staff. There may be several factors that contribute to these findings. For example, women's corrections may not have the job appeal to white women that men's corrections has to white men. Furthermore, security positions in women's prisons may be seen as an accessible opportunity by those minorities who have traditionally been limited to lower paying tax-supported occupations. Another possibility is that many black and Hispanic families do not enjoy the option of having only one member responsible for household income. Finally, while Bedford Hills is located within an upper-income area in upstate New York, it remains within commuting distance of New York City, which is seen by most racial minorities as being a more desirable residential area.

As shown in table 3-2, a very small number of female guards were employed at the four male maximum-security prisons. A survey cited in *Corrections Magazine* reveals that, with the exception of California, very few women guards hold unlimited security positions in male state prisons.[57] Currently, California has one of the most widely acclaimed affirmative action efforts aimed at expanding the role of opportunities for women guards in male prisons. During the period of the study in California, we observed a substantial number of women employed in front-line custodial positions. However, the remaining male maximum-security prisons in the study appeared to offer only limited front-line opportunities to women.

Several additional demographic characteristics reveal differences between samples. For example, a substantially large proportion of all male guards were military veterans, with OSP guards having the greatest proportion (80 percent). Furthermore, approximately one-third of all veterans had served as military police. Of the three male guards employed at Bedford Hills, two were military veterans. However, only two women, or 4 percent of the Befford Hills sample, were veterans of military service.

Table 3-2 also indicates that Bedford Hills had the least proportion of married guards currently living with their respective families. For example, 34 percent of the Bedford Hills guards, compared to 65 percent of the Rahway guards, 70 percent of the Folsom guards, and 78 percent of the OSP guards were married and maintained intact family units. Consequently, Bedford Hills guards revealed a high proportion of single (never married) and separated or divorced (split family) staff. Only Rahway and Stillwater revealed a similar proportion of nonmarried guards among the front line. The underlying reasons for these differences between male and female guards is not readily apparent from our data. However, when we consider age, length of correctional career, and traditional work and sex roles, it appears that women guards tend to experience a substantially different social impact from their employment in prisons than men. For example, traditional sex-role sterotypes, for example, "wife and homemaker" and "mother," are in marked contrast to the guard role. In addition, the social image of prison matron, created largely by the media and popular literature, still lingers in the minds of many members of the free community in spite of substantial changes in women's corrections during the past decade.

Occupational Concerns of the Front Line

As noted earlier in this chapter, guard's work-related concerns have not been widely communicated outside the relatively closed circle of their peer group. This problem has its roots in the organizational structure of the prison. Guards occupy the lowest stratum within the prison organizational hierarchy. Hence, their concerns are not easily communicated upward through the chain of authority to prison management. It has only been since the advent of union representation and collective bargaining that work-related concerns of front-life staff have been translated into organizational language intended to facilitate resolution.

Previously, most guard concerns tended to be individualized and/or communicated informally to line supervisors and other lower-management personnel. As prisoner populations continue to increase and public-servant salaries, status, and job opportunities decrease, guard concerns may be expected to become stronger and more specialized.

Our objective was to identify and assess the relative strength and importance of guard work-related concerns at each of the five maximum-security prisons included in the study. The survey instrument, a Correctional Officer Occupational Concern (COOCS) Scale,[58] was made of six interrelated thematic dimensions; communications and support, control, power, resistance to change, racism-sexism, and safety. Each scale dimension was composed of five items reflecting a range of guard concerns specific to each theme. The design of the instrument was intended to provide symmetry across each scale dimension and make the difficult problem of intrascale interpretation more straightforward. The findings have been organized in descending rank order of mean values to allow easy identification of those items or scale dimensions that reflect the most salient concerns of each sample. As a result, the nature and implications of the findings are presented in the following order: power, control, safety, communications and support, resistance to change, and racism-sexism. Representative interview excerpts, illustrating the personal experiences and impressions of front line workers, are included with the analysis of questionnaire responses to provide a more accurate and realistic picture of the guard's role and relationship within the prison organizational structure.

Power

The data reveal that power concerns ranked first among all guard samples. *Power,* as operationalized for the purpose of this study, was defined as a concern about a continuing decrease in correctional officers' power within the prison organization. Correctional officers may perceive this loss of power as having a direct impact of their ability to influence correctional policy, the selection (and survival) of top management, and their wages and employee benefits.

Table 3-3 presents the arithmetic mean and standard deviation values for the power items for each of the samples.[59] The items were stated as follows:

Power Scale Items

8 Correctional officers need unions because top management too often ignores the views of custody staff.

12 Most of the custody staff I know have very little confidence in the direction set by the central department up in the state capitol.

18 Correctional officers will never get an even deal until they gain more direct input into top management decisions.

Table 3-3
Power Scores Rank Ordered by Item Means

	Folsom			Stillwater			Rahway			OSP			Bedford Hills		
Item No.	$\overline{X}$	S.D.	Item No.	$\overline{X}$	S.D.	Item No.	$\overline{X}$	S.D.	Item No.	$\overline{X}$	S.D.	Item No.	$\overline{X}$	S.D.	
(20)	4.67	.72	(8)	4.46	.77	(20)	4.50	.88	(20)	4.37	.98	(20)	4.49	.91	
(12)	4.42	.91	(20)	4.11	1.19	(8)	4.36	.91	(8)	4.10	1.22	(8)	4.34	1.12	
(8)	3.81	1.40	(18)	4.02	.98	(18)	4.00	1.22	(18)	3.75	1.25	(18)	4.21	1.00	
(29)	3.79	1.36	(29)	3.89	1.25	(29)	3.93	1.18	(12)	3.72	1.24	(29)	3.71	1.36	
(18)	3.69	1.12	(12)	3.63	1.15	(12)	3.61	1.07	(29)	3.36	1.45	(12)	3.44	1.09	
Scale Mean	4.08	.58		4.02	.44		4.08	.35		3.86	.54		4.04	.44	

Note: $\overline{X}$ = Arithmetic mean.
S.D. = Standard deviation of the mean.

20 Correctional officer salaries will always be inadequate until they acquire the
    power to negotiate rates equal to state highway patrol or city policy officers.
29 Correctional officer employee organizations and unions should be given the
    right to express their vote of confidence before final decisions are made on
    the selection of middle and top prison managers.

As shown in table 3-3 the specific varieties of power concerns and their relative
strength differed only slightly among front-line staff at the five prisons studied.
The data reveal nearly uniform high mean values (4.67 to 4.37) for the view that
greater power is needed to negotiate wages comparable to those found for equiv-
alent state law-enforcement positions (item 20). While responses were similar
for this item, Stillwater guards tended to see the need for correctional officer
unions (item 8) as being a slightly more important power concern than guards at
the remaining sites. With the exception of Folsom guards, who placed a greater
emphasis on their lack of confidence in central management (item 12), most
guards felt that they would never get a fair shake until they gained more input
into top management decisions (item 18).

It appears that power concerns were affected only slightly by differences in
geographic location of the prison, the type of institutional and department
policy, and the demographic characteristics of the front-line staff. As the interviews will illustrate, power concerns are an integral part of the shared experiences and expectations of maximum-security guards. This is best illustrated by
the growth of correctional officer unions during the past two decades.[60] With
the exception of California guards (who had received legislative authorization to
organize for collective bargaining during the study period), the front line at each
remaining site had formal union representation and collective bargaining. However, the extent of power and influence wielded by these unions and their ability
to directly influence institutional decisions and policies varied substantially from
state to state. While unions were able to address collective concerns such as
wages and benefits, issues evolving from guard safety and communications within the organization often remained outside the scope of the union's power and
authority. As a result, many guards were sensitive to their limited role and influence within the prison organizational hierarchy and often expressed a need to
have their union take a much more active stance in protecting their interests.

A former union officer at OSP told us that before any significant changes
can be made, the union must meet with top management to clarify the role of
correctional officers within the organizational structure. He also saw the bureaucratic structure surrounding the Oregon Department of Human Resources as
being the major obstacle to acceptance of the guard as a professional worker:

> I would like to see the employee organization and the management take
> the time to sit down and go over the roles a little bit better, better de-
> fine the roles, and have management accept the fact that the correc-
> tional officer is a little more professional. I don't think that our basic

problem is with our management in corrections, I think you have to look at Human Resources and then on to the executive department and the legislature, for the simple fact that all of the people in corrections in this state have been in the institution. But the people who have the power to change, the Human Resources Department, the executive department and the legislature, that's where the real changes have to be made. Those are people who have to realize that we do something besides stand out there and knock heads together, you know, the TV image of the prison guard. (OSP-OF-44)[61]

Another Oregon guard said that many rank and file members are reluctant to challenge management's authority. In his view, guards will continue to have the same basic relationship with management until the union gains greater strength and solidarity:

The officers here, some of them are scared of the administration's retaliation. Others don't go to the meetings, they don't vote on the important issues, and then when something comes down that they don't like they drop out, they quit, or they scream and yell that it's the union's fault. They don't realize that *they* are the union, and this is our biggest problem. We've got to get interest in the union generated. I think there's got to be a union, but if the union gets too strong then everybody loses there, too. But I think here the union needs to be a little stronger than most places, a whole lot stronger than it is. (OSP-OF-20R)

Many guards felt that their union was merely a vehicle for asserting a collective voice within the prison bureaucracy. Others, however, viewed their union in an active political role intended to influence decisions at higher levels. For example, one Rahway guard viewed his union (P.B.A.) as having substantial power within the state political bureacracy as well as within the organizational context of the prison:

The union has got a lot of power. We've got close to 1,300 members. Not just in this institution, but throughout all the institutions. If you have everybody voting for a politician, multiply that by three for each family. You have a powerful organization there. We're struggling and a politician won't do anything unless you get him elected. In the past the union wasn't really that much involved,but if it involves security, officer's complaints, or if it's going to cause a problem, then the union will sit down and talk it over with the administration. (NJ-OF-10A)

It should be noted that a substantial number of front-line staff at each prison felt that their union was often unresponsive to individual problems. They told us that there were a wide range of personal conflicts with management that were ignored by their union leadership. In these guards' view, membership and payment of union dues entitled them to support and assistance in formal disputes.

For example, one Stillwater guard saw their union's (Teamsters) role as being supportive of guards who were the target of prisoner litigation:

> I think that's essentially what's involving the Teamsters now. I think in this day and age in the prison context, the lives of inmates have been really focused. Therefore, we are saying as staff that we have to be really careful what we do to inmates, and how we process inmates, and how we deal with inmates. Because if we don't, we're going for criminal cases, OK? So we want some more support from the Teamsters in regard to an attorney, to our rights. If I go into a cell and have to subdue an inmate and in subduing that inmate I break his jaw or really severely hurt that guy, I want to be able to feel comforable that the union or the state is going to provide me with legal assistance. (MSP-OF-39)

Quite often the union leadership was accused of promoting a service-oriented approach to obtain a broader base of membership support and then failing to honor its agreements. We found that a large number of front-line staff members were unsure of the appropriate or legitimate role of their union and how it served individual members. It appears that the relatively new experience of correctional officers with union representation has stimulated some confusion and unfilled expectations among their rank and file membership.

Control

Control, a dimension focused primarily on internal order and regulation of prisoner conduct, was defined as a concern over the expansion of personal freedoms of prisoners arising from an increase in special privileges, program opportunities or court-mandated rights. These freedoms may be perceived as a threat to the security and custody interests of correctional officers and/or disruptive to institutional routine.

The control scale items were presented as follows:

Control Scale Items

3 With few exceptions, the involvement of outside groups supporting inmate organizations is an invitation to disorder in a high security prison.

4 Prisons would be much easier to operate if prisoners who simply didn't want to cooperate with the system were locked up.

17 Tight security and close supervision are absolutely necessary because too many prisoners take advantage of the opportunities given to them.

19[a] Very few inmates use their special passes or privileges to engage in unauthorized activities.

27[a] In this institution we rarely depend on coercive procedures to keep the peace.

[a]Polarity of scale was reversed during analysis.

Table 3-4 presents the rank-ordered control means and standard deviations for each sample. As shown, there appear to be more similarities than dissimilarities across front-line staff-member responses. The data indicate that guards at all five prisons have strong concern over a need for tight security and close supervision of prisoners, which, in their view, is needed because too many prisoners take advantage of the opportunities given to them (item 17). In addition, most front-line staff who favor strict custodial approaches in dealing with prisoners perceived as being uncooperative with official institutional guards are primarily oriented toward control and restraint in their supervision of maximum-security prisoners. However, guards at each site appeared to place little emphasis on the use of coercive restraints to maintain control over their respective prisoner populations (item 27). The lower emphasis on coercive methods may be related to the growth and popularity among corrections workers of special tactical or security squads made of guards trained in the strategic use of force and special search methods. Commonly known as *S-Squads,* these units typically represent elite officers who tend to be oriented toward law-enforcement roles. Although their operations are usually limited by official policy and procedural guidelines, they have assumed much of the discretion traditionally associated with maintaining institutional security and control. Hence, front-line officers may not hold strong views for a need for personal coercive restraint with the availability of these units.

Thus far, front-line custodial staff at the five state maximum-security prisons tend to be very similar in their control concerns. Differences in both the relative strength (as revealed by the item mean values) and importance (as revealed by the rank order of these values) of control concerns appear to be related more to specific features of each institutional policy concerning prisoner activities than to differences in guard perspectives toward their responsibility for maintaining institutional security. For example, we observed a much greater use of restrictive confinement, that is, segregation, for prisoners viewed as troublemakers at Folsom, OSP, and Stillwater, respectively, than we did at either Rahway or Bedford Hills. Our personal observations during contacts with management and security personnel are consistent with both questionnaire and interview responses at each site. However, guard's concern for control within the prison took a number of different forms. For example, some guards saw the erosion of their control stemming primarily from the articulation, or in some perspectives, the expansion of prisoner's rights by the courts. Others saw their control concerns as being related to increasingly unacceptable prisoner-guard relations and inadequate security procedures and policies. Regardless of the specific cause of these concerns (which were most often linked to current security issues), guards at each prison saw their authority and power for exercising control being weakened by decisions and policies they were expected to enforce, but which overlooked their interests and specialized concerns.

One guard at OSP told us that the role of the correctional officer is being undermined by outside liberals who fail to recognize the inherent danger in lessening institutional control:

Table 3-4
Control Scores Rank Ordered by Item Means

	Folsom			Stillwater			Rahway			OSP			Bedford Hills		
	Item No.	$\overline{X}$	S.D.	Item No.	$\overline{X}$	S.D.	Item No.	$\overline{X}$	S.D.	Item No.	$\overline{X}$	S.D.	Item No.	$\overline{X}$	S.D.
	(17)	4.42	.85	(17)	4.09	1.03	(17)	4.25	1.01	(17)	4.49	.82	(17)	4.15	1.06
	(4)	4.16	.95	(4)	3.76	1.23	(19)	3.68	1.02	(4)	3.93	1.29	(3)	3.59	1.13
	(3)	3.91	1.21	(3)	3.28	1.35	(4)	3.64	1.45	(3)	3.61	1.22	(4)	3.37	1.22
	(19)	3.77	1.07	(19)	3.28	1.16	(3)	3.00	1.09	(19)	3.42	1.22	(19)	3.11	1.17
	(27)	2.86	1.04	(27)	2.72	1.10	(27)	2.74	1.35	(27)	2.50	1.25	(27)	2.85	1.39
Scale mean	3.82	.63		3.42	.68		3.47	.74		3.59	.64		3.36	.58	

Note: $\overline{X}$ = Arithmetic mean.
        S.D. = Standard deviation of the mean.

One of our concerns is losing complete control over the inmates, as far as being able to control them as well as we'd like. Such as in a case of violence, to be able to subdue him or put him where he's supposed to be. I think this is one of our concerns, that inmates could probably do something to you and they would not get anything from it. There's so much of these "bleeding hearts" from the outside that don't understand that some of these men need help. And just because we have them here doesn't mean that we're picking on them. But you can't let them walk all over you. I think this is the main concern of the officers, losing complete control, to being just plain guards, just plain dummies, standing there so that anybody can throw a rock at them if he wants to. And if he can do it good enough, he can get away with it. Of course, we always worry about if they're going to lessen up on the security in the area. In other words, we don't want them to downgrade it, we want to keep it as tight as it is . . . for our own protection. (OSP-OF-40)

However, a lieutenant at Bedford Hills provided a broader perspective. She described the dynamics surrounding the silent abdication of guards' responsibility for control during a period in which prisoners sought legal clarification of the legitimacy of official power:

Well, of course the controls have diminished. The rules have changed through the years quite a bit. I was talking to an officer, she said, "Inmates have so many rights you can't do anything because they've got all their constitutional rights, and the courts have given them these rights." I said, "Now, wait a minute, wait a minute, they've always had rights. And that's what you've failed to realize, it's never been taking rights away from inmates; their rights have never been taken away from them. The few rights that were taken were very specific; they couldn't vote, they couldn't hold a driver's license, and maybe a few others," I said. And you know, the court says an inmate is entitled to every privilege that's not specifically taken from her or him by law. And when inmates began to realize that they weren't dead citizens after all, they began to assert themselves. I think that staff hostility—that might be too strong a word to use, maybe resentment is better—probably stemmed from the fact that they, too, were not aware of the rights that existed. I think they were afraid that it might change, they were really afraid. The inmates saw that the officers were being passive during the period of change and they took advantage of it and they became stronger. The officers didn't really know what they should do and what they shouldn't do because the whole staff was in sort of a chaotic condition at the time. Guidelines weren't coming down the way they should have and everybody just came and worked with what they had. Nobody wanted to upset the inmates, I think that's caused the problem. (BH-OF-32)

Many of the control concerns raised by front-line staff appeared to stem from work-related issues that, in their opinion, had not been adequately addressed by security management. The guards tended to view themselves as being the front-line observer of needed security modifications but were unable to communicate the importance of the problem to prison management. Consequently, many guards directed their frustration back to the source (the prisoners) of the problem rather than seeking a more effective channel of communication.

One guard at Rahway told us that the movement of large numbers of prisoners within the institution presented an undesirable risk to staff. He felt that given the current staff-prisoner ratios, prisoner traffic should be severely limited and prisoners should be locked up whenever they are not engaged in structured activities:

> You can't have too much control on the mass movement because you've got a lot of inmates going back and forth. At any given shift, take the first shift, maybe fifty or fifty-five officers with all those inmates—what are you going to do? The ratio is about ten to one. Sure it's dangerous, you have no control. You can't run tier by tier, the only time we run that procedure is when we have problems in the jail. Other than that, we run a wing at a time. You've got to have mass movement to the mess hall, to the yard, or to the shop area, but as far as other freedoms, I feel this way: a man who is not working, or not eating, or is not in recreation, he should be locked up. (NJ-OF-38)

A Bedford Hills guard expressed feelings of indecisiveness emerging from a perceived fear of prisoner-initiated litigation. She told us that staff and management are reluctant to respond with traditional control techniques to avoid legal implications:

> Well, it has gotten to the point now—I can't say the law has done it, but it seems that the facility is a little bit leery to do certain things. A fear that—a lawsuit is the basic thing now. Everybody's afraid of a lawsuit. So I feel they're bending over backwards to avoid being sued. So in the meantime they lose control, because you're not even using the—well, the basic things you can do—we're kind of sitting on the fence and really not knowing what we can do for the inmate. (BH-OF-27)

While prisoner litigation may have increased during the decade following the Supreme Court decision in *Johnson* v. *Avery*,[62] there is little evidence that suggests that it has directly reduced the correctional officer's ability to pursue legitimate control interests. Most apprehension appears to be related to the fear of being held personally liable, an unlikely decision unless malicious intent was demonstrated. Furthermore, federal courts once again appear to be unwilling to interfere with legitimate state interests, unless gross violations of prisoner's constitutional rights is demonstrated. Hence, guard concern about being the target of litigation is more likely to be related to their relative lack of knowledge and understanding of the legal process.

Safety

Personal safety within the institution, according to many guards, is a highly individualized form of adaptation to prison work. Many front-line staff told us that confidence, alertness, knowledge of the dynamics surrounding the escalation of conflict, and strategic use of authority were among the factors that determined the relative safety of an individual guard. However, most felt that greatest concern for safety came from unpredictable incidents of collective violence and destruction. As will be shown in the following discussion, guard's safety concerns tend to be quite similar. Some differences appeared to be explained by demographic characteristics of the front line or formal policies of prison management toward institutional security.

Safety was defined as a concern about increasing instability and volatility of prison populations and the impact it may have on correctional officers' safety. This concern may be accompanied by a perceived decline in the emphasis and priority given to security and discipline by prison management.

The items of the scale were:

Safety Scale Items

2[a] Legitimate prisoner organizations with clearly stated objectives can make the correctional officer's work much easier.
13 Correctional officers should be considered peace officers and be allowed to carry weapons while off duty, the same as police do.
21 If it weren't for information given by inmate informers, correctional officers would be faced with many more situations involving prisoner-made weapons.
23 Correctional officers are not safe here because certain inmate groups and gangs have gained too much power.
30 More personal safety for correctional officers ultimately depends on the priority given to institutional security.

[a]Polarity of scale reversed during analysis.

Table 3-5 presents the mean and standard deviation values for the safety items. As indicated, few substantial differences were found among samples, although Stillwater guards appeared to place slightly less emphasis on safety than those in other prisons. However, guards at all five prisons saw institutional security as the most important safety concern (item 30). Several slight differences were revealed among guard samples for other safety items. For example, Folsom, Rahway, and Bedford Hills guards placed substantial importance on the belief that they should be authorized to carry firearms during off-duty hours (item 13), suggesting that these guards may extend their concern for personal safety outside the immediate work environment and strongly identify with law enforcement roles and responsibilities.

Table 3-5
Safety Scores Rank Ordered by Item Means

	Folsom			Stillwater			Rahway			OSP			Bedford Hills		
Item No.	$\overline{X}$	S.D.	Item No.	$\overline{X}$	S.D.	Item No.	$\overline{X}$	S.D.	Item No.	$\overline{X}$	S.D.	Item No.	$\overline{X}$	S.D.
(30)	4.53	.70	(30)	4.44	.66	(30)	4.63	.49	(30)	4.64	.67	(30)	4.46	.76
(13)	4.35	.97	(21)	3.13	1.40	(13)	4.39	.92	(21)	4.18	1.01	(13)	4.07	1.25
(21)	3.74	1.12	(23)	2.83	1.29	(21)	3.93	1.02	(2)	2.86	1.29	(21)	3.51	1.18
(23)	3.19	1.11	(13)	2.76	1.78	(23)	3.07	1.18	(13)	2.77	1.66	(2)	2.72	1.14
(2)	3.02	.96	(2)	2.24	.95	(2)	2.64	1.03	(23)	2.01	1.11	(23)	2.54	1.21
Scale mean	3.77	.46		3.08	.65		3.73	.38		3.29	.59		3.46	.51

Note: $\overline{X}$ = Arithmetic mean.
         S.D. = Standard deviation of the mean.

Guards in each sample also expressed concern about prisoner weapons (item 21) and relied on snitches as a safeguard against personal injury. However, field observations and records inspection indicate that the frequency of prisoner attacks on guards has little to do with the formation of these views. Very few cases were recorded of prisoners using weapons against guards at any of the five prisons studied.[63] It appears that guards were more likely to be concerned about weapons being acquired by prisoners who were either unpredictable or who held hostile views toward prison policies.

Several slight differences were also revealed among samples for other safety concerns. For example, one Rahway guard told us that his concern for personal safety arises from widespread availability of special machinery and equipment that prisoners use to manufacture sophisticated weapons. He sees a relationship between guard safety and institutional security procedures:

> Your safety is on the line all the time. When you're in an environment where shops are open to the inmates to the degree you see here, and inmates have access to machinery and other equipment, they can manufacture anything they want. Then your life is on the line all the time. Nobody really talks about it. One of our guys went down to the shops and found a couple of shotguns that were manufactured by the inmates. Last year we found a guy who was making a fifteen-foot ladder who had a shotgun. He even took it across the street and test fired it. There are revolvers being made, and I've seen automatic and semiautomatic weapons. I don't think it's going to be solved unless they change the whole structure of this institution, security-wise. They call it rehabilitation. The shops are open to the inmates and there are not that many security officers down there for supervision. (NJ-OF-10A)

Another guard at OSP informed us that safety concerns are not limited to staff. He expressed a commonly stated fear that a major disturbance may occur while they are on duty and viewed the majority of prisoners as being caught up in situations they would personally choose to avoid:

> There's apprehension not only in staff, but in inmates alike. There's a lot of inmates out there who don't want to see any trouble. But being the inmate population, if anything does come down, they're going to have to be part of it whether they want to or not. Then you have apprehension and it's been voiced many times, "Hey, man, I hope to hell if anything does come down that I ain't on duty." It's a poor way to feel for a man who has picked this type of business as a career, but there is a lot of apprehension, a lot of it. (OSP-OF-38)

A woman guard at Stillwater, recognizing that personal safety can never be assured in prison, told us that safety is primarily related to the manner in which guards treat prisoners:

The safety of an officer here, well, you can never say—You may walk in
the building, you can never say, will I walk out that door? And that's
the point, you never know what will happen. You could fall off one of
the tiers, you could fall down the stairs. And then again, your safety
comes from how you treat people. That has a lot do with it. You can be
an asshole, or whatever you want to be, and I think that has a lot to do
with your safety, walking in here and being an asshole. You don't have
to cater to the inmates, but you can treat them like human beings.
(MSP-OF–41)

In general our findings suggest that most guards viewed personal safety as
being primarily related to greater institutional security and expansion (or re-
definition) of their law-enforcement powers.

Another safety concern, not clearly revealed by questionnaire responses,
was the activities of organized prisoner groups.[64] Stillwater guards, in particular,
were uneasy about the increasingly militant stance taken by Native American
prisoners. Similar views were shared by Folsom and Rahway guards toward
blacks or Hispanics. The least concern regarding prisoner group activity was revealed by Oregon guards. This finding was expected as OSP management had an
official policy restricting all unauthorized prisoner collective activity and, at the
same time, offered the broadest range of opportunities for participation in clubs
or organizations authorized and supervised directly by management. The few
prisoner groups that fell outside of this criteria, such as a informal cliques based
on California residence, were monitered closely and not allowed to evolve a collective voice. The remaining prisons in the study did not pursue as tight a measure in discouraging unity among prisoners.

Communications and Support

This concern ranked fourth among all correctional officer concerns measured
with our instrument. This was a slight surprise as the literature suggested that it
would be among the most important issues raised by line custodial workers in
maximum-security settings.

Just as responses to power items tended to illustrate guard concern about
their diminished role and influence within the organization, responses to communications and support items reveal frustration stemming from a perceived
reduction in support by prison management and a disregard for the front-line
worker's viewpoint on custodial practices within the institution.

The *communications and support* theme was defined as a concern about the
correctional officer's ability to communicate effectively with supervisors and
prison management. These concerns may arise from a feeling of being denied
important information related to specific job duties. Correctional officers may
also view themselves as having little support from supervisory and management
staff on their discretionary judgments.

The list of communications and support scale items follows.

Communications and Support Scale Items

1   Correctional officers can nearly always count on the support of supervisors and management to uphold officers' decisions and judgments.

10 Conditions of work and morale have deteriorated in this institution because management has gradually reduced the importance of the correctional officer's point of view.

14 It seems like the supervisors here pay more attention to what an inmate has to say than to what a line officer says.

25 The only way correctional officers can be sure of what has happened during the last shift is to develop their own intelligence network.

26 Most correctional officers feel supported by management in the administration of prison discipline.

Table 3-6 illustrates the different mean values for communications and support. The data reveal that guards at each site saw their working conditions and morale as having been deteriorated because management has gradually reduced the importance of the line worker's point of view (item 10). While primary communications and support concerns were similar, slight differences were found among samples for secondary concerns. For example, Folsom, Rahway, and Oregon guards pointed to a communications vacuum during shift changes, which required the development of private networks (item 25). However, Bedford Hills and Stillwater guards saw greater concern resulting from more attention being paid to prisoner's interests than to those of the front line (item 14).

Folsom, Rahway, and Oregon officers revealed the highest scale values while Stillwater had the lowest, suggesting that Stillwater custodial staff may have enjoyed greater management support. It should be noted that line custodial workers at any total institution may never be able to experience a desired level of communication within the organization. They may never be able to feel fully supported by their respective supervisors, particularly in situations involving the use of discretionary judgment. Court decisions have markedly changed the nature of the relationship between guards and prisoners as well as between guards and managment. This is particularly evident with the requirements of providing written, accurate information describing prisoner misconduct. When an institutional disciplinary committee finds that a report did not contain sufficient detail to justify the alleged infraction, an individual officer may feel betrayed by management or supervisors who are perceived as favoring prisoners.

Prison management has not been entirely responsive to these organizational problems. In particular, they have not invested in the development of mechanisms for extending their recognition of the importance of the line worker's contribution to organizational goals. Consequently, many guards felt in competition with prisoners in their relationship with management. They, like prisoners,

Table 3-6
Communications and Support Scores Rank Ordered by Item Means

	Folsom			Stillwater			Rahway			OSP			Bedford Hills		
Item No.	$\overline{X}$	S.D.	Item No.	$\overline{X}$	S.D.	Item No.	$\overline{X}$	S.D.	Item No.	$\overline{X}$	S.D.	Item No.	$\overline{X}$	S.D.	
(10)	3.74	1.14	(10)	3.20	1.39	(10)	4.21	.96	(10)	3.63	1.42	(10)	4.18	.99	
(25)	3.54	1.32	(14)	3.19	1.47	(25)	3.57	1.35	(25)	3.29	1.48	(14)	3.54	1.28	
(1)	3.33	1.04	(25)	3.00	1.41	(14)	3.32	1.39	(14)	3.28	1.44	(26)	2.85	1.25	
(26)	3.07	1.22	(1)	2.96	1.20	(1)	2.70	1.17	(1)	3.19	1.21	(1)	2.56	1.15	
(14)	2.71	1.19	(26)	2.56	1.37	(26)	2.32	1.12	(26)	2.83	1.34	(25)	2.48	1.36	
Scale mean	3.28	.39		2.98	.46		3.24	.49		3.25	.52		3.14	.49	

Note: $\overline{X}$ = Arithmetic mean.
S.D. = Standard deviation of the mean.

have realized that the squeaky wheel gets the grease and that collective voices are much louder than any single outcry of dissatisfaction or frustration.

Our interviewees at each site expressed this point vividly. Frequently, guards pointed to a lack of certainty of support for judgments made in the exercise of authority over prisoners. Many of these guards saw their frustration stemming from the ambiguity of their discretionary powers, the inconsistency of responses from various supervisors, and the frequent dismissal of disciplinary charges against prisoners. Some guards pointed to ineffective communications from prison management regarding rule changes and guidelines for prisoner conduct. Others felt that the "new way" of handling disciplinary proceedings tended to undermine their traditional authority and power.

Communications and support concerns varied among guards to a far greater extent than any of the other work-related themes. For example, while some guards saw their supervisors as failing to provide support for their decisions, others viewed supervisory staff as extending oustanding support and leadership. Similarly, some guards viewed themselves as being outside the flow of information essential to their posts, while others felt that the amount of information available to line workers was sufficient. These differences in perspective appeared to be related to their ability to develop positive working relationships with fellow workers and prisoners. Many of the line supervisors interviewed told us that those guards who frequently extended their range of discretionary powers beyond acceptable limits were not likely to receive consistent support. For example, a sergeant at OSP with nine years of line experience told us that lieutenants and captains provided support for sergeant's decisions in nearly all instances except when very poor judgment was used:

> With two exceptions, I've worked with every captain or lieutenant in here at one time or another, and while they may not always agree with me, and we may sit down and have a talk about it later, at the point that it happens, especially if there's inmates standing there that are involved in it, they'll back you. And then they may tell you later that they felt you were wrong, and leave it up to you to get the situation straightened out, which is fine. I think we get very good backing. As long as you use some common sense when you're making the decisions. If you go off half-cocked and you've got a chip on your shoulder, chances are that you're not going to get any backing. (OSP-OF-44)

Another Oregon sergeant, asserting his own position, told us that his practice was to give his front line support for action requiring immediate judgments and that he would accept responsibility of shielding them during an investigation by higher ranking supervisors:

> Well, speaking for myself, any staff member that is working under me, if he makes the decision that, all right, it has to be done this way, it's a situation that has to be handled now, I will back him all the way. We

have run into problems with higher supervisors that say, "That was wrong, you should have handled it that way," and they don't back the man up at all, I've seen this. And I wouldn't do it. I don't believe in it. Like I say, whether it was a right or wrong decision, the man had to make it. I'll back him up and if any heat comes down from the supervisors above me, I'll say, "Okay you blame me. That was that man's decision, and as far as I'm concerned it was a correct decision. So you get me; you don't get him." (OSP-OF-38)

However, approximately one-half of the guards we interviewed at each prison saw their relationship with supervisors quite differently. One Stillwater guard explained that the amount of support given to guards depends on how much risk any given supervisor is willing to take in each situation. He told us that his supervisors consider the impression their support will make on their own image and reputation:

I mean if it won't look bad on them, they will back you up. But if it's gonna look bad on them, maybe a rule that they put out and I have to go enforce it, if it's gonna cause a stink, they won't back you. They are going to protect their name. You talk to anyone, you ask this next guy who's coming in, I think he will tell you the same thing You don't know who will back you or what they want. And we get so many new guys here, that don't even know what's going on. So if you boil it down to these few older guys—if it don't affect their job, they will probably back you up, but they are going to protect their own hide first. (MSP-OF-21)

Guards commonly referred to this as an unwritten standard of C.Y.O.A. or cover you own ass (first). Even guards who worked closely together assumed that individuals had the burden of defending their own action whenever their decisions were reviewed by lower management.

Communications within the organization appeared to be closely linked to the amount of support from supervisors. For example, when institutional rules and policies were seen as being clearly communicated, line supervisors tended to be more supportive. However, ambiguity and inconsistency often fostered a reluctance on behalf of the guards in enforcing rules regulating prisoner conduct:

One thing that is one of the biggest problems, I think, is just communication. For a new officer, it makes it tough because none of the supervisors work alike. You can get away with one thing with one captain or lieutenant or watch commander, and the other one you can't. You've got to learn by mistakes; nobody tells you anything. There is definitely a communications gap in this place. It's a big one, too. A lot of times they just stick you on a post, you never worked it before, you've got to learn all about the post just by working it, nobody is going to tell you what the hell to do. There's no consistency, that't another communication gap, too. (OSP-OF-43)

Another guard told us that line staff cannot respond appropriately to their daily responsibilities:

> That's one thing at this institution here. And the administration knows it; everybody knows it. The line of communication is almost nil. It needs to be looked at very, very seriously. Something has to be done because the convicts know a lot of times before you do what's happening. They're better informed than the staff is. And this is not a good way to run a ship. If your staff is not kept informed properly and your line of communications is not what it should be, then your staff is not going to respond. They can't respond properly. (OSP-OF-38)

Front-line workers' perception of the need for more and better communications tended to cover a very broad range. Among the areas mentioned as needing improvement were more guard input into larger organizational decisions and more effective information sharing for security posts inside the institution.

One sergeant told us that many rule and policy changes were first seen by officers as "orders to be carried out," rather than as problems for which they provided some perspective. He viewed lower management as being the only organizational element with an opportunity to influence policy:

> It's your line of communications. It's shot down the drain. I have never been—in the ten years I've been here—I have never been questioned as to my feelings about any policy, what my thoughts were, what I would think about this policy being changed and so on. The policy goes in where the committees, captains, lieutenants, superintendents, assistant superintendents—they meet and change policy. The next thing you know, the change comes out, you don't know what brought it on, you don't know when the meeting was, you've never been given prior information. All you know is you walk into work, say in one of the big blocks, and the man you relieve says, "All right, this is the new policy." You say, "Where in hell did this come from, when did this come from, when did this change?" And it just keeps your staff in a turmoil; they don't know which way to jump; they don't know what to do. (OSP-OF-38)

Effective communications within the organization are essential in obtaining maximum compliance to stated organizational goals. In addition, worker compliance, beyond blind loyalty, would appear to be best mobilized when front-line workers are involved in many stages of goal setting as well as being directly involved in the evaluation of new policies and security procedures. Most correctional officers understood that their status and role did not afford the privilege of influencing decisions that affected them indirectly. However, they were acutely aware that their closeness to many security problems was consistently overlooked by management. Top management argued that their sergeants and lieutenants served this function and that line staff merely needed to report their observations to the appropriate supervisor. However, many front-line staff felt that supervisors often either ignored the importance of their input or used the information to gain favor with upper management. In either case, correctional officers expressed a growing sense of alienation and isolation.

The structured observations of relations between line workers and their supervisors tend to support many of the expressed contentions of guards. The degree of support shown by line supervisors and the extent of communications within the security hierarchy appeared to be most affected by management's expressed willingness to include line staff in policy decisions. However, management's interest in worker involvement was frequently tempered by their relationship with the correctional officers' union. Where unions pursued adversary relations with management, there was substantially less effort by management to open new channels of communication or opportunities for participation in institutional decisions. However, the absence of union assertiveness did not necessarily improve the flow of communications between guards and management.

Resistance to Change

As indicated in chapter 2, top (executive) prison management has primary responsibility for facilitating organizational change. While the actual setting of various change goals may be shared with central (statewide) management, only prison management has the accuracy of information and familiarity required for construction of an organizational climate supportive of change. This particularly involves obtaining the cooperation of custodial staff, front-line supervisors, and, to a lesser extent, the prisoner community. Failure to obtain support from lower organizational members is a common reason for the failure to effectively mobilize organizational resources to achieve stated change goals. Lower-level staff resistance, in particular, has the potential of not only rendering change initiatives virtually dysfunctional but also increasing the risk of the change producing an unintended result.

Without front-line support, organizational change is nearly impossible. In many instances, custodial staff may attempt to undermine management efforts merely to demonstrate their power or block changes viewed as threatening long-term needs and interests. Hence, it becomes essential to develop some level of cooperative relationship with lower organizational participants before committing resources to a stated change objective. In addition, prison management has the extra burden of obtaining prisoner cooperation and support, unless they view coercive strategies as being consistent with their intended change.

The *resistance to change* theme was defined as a concern resulting from a perceived erosion and decay of the traditional roles and responsibilities of the correctional officer. These concerns may produce staff resistance to change strategies and may signal a personal commitment to maintaining the traditional custodial functions of institutional corrections.

The items in the resistance to change scale were:

Resistance to Change Scale Items

6^a Prison reform should be given a higher priority by our justice system.

7^a Prisoners in this institution should be given much more say in decisions which affect their lives in confinement.

9^a Correctional officers should be working with prisoners' personal growth and development rather than acting exclusively as guards and performing strictly custodial tasks.

15   Given the number of studies indicating that prison rehabilitation programs are a failure, it makes more sense to use prison solely as a means of isolating offenders from society.

22^a Well-staffed alternative and community corrections programs offer more effective approaches to correcting criminal behavior than large institutions.

^{a}Polarity of scale reversed during analysis.

The findings in table 3-7 illustrate the extent to which front-line workers at each of the five maximum-security prisons expressed agreement with organizational change proposals and perspectives that have potential for affecting their role and scope of authority within the prison. Included were change initiatives setting system-level priorities (for example, reform or restraint), and changes altering relationships between guards and prisoners, (for example, extending greater participatory powers to prisoners or pursuing treatment rather than control goals.)

The data indicate that guards uniformly oppose greater prisoner participation in decision making, including decisions that may directly affect their lives in confinement (item 7). Folsom, Stillwater, and Oregon guards had strong views that prisons should be used solely as a means of isolating prisoners from society rather than providing programs, which were seen as being obsolete or ineffective (item 15). Rahway guards saw community corrections as being less effective in correcting criminal behavior than large correctional institutions (item 22), suggesting that they had a strong commitment to institutional corrections. To a slightly lesser degree this view was shared by other samples. The data also indicate that prison guards strongly reject the notion that prison reform should be given a higher priority in the development of a more effective system of justice (item 6). Folsom and Oregon correctional officers revealed the strongest resistance to change, suggesting that they were less likely than other guards to be supportive of change initiatives that may alter their custodial roles.

It appears that resistance to organizational change, in part, stems from guards' attitudes toward crime and its correction. A substantial number of the guards interviewed were strongly supportive of the contemporary trend toward retributive justice. The advocacy of punishment, rather than rehabilitation, was usually equated with a desire for greater restriction of prisoners' rights and privileges. For example, a female guard at Stillwater told us that prisons have become too permissive and that convicted felons have abdicated their claim to

Table 3-7
Resistance to Change Scores Rank Ordered by Item Means

	Folsom			Stillwater			Rahway			OSP			Bedford Hills	
Item No.	$\overline{X}$	S.D.	Item No.	$\overline{X}$	S.D.	Item No.	$\overline{X}$	S.D.	Item No.	$\overline{X}$	S.D.	Item No.	$\overline{X}$	S.D.
(15)	4.16	1.13	(7)	4.17	.99	(7)	4.14	1.08	(7)	4.54	178	(7)	4.33	.80
(7)	4.14	1.10	(15)	3.04	1.37	(22)	3.11	1.29	(15)	3.24	1.40	(22)	2.74	1.15
(9)	3.16	1.54	(22)	2.61	1.19	(9)	2.75	1.35	(9)	2.94	1.48	(15)	2.56	1.29
(22)	3.21	1.23	(6)	2.40	1.15	(15)	2.71	1.21	(22)	2.79	1.30	(9)	2.38	1.37
(6)	2.74	1.51	(9)	2.39	1.16	(6)	2.04	1.11	(6)	2.64	1.34	(6)	2.30	1.36
Scale mean	3.48	.83		2.91	.74		2.95	.68		3.23	.82		2.87	.66

Note:　$\overline{X}$ = Arithmetic mean.
　　　S.D. = Standard deviation of the mean.

civil and constitutional rights. She also saw prisoners as having a higher quality existence during confinement than in their respective communities:

I think the overall opinion of most of the staff members is that the prison environment has changed drastically throughout the years. We've completely done away with the whole idea of punishing the inmate. When he's been sentenced, he has given up his right to freedom, he has to give all of his rights. He is in a controlled environment, and even though we have control, we don't have too much. The inmates have so much power here that I think the inmates have completely forgotten why they were put here. These inmates are better fed than normal people on the outside. They've got excellent hospital care. I believe the inmates, even though they don't want to realize it, they've got it a whole lot better than they did on the outside. And I don't know, we all feel very strongly that we'd like to see that pendulum swing back so that the inmate does realize that he's here for a reason. They're not appreciating all of the things that they do have, in comparison to how little care they did receive many years ago. (MSP-OF-05)

In a similar vein, a Bedford Hills guard viewed a relatively new psychological services program as being too lenient. She told us that women prisoners with adjustment problems were merely being recycled through the program:

They've got this new thing someone thought up called a "satellite," and they have a color TV up there, and they've got the women, you know, they're not locked up. So when the inmates feel they need a rest they go up there, and they keep them there for a couple of days. But there's nothing wrong with them, they just want to get away, so they go, that's fine. But what I resent about it is that, what are you doing for this person? Why are you just letting her come and stay a couple of days, and, okay, so she'll talk to a psychiatrist, big deal, what is the psychiatrist to evolve? She's gonna go back on campus and raise hell again, and they're going to send her back up there. (BH-OF-07)

Change that results in greater benefits and opportunities to prisoners was viewed with caution and disregarded by many guards. However, when these changes also were seen as resulting in a greater burden on guards, they were resented by the vast majority of the front-line custodial staff.

Another Bedford Hills guard who, like many of her fellow workers, was subject to mandatory overtime assignments, told us that she would be much more supportive of prisoner programs if adequate security coverage was provided. In her opinion, too little attention was given to the guards' time and interests:

I'm not against programs, don't misunderstand me by any means. I am against trying to have a program on Saturday morning, a movie on Saturday afternoon, and something else going on Saturday evening. I'm

against having to pay all of us overtime, and make officers work overtime every other night or something so that these women can be kept
busy every day. I cannot see it. They've lost sight of the fact that they
have committed a crime to get here. Now they have great big plans for
the holidays for them, wonderful. But it's also a holiday for the staff.
They will cram everything they possibly can in the holidays to keep the
little darlings happy. I feel that's wrong. I think they should have programs, but if you're going to have the programs, I think they should
have the coverage for them. (BH-OF-45)

There were several guards, particularly those in supervisory positions, who
saw the change as a desirable and inevitable aspect of prison operations. Their
concerns were most frequently centered around the process for determining the
nature of any given change and the procedures for its implementation. To a large
extent, these guards expressed concerns emerging from the relationship between
change and communications within the organization, rather than simple resistance to organizational change initiatives.

The following Rahway guard provided a broad perspective on the dynamics
surrounding officer resistance to change and the problems in implementing
policy changes within the organization:

I think one of the cries of the younger officers is how come the inmates
have so much. But they don't understand, first place, that the inmates
are entitled to it by law, and we don't make the law. We only carry it
out. They don't understand that, and the courts have handed down
verdicts in late years which forced us to change our method of doing business. No question, we have to change, we have to respond. The superintendent is responsible and he issues the order, and we do it. And it's
going to be done and there may be flaws and all that; nothing is perfect,
but basically the drive is to give the inmates what they're entitled to by
law. I think the officers here are just like anybody else in any organization. If there is a change, they just resist the change. You know, "Why
do we have to do it that way?" It takes time to get across a change, but
they get across. And you'll hear guys gripe about things, but they'll do
them. I would say that it would be the same in any large organization
where people don't fully understand the reason for change or how to
implement the change. A lot of times you get change that are policy
changes, and in the process of doing the mechanical part of the change,
conflict arises and has to be ironed out and a different tack tried and
so on. (NJ-OF-39A)

Racism and Sexism

As indicated earlier, the problem of race relations in prisons is intricately linked
to the attitudes and values of front-line custodial staff. While racist attitudes and
conduct of some guards may not be the sole reason for racial conflict, their actions often serve as a triggering mechanism for the release of accumulated feelings

of racial injustice held by many black prisoners. White guards often become a convenient and highly visible symbol of white economic dominance and authority over blacks lacking the footing to gain equality. Hence, the measurement of racial attitudes of prison guards was essential to our attempt to understand the nature and extent of personal and structural racism and racial conflict within the prison.

Equally important, and possibly closely associated, was the attitudes of male guards toward the employment of female officers. At the time of the study, women guards were being considered for a greater number of custodial roles, including assignments in cell blocks, special housing, and other contact posts.[65] In this context, we viewed male guard resistance as an important variable in developing more effective and harmonious relationships among members at all levels of the organizational structure.

Presently, there is little theoretical or empirical work that addresses the relationships between racist and sexist attitudes or values. However, it was our judgment that these two attitudinal dimensions could be conceptualized as being within the same theme; rejecting those who represent different physical characteristics, social values, cultural perspectives, and personal needs. In this regard, the data presented from this correctional officer concern scale dimension are intended to explore the nature and implications of sexual or racial rejection rather than offer a new theoretical model.

The *racism-sexism* theme was defined as a concern stemming from changes in employment patterns that may be perceived as favoring minotiry races, ethnic groups, and women. These concerns may also extend to questions about the performance capabilities of these groups and the possibility that they will be given preferred assignments and promotions based primarily on their physical characteristics.

The items of the racism-sexism scale were:

Racism-Sexism Scale Items

5 The use of female (male) correctional officers in male (female) prisons tends to put more work and responsibility on the male (female) correctional officers and supervisors.[a]

11[b] Nearly all black correctional officers I know perform their duties in a very capable and professional manner.

16 Except for language, Hispanic correctional officers are no more effective than black or white officers in dealing with Hispanic prisoners.

24 Female (male) officers' assignments should be restricted to non-security posts.

28 Male (female) correctional officers and supervisors should be given more consideration than females (males) on job assignments.

[a]Items reflecting gender were adjusted to correspond to male and female prisons.
[b]Polarity of scale was reversed during analysis.

Table 3-8 presents the distribution of racism-sexism item mean values for each of the five correctional officer samples. As indicated, Bedford Hills guards differed substantially from other guard samples in their views toward the use of opposite sex officers. Male guards expressed strong disapproval of female guards, asserting that women officers tend to put more work and responsibility on male officers and supervisors (item 5). Hence, women tended to express much less concern about male guards' employment in female prisons than male guards did regarding the use of women correctional officers in male institutitons. It should be noted that a substantial proportion (11 percent) of the Stillwater sample was women, whereas fewer women were included in other officer samples drawn from male prisons. The Stillwater female guard views, strongly in favor of expanding roles and opportunities of women officers, tended to result in lower values for those items specifically related to sexism concerns.

These data also indicate that Bedford Hills guards strongly disagreed with decisions that gave post and position preference to male officers (item 24 and 28). Many male officers told us that they should have such preferences because they were responsible for their families. This perspective failed to recognize that many (at Bedford Hills, the majority) women officers were head of household and, subsequently, were singularly responsible for family income.

All guard samples tended to view Hispanic officers as no better or worse than black or white officers in their relationships with Hispanic prisoners (item 16). Essentially, their perspective acknowledges the advantage of Spanish-speaking officers in this situation but does not recognize any additional social or cultural advantages. None of the five guard samples revealed strong concern about the performance of black guards, although male guards tended to accept blacks and other racial minorities more readily than they accepted women.

Overall, OSP and Folsom officers reflected the strongest racism-sexism perspectives and concerns. Expectedly, Bedford Hills guards revealed less concern about these issues, which in all likelihood is related to their greater representation of racial and ethnic minorities in addition to being an essentially all-female workforce. These findings were not a surprise, as women guards have only recently been introduced into the security force of male prisons. Previously, women at Stillwater and OSP were limited to special posts such as the switchboard, the visiting room, and the front desk where they provided a good public image to official visitors of the prison. Consequently, these posts tended to be viewed as female posts by the vast majority of male guards who had little or no previous experience in working with women.

The transitional period in which women entered the security force tended to evoke very similar male attitudes and responses. For example, one common pattern we observed was the casual use of the term *girls* when male guards addressed or gave reference to their female colleagues. Many males we interviewed also tended to avoid direct reference to women by the almost constant use of *they* or *them*. Other male responses were more salient and, in our judgment,

Table 3-8
Racism–Sexism Scores Rank Ordered by Item Means

	Folsom			Stillwater			Rahway			OSP			Bedford Hills		
	Item No.	$\overline{X}$	S.D.	Item No.	$\overline{X}$	S.D.	Item No.	$\overline{X}$	S.D.	Item No.	$\overline{X}$	S.D.	Item No.	$\overline{X}$	S.D.
	(5)	4.63	.82	(5)	3.46	1.53	(5)	4.07	1.15	(5)	4.15	1.24	(16)	3.56	1.37
	(16)	3.67	1.11	(24)	3.32	1.62	(16)	3.29	1.24	(24)	3.59	1.56	(5)	2.47	1.20
	(24)	3.05	1.75	(16)	3.15	1.17	(24)	3.25	1.58	(16)	3.58	1.22	(11)	2.30	1.10
	(28)	2.95	1.52	(28)	2.69	1.43	(28)	2.82	1.49	(28)	3.04	1.51	(24)	1.39	.73
	(11)	2.42	1.14	(11)	2.19	.91	(11)	1.75	.84	(11)	2.42	1.23	(28)	1.32	.79
Scale mean		3.33	.83		2.96	.92		3.04	.65		3.35	.78		2.21	.45

Note: $\overline{X}$ = Arithmetic mean.
S.D. = Standard deviation of the mean.

much more consequential. For example, a substantial majority of the male guards interviewed felt that the presence of women guards inside the prison increased the risks of personal injury. Some saw this likelihood as stemming from a need to come to their aid when they would inevitably be sexually assaulted by prisoners. Others saw women as providing a sexual stimulus in an environment becoming increasingly more unstable.

Concerns about women and the performance expectations of blacks and other racial minorities were much more sharply illustrated by the interviewees than by questionnaire responses. The most frequent justification given by male guards was their doubt that women could perform comparably during crisis situations. For example, a sergeant at Stillwater who experienced an early riot, arbitrarily imposed a standard of performance used to measure the capability of women during collective disturbances:

> Women are good in their place. When I got taken hostage, I was sure glad I didn't have to ask for a female to come and help me. They might be smarter than men, and they can do a lot of other things that men can't do, but when it comes to physical stamina like a man has, not too many women have that physical ability to outmaneuver a man. (MSP-OF-31)

Another guard with a long work history at Oregon State Penitentiary expressed a similar concern. He told us that women would be of little assistance if he encountered a group of prisoners intending to inflict personal injury:

> I don't believe a woman should hold down a correctional officer's job that means coming in contact with prisoners. If I'm in trouble out here, particularly in the yard, and I've got four inmates who are going to jump me, and I blow my whistle and here comes some woman running up to me, this isn't a very good help at all, and I don't care whether she's black belt or not. As you well know, if somebody slapped her on the jaw it would probably bust up her face. She doesn't have the strength, number one. Number two, some of these men—and I'm sure I would feel the same way after being here so long, and actually have the urge, they haven't been around women. I think it's just a temptation to put a sexy looking broad working around them. (OSP-OF-40)

Male guards' concern about female counterparts' ability to defend themselves against physical attack or respond during a crisis is somewhat unrealistic and fails to consider the physical strength and ability of many males (some of whom by virtue of age, weight, and lack of exercise have few defensive skills). Women guards' behavior was consistently subjected to critical evaluation, while the responsiveness of men during crisis was assumed without doubt to be exemplary. This view, however, was not held by all male guards. Our observations suggest that guards who have been recently hired by the department, and those with academic as well as on-the-job knowledge, tended to be less concerned with this issue.

A guard at Stillwater expressed an awareness of the probability of either sex being the victim during collective disturbances. Nevertheless, he saw women as the principle target of prisoners' sexual aggression:

Some of the officers are concerned that women officers are making their jobs harder because they have to watch for women as well as the other—you know. If the woman's in the block, they have to worry that she might be taken or something. Personally, I feel that any one of us could be in the same position.

That these women are good looking and pretty, eventually, these inmates are going to find out that they don't have anything to lose by taking one of these women. Because if you are doing life, obviously by taking a woman and raping her, or whatever, in a cell block—what are they going to do, put him in a hole for a year? What does he have to lose by doing it? (MSP-OF-19)

A Rahway guard saw women as "susceptible" to male sexual manipulation, as indicated by the recent resignation of a female guard:

Well, look at it like this—in a prison atmosphere where you bring a female in to work, and we'll say you have 500 inmates, the only contact they've had in the past two years with the outside world is through letters and restricted visits. Now we have a female officer who, at times, is going to be in areas out of sight of fellow officers. I'm going to tell it just like it is, if I were an inmate and a female correctional officer was in my area, as the word goes, I'd rap to her, and if she got weak, well, then we'd do our thing. The guys are going to talk to her, and they've got to be strong enough to keep their distance, or they're going to get burned. I say this because we've had a couple of incidents here. We just recently had one officer resign, she was fooling around with an inmate. And we had another officer, maybe six months ago, who was given an alternative, either face charges or resign, and she resigned. I won't say that she initiated it and I don't think there's a female who would want to be a correctional officer with the thought in mind that, gee, I'm going into the institution, there's going to be lots of them, and I'm going to pick who I want. I don't think they'd come here with that attitude. I think what it is, after they're here awhile, they might see about it, and this is normal. Males and females were born and bred to either like or dislike, and if a girl sees an inmate she likes, she's more susceptible, I believe, to possibly do favors for him. (NJ-OF-11)

The concern for the "sexual safety" of women was not as clearcut as many male officers were willing to admit openly. It is possible that this male concern may evolve from a linking of their attitudes toward women in the free community and their attitudes toward prisoners (and other social deviants). One possible interpretation is that male guards' perception of prisoners' "uncontrollable sexual desire" is in part a reflection of their own sexual appetites (inhibited by organizational and social restraints). The prisoner, in this scheme, become a handy mirror for revealing male guards' sexual fantasies.

The psychological impacts of an environment lacking normal patterns of social and sexual interaction may influence the conduct of guards as well as prisoners. In our view, the behavioral dynamics within the prison would become more like those within the free community once women represent a larger proportion of the security force and more experience has been gained by their presence in male prisons.

The male concern for the safety of women was not shared by a majority of female guards. Many female guards saw the potential of sexual assault as a risk that they accepted in corrections work; therefore, they were much less concerned about sexual abuse by prisoners than their male counterparts. Several of the women told us that fear of sexual violence was a constant threat in prison or in the free community that was long ago accepted as the social reality of womanhood. One female officer at Stillwater identified an attitude among male guards that she viewed as potentially dangerous to all women. She told us that men react inappropriately to the likelihood of sexual abuse and fail to consider the potential of their own victimization:

> There is a mind set of officer here who feel that women don't belong at Stillwater and they are waiting for one of us to get sexually assaulted because then we will all leave. They think that we will make a mass exodus. And what concerns me is that they (the male officers) might in some way, inadvertantly, set it up or allow the situation to escalate; I might not have the back-up I need just because I am a woman officer. It's a test to see what kind of stuff we are made of, not on an individual basis, but as women officers. As far as that goes, fear of sexual assault is all around us. It goes into the territory of walking down the street, too. I would personally rather be in a sexual assault situation that I could live through, than to have my throat cut. The worst thing that could happen to me here would not be a sexual assault, it would be being killed. And that particular mind set of officer doesn't consider that. They see the worst thing that can happen to a woman as some kind of sexual violation. (MSP-OF-28)

It appears that most male guards fail to completely understand the implications of their setups intended to test the performance capability of women. According to our observations, these actions (unsanctioned by prison management) occasionally subjected women to unnecessary security risks and personal humiliation. For example, at one research site, there were official reports that prisoners and guards had attempted to stage a "game" that would have seriously jeopardized the personal safety of a female guard. Nearly all the women interviewed at the field study sites were qualified, intelligent, street-wise guards who approached their work in a professional manner. One of the most oustanding traits observed among female officers was their ability to withstand varying degrees of harassment and intimidation from both prisoners and male guards. Nearly all women stated that their primary source of irritation came from male coworkers, not prisoners. The self-control and discipline we observed among women guards appeared to be an unnecessary and counterproductive utilization of human energy, which is useful only for self-survival in a hostile work environment. Women, under these circumstances, are forced to submit to the male-established norm of "only the strong survive" or accept posts or positions that carry little opportunity for professional advancement.

Women who endure the gauntlet of male performance measures appear to be extremely determined workers with a feminist perspective of the organization. This is not to say that all female guards may be classified as feminist but that many women interviewed expressed an awareness of male socialization and it's impact on the formation of barriers to women within correctional officer ranks. For example, a woman at Oregon told us that she did not expect equal treatment because OSP was a traditional male institution. As a career correctional officer she saw herself as representing a different image of women. She also felt that many men cannot make an easy transition to a heterosexual work environment.

> First of all, you've got to understand that this has been a male institution for a long time, so they're very much into their macho, into their male-identified place here. So I'm very much a threat to that, and all their wives are at home or they're doing something, but it's not quite as important so to speak. So for me to come in and expect to be just on the same level as anybody else and to be treated just the same is an impossibility. We have a very conservative penitentiary as far as attitudes and ideals are concerned, and most of the men around here can't relate to a woman other than as a sex object or in stereotypical terms of some sort, and so it has to take a lot of consciousness raising for them. (OSP-OF-03)

She also describes two reactions by males, possibly assumed by males to be harmless and playful, but which had the potential for undermining her role and authority as a guard:

> There was one sergeant who always used to say, "Hi, babe," when we'd come down. Well, that's not appropriate for this place. On the outside, well, big deal. But down here, the inmates reflect the attitudes of the male officers and for the sergeant to be putting me in that kind of a category, I was no longer an officer, I was a toy. And I have to bring out those kinds of setups that maybe a lot of times they don't even realize, because it just comes off as a natural part of their socialization or whatever.

> Another time when I was out in the yard, I was working on the shake-down line, and on the shakedown line you have four officers lined up. And as inmates come down a line, you pick them out at random to give them a shakedown. And you have the watch commander standing behind, viewing the whole line. Well, this one particular morning when I was shaking down this one inmate, they worked with him closely out with the yard crew or something, and since I had only been out there a

week or two I was getting a lot of razzing and stuff. I was trying to be very professional, not emotional, and I was shaking him down and the officer and the lieutenant started smirking behind my back at the inmate, kind of making fun of me shaking that inmate down, which not only made me look like a fool and as a joke, but also intimidated the inmate because the inmate has a very male-identified ego, and for a woman to be shaking him down. It really humiliated him, along with making me look like my shaking down was just a joke. And that happened a couple of times when I was on the shakedown line until I turned around one day and just walked over to the lieutenant and the officer and pointed out the situation to them. I was really angry so they quit doing it. (OSP-OF-03)

While the questionnaire responses do not clearly identify strong negative attitudes toward blacks and other minorities, our interviews with both white and minority guards suggest that many whites either carry a basic misunderstanding about minorities or harbor feelings of resentment or distrust. As indicated earlier, attitudes toward racial and ethnic minorities do not manifest themselves as openly or as pointedly as attitudes toward women. In part, this may result from the ability of male minority guards to counter hostility on a more equal footing than women. Furthermore, as prisoner populations in those states that reflected a nonwhite majority, black and other racial minority guards may have a consistency among prisoners, if not among fellow workers. This may alter the balance of power and may inhibit blatant acts of racism. The potential for alliances between minority prisoners and guards may also soften many of the perspectives white males hold toward their minority colleagues.

Several distinct negative perspectives were observed among guards. For example, some whites, particularly those who had lengthy careers as correctional officers, doubted the performance ability of blacks, suggesting that they were unable to maintain the level of dependability required for the job. Others indicated that racial and ethnic minorities were more likely to traffic contraband for prisoners. While these views tended to be relatively low-key and were not held by the vast majority of guards, they nevertheless raised a number of important concerns about race relations among prison staff.

Reflecting the viewpoint of a small but salient group of whites who question the performance of blacks, one guard told us that blacks are more vulnerable to the pressures and temptations of easy money and fail to measure up to the standards imposed by line workers:

A lot of the problem is that many of the minority staff come up here and for some reason or other, having nothing to do with the fact that they're a minority, they are either lazy officers, lousy as far as their approach with people, or they're on the take. They're bringing in drugs, or bringing in money for the inmates, or something like that. But there's another side of it, too, because finally they say, "Well, it's practically like I'm being accused of being on the take anyway, so there's no reason why I shouldn't do it." It's a real struggle for a minority officer to make it here, I'm going to say that, too. I want to give you both sides of the picture. (MSP-OF-45)

He also told us that the acquisition of large cars and other material goods make minorities suspect:

I remember several instances of a black officer coming to work here, he'd go through the training academy, he'd take his courses, get to be a CCII [Correctional Counselor II], and next thing you know, he's driving a brand-new big car and all this other stuff. And the next thing you know, the guy gets caught trading off money with an inmate or something. And you wonder, what's been going on, have I been blind? How did he get that new car, he came in here with a junker, and all of a sudden he got rich overnight and he's driving a Cadillac. The same thing has happened with one of the Native American fellows who was here. (MSP-OF-45)

Disgruntlement over the influx of women and racial and ethnic minorities is a counterproductive but predictable reaction in an employment area traditionally dominated by white males. California may well have the edge on most other states in fulfillment of its commitment to affirmative-action principles, but this policy has not been generously accepted by line staff who feel threatened by a recently "advantaged" minority. For example, one guard in California told us that the Department of Correction plays ethnic politics with promotion and career enhancement:

There are too much politics in the Department of Corrections—too liberal. If you don't believe me, examine the turnover rates at CTF-Central over the past five years. Why do so many C.O.s quit? And look who is getting promoted, qualified people, no! Promotion is based on who gets along, by what race you are, black Mexican, and lately, sex. Females working only a few years become lieutenants, sergeants, and associate superintendents. (SO-OF-11)

Affirmative action in corrections is an extremely complex issue and it appears that equitable solutions are difficult to evolve. Employment practices and promotional policies resulting from efforts to correct historical imbalances smacks of short-term injustice to some guards. This perspective was adamantly expressed by one guard whose father also worked as a career correctional officer:

I'm speaking of whites now, we recognize a need for minorities in the prison system and into other areas, and we recognize their right to gainful employment. However, we had to work our way up to it, nobody came in an handed me the silver platter and said, "go to it." I had to earn what I got, but to see females or minorities come in and just be handed it (jobs and opportunities) is very depressing. Not only that, the quality of people they select is an atrocity. I don't know where they get off going down and recruiting at an unemployment office, he's down there because he's lame, he can't hold a job as a dishwasher. So why the hell recruit him to work in a prison? It's ridiculous. (SO-OF-16)

Racial and cultural differences between guards and prisoners and among guards appeared to promote a greater reliance on coercive methods of control. Many white guards, inexperienced in social relationships with blacks from urban communities, lacked the flexibility to develop effective working relationships with their black fellow workers. In addition, their relationships with black prisoners, in many instances, was based on the use of coercive force rather than on human concern and understanding. White officers tended to see black prisoners and social misfits as one and the same because their observation of black culture has been largely tempered by their direct power and control over convicted offenders. As a result, many of the problems in race relations with prisoners, as well as with fellow guards, stems from an ignorance of black culture and social dynamics.

During the study, we learned that minority guards often experienced many of the same tests that females do in working as a guard. Many black and white guards told us that blacks were often asked to intervene in a potentially volatile situation involving black prisoners because "blacks are more effective in dealing with hostile prisoners." It was common for whites to admit their inability to respond effectively to hostile black prisoners. They pointed to a need for more blacks but their motives often departed from support for affirmative action principles:

> We have several black sergeants and a black lieutenant, and simply because they are black and have grown up in a situation that's very familiar to most of the inmates, their ability to calm down a cell hall, especially at a time when there's a black uprising or unrest, is incredible. And I think they're needed very much because they can go in and say a few words like, "Look you motherfuckers, calm that shit down, the shit stops now or we'll bring . . ." And I can say these things, but I have trouble getting the rap down. They don't, so they're very effective people. (MSP-OF-45)

Blacks, who were willing to express their candid observations and impressions about fellow workers, saw the same picture but from a different perspective. We discovered that younger blacks were more willing to share their experiences, while older blacks who had been guards for lengthy periods were somewhat reluctant to draw similar conclusions.

One black officer, interviewed outside of the prison for fear of being identified, was very blunt about his experiences with whites. He told us that he was aware of racial prejudices and different role expectations since the early weeks of his training. He felt that whites were always ready to pit him against hostile black prisoners to test his effectiveness:

From my account, I saw that I was going to be the "token," even when I was in training. The guy I worked for eventually made statements to the effect that he thought that I was too slow, which was brought to my attention by other people. So already, it was happening when I got here. What they used to do was, the guys who were established were trying to set me up in situations, hoping that I would fail, that I would look bad in these situations. It didn't work that way, they didn't have enough yang to set me up, period. Like so and so would be on the phone too long, and they would say, "You go down there and tell him to get off the phone." They expected this guy to blow up, and I'd just go down there and tell him, "Look here, time's up, and you have to go," No problem, see, being black, I really had an edge on them. They (the white officers) are looked at as the "system." I'm looked at as "what the fuck are *you* doing here?" I just told them quite frankly how I felt about the whole thing, "Were I not here, you would have a harder way to go." (MSP-OF-35)

The perspectives and personal experiences of female and black officers interviewed at the four male prisons suggest that the normative system of the predominantly white, male custodial staff is a major obstacle to organizational effectiveness. For example, it is unlikely that guards can substantially increase their effectiveness in dealing with prisoners, particularly blacks and other racial minorities, until they are able to evolve better race relations within their own ranks. The data examined thus far strongly suggests that concerns such as control, power, and officer safety are closely linked to human relations within the organization.

Harassment of female officers in the workplace and giving assignments based on stereotypes, such as sending a black officer to "cool out" rowdy black prisoners, are clearly detrimental to management's interests and may jeopardize institutional security. It is ironic that the strong control concerns expressed by guards can easily be discarded for the personal amusement of those who identify with racist and sexist values. Until racism and sexism are no longer accepted as a part of the prison-workers normative system, we cannot realistically expect a reduction in racial conflict and violence among prisoners.

Table 3-9 presents a summary of the mean values for the six Correctional Officer Occupational Concern Scale dimensions. As shown, few differences were revealed among samples for control, power, and safety concerns, indicating that these common job-related cares were shared by most maximum-security guards. Similar agreement is also revealed for communications and support. However, Stillwater guards expressed considerably less concern about their quality of communications with supervisors or support by management. As indicated earlier, unit management may have played a role in shaping the Stillwater line staffs perception of institutional communications and support.

The greatest differences among officer samples were revealed for resistance to change and racism-sexism. It is possible that many guards shared common concerns about control, power, and safety but maintained personalized concerns about the role of racial minorities or women within the organization. This

Table 3-9
Summary of Correctional Officer Occupational Concern Scale Scores

Scale Dimension	Folsom		Stillwater		Rahway		OSP		Bedford Hills	
	$\overline{X}$	S.D.	$\overline{X}$	S.D.	$\overline{X}$	S.D.	$\overline{X}$	S.D.	$\overline{X}$	S.D.
Power	4.08	.58	4.02	.44	4.08	.35	3.86	.54	4.04	.44
Control	3.82	.63	3.42	.68	3.47	.74	3.59	.64	3.36	.58
Safety	3.77	.46	3.08	.65	3.73	.38	3.29	.59	3.46	.51
Communications and support	3.28	.39	2.98	.46	3.24	.49	3.25	.52	3.14	.49
Resistance to change	3.48	.83	2.91	.74	2.95	.68	3.23	.82	2.87	.66
Racism-Sexism	3.33	.83	2.96	.92	3.04	.65	3.35	.78	2.21	.45

Note: $\overline{X}$ = Arithmetic mean.
       S.D. = Standard deviation of the mean.

specialization of attitudes and values may also be reflected in their perception of the desirability of organizational change, particularly those changes that carry the potential of extending greater privileges or rights to prisoners.

Earlier in this chapter it was stated that at least one questionnaire sample (Rahway) did not appear to be completely representative of its respective security force. Recognizing the relatively small samples obtained at each of the other three male prisons, we made a special effort to obtain a much larger correctional officer sample in Oregon. This coincided with favorable conditions such as a highly cooperative line staff and a supportive management team. Consequently, we obtained data from nearly 98 percent of all OSP security personnel. We anticipated that differences in sample size, as well as in prison policy, security procedures, and demographic characteristics, would be reflected in responses to COOCS items. Obviously, with two or more sets of influences it is extremely difficult to accurately determine the source of measurement differences. However, such a dilemma did not present itself as the data convincingly indicated (with the exception of the issue stemming from the employment of female officers) that correctional officer concerns were very similar regardless of sample size or demographic differences. These findings suggest that the work experiences of prison guards promote common values and attitudes.

As illustrated in chapter 4, the work-related concerns of prison guards are in marked contrast to those held by prisoners, particularly concerns directly related to control and personal safety. It is unlikely that front-line custodians will accept increased prisoner participation in organizational decision making or expanded participatory roles in prison operations unless they receive strong assurances from management that security and control interests are strengthened.

Notes

1. The official title of *correctional officer* appears to have evolved out of deliberate attempts to professionalize the job responsibilities of prison custodial personnel. The most widely recognized literature outlining this effort is found within the various reports to the President's Commission on Law Enforcement and the Administration of Justice. See especially: the *Task Force Report: Corrections* (Washington, D.C.: U.S. Government Printing Office, 1967). However, in spite of these efforts, and nearly two decades of organizational change in corrections, most front-line staff continue to view their jobs, primarily, as guarding. Hence, our use of the term *guard* is intended to characterize the most widely recognized job title and is used interchangably with correctional officer and other descriptive terms used by custodial personnel.

2. J. Jacobs and H. Retsky, "Prison Guard," *Urban Life and Culture* 4(April 1975):10. Also see: Roger Martin, *Pigs and Other Animals* (Arcadia: Myro Publishing House, 1980).

3. In spite of several innovative management strategies, such as unit or team management, line custodial personnel continue to devote nearly all of their time to order maintenance and social-control tasks. For a discussion of formal mechanisms of social control and the manner in which social-control systems produce the behavior they intended to avert, see: Richard Cloward, "Social Control in the Prison," *Theoretical Studies in Social Organization of the Prison* Pamphlet no. 15 (New York: Social Science Research Council, March 1960), pp. 20-48.

4. Donald Cressey, "Contradictory Directives in Complex Organizations: The Case of the Prison," *Prison Within Society,* ed., Lawrence Hazelrigg (Garden City, N.J.: Anchor Books, 1968), pp. 477-496.

5. Ibid., p. 483.

6. Hans Toch, *Men in Crisis: Human Breakdowns in Prison* (Chicago: Aldine Publishing Company, 1975).

7. C. Bartollas and S. Miller, *Correctional Administration: Theory and Practice* (New York: McGraw-Hill Book Company, 1978), p. 169.

8. Robert Johnson, "Ameliorating Prison Stress: Some Helping Roles for Custodial Personnel," *International Journal of Criminology and Penology* 5(August 1977):263-273.

9. Robert Johnson, "Informal Helping Networks in Prison: The Shape of Grassroots Correctional Intervention," *Journal of Criminal Justice* 7(Spring 1979):53-70.

10. Ibid., p. 56.

11. Ibid., p. 56.

12. One of the earlier articles describing these relationships was by L. McCorkle and R. Korn, "Resocialization With Walls," *The Annals* (May 1954). Also see: Gresham Sykes, *The Society of Captives: A Study of a Maximum Security Prison* (Princeton, N.J.: Princeton University Press, 1958).

13. The double risks associated with departures from routine social relations with prisoners may result in most guards electing to follow closely established work-related norms. Expressions of friendliness may invite offers to transport drugs or other contraband goods, while strict rule enforcement may result in prisoners escalating situational conflict.

14. For an example of early descriptions of the social relations among correctional workers, see: R. Esselstyn, "The Social System of Correctional Workers," *Journal of Research in Crime and Delinquency* 12(April 1966): 117-124.

15. More recent views on prison guards include: David Duffee, "The Correctional Officer Subculture and Organizational Change," *Journal of Research in Crime and Delinquency* 2(July 1974):155-172; Jacobs and Retsky, "Prison Guard," pp. 5-29; B. Shamir and A. Drory, "Some Correlates of Prison Guards' Beliefs," *Criminal Justice and Behavior* 8(June 1981):233-249.

16. C. Bartollas, S. Miller, and S. Dinitz, *Juvenile Victimization: The Institutional Paradox* (New York: Halsted Press, 1976).

17. Ibid., pp. 200-205.

18. Ibid., p. 200.

19. David Duffee, "Correctional Officer Subculture," pp. 155-172.

20. David Duffee, *Correctional Management: Change and Control in Correctional Organizations* (Englewood Cliffs, N.J.: Prentice-Hall, 1980), pp. 205-207.

21. Lucien Lombardo, *Guards Imprisoned: Correctional Officers at Work* (New York: Elsevier, 1981), p. 103.

22. Ibid., p. 108.

23. See: B. Margolis, W. Kroes, and R. Quinn, "Job Stress: An Unlisted Occupational Hazard," *Journal of Occupational Medicine,* vol. 16, no. 10 (1974):659-661; G. Kelling and T. Pate, "Job Stress Among Police Officers," HEW prepublication no. 7604228 (Cincinnati: National Institute for Occupational Safety and Health, 1977); and W. Kroes and J. Hurrell, Jr., *Job Stress and the Police Officer: Identifying Stress Reduction Techniques,* HEW publication no. NIOSH 76-187 (Cincinnati: National Institute for Occupational Safety and Health, 1975).

24. F. Cheek and M. Miller, "The Experience of Stress for Correctional Officers." Paper presented at the annual meeting of the American Academy of Criminal Justice Sciences, Cincinnati, Ohio, March 1979.

25. Ibid., p. 23.

26. Ibid., p. 22.

27. See: S. Kronstadt, "The Prison Guards; An Unhappy Lot," *New York Affairs* (Fall 1974):60-77; E. May, "Prison Guards in America: The Inside Story," *Corrections Magazine* 11(December 1976):3-12.

28. Kronstadt, "Prison Guards," pp. 60-77.

29. May, "Prison Guards in America," pp. 3-12.

30. Lombardo, *Guards Imprisoned,* p. 13.

31. Ibid., pp. 113-114.

32. Ibid., p. 114.

33. Leo Carroll, *Hacks, Blacks, and Cons: Race Relations in a Maximum Security Prison* (Lexington, Mass.: Lexington Books, D.C. Heath, (1974).

34. Ibid., p. 53.

35. Ibid., p. 59.

36. John Wynne, Jr., *Prison Employee Unionism: The Impact on Correctional Administration and Programs* (Sacramento, Calif.: The American Justice Institute, 1977).

37. Ben Crouch, *The Keepers: Prison Guards and Contemporary Corrections* (Springfield, Ill.: Charles C. Thomas, 1980), p. 6.

38. Ibid., p. 25.

39. Ibid., pp. 27-33.

40. Ibid., p. 33.

41. For a discussion of the development of this movement in prison settings, see: Carroll, *Hacks, Blacks, and Cons,* pp. 91-113; Jacobs, *Stateville: The Penitentiary in Mass Society* (Chicago: The University of Chicago Press, 1977), pp. 59-62; and John Irwin, *Prisons In Turmoil* (Boston: Little, Brown and Company, 1980), pp. 66-88.

42. See: *Prison Law Monitor* 1 (March 1979); Scott Christianson, "Our Black Prisons," *Crime and Delinquency* 27(July 1981):364-375; Scott Christianson, "Racial Discrimination and Prison Confinement," *Criminal Law Bulletin* (November-December 1980):616-621. As indicated in chapter 1, black incarceration rates exceed white rates by over eight to one. See: Christianson, "Our Black Prisons," p. 365.

43. See: Carroll, *Hacks, Blacks, and Cons,* pp. 197-221; James Jacobs, "Race Relations and the Prisoner Subculture," *Crime and Justice: An Annual Review of Research,* vol. 1, ed. N. Morris and M. Tonry (Chicago: The University of Chicago Press 1979), pp. 19-24.

44. Lombardo, *Guards Imprisoned,* pp. 95-96.

45. Ibid., p. 95.

46. Racial differences among guards, differential responses to prisoners by different racial groups, and the dynamics of institutional racism, were completely ignored in an otherwise outstanding study of prison guards.

47. The use of the term *social distance* has taken several forms in the prison research literature. Most frequent applications include the use of *cooperative relationships* and *corruption of authority.* Lombardo, *Guards Imprisoned,* pp. 60-72, used *sympathetic understanding* to operationally define social distance between Auburn guards and prisoners. For an early empirical approach see: Emory Bogardus, "A Social Distance Scale," *Sociology and Social Research* 17(1933).

48. See: Sykes, *Society of Captives,* pp. 52-53. Also see: Gresham Sykes, "The Corruption of Authority and Rehabilitation," *Social Forces,* 34(March 1956):257-262; and Carroll, *Hacks, Blacks, and Cons,* p. 58.

49. During the pilot studies at Soledad (CTF-Central), we observed a disproportionate number of white prisoners in protective custody. On 30 June 1977, the CTF-Central prisoner population was comprised of 39 percent white, 33 percent black, and 27 percent Chicano prisoners. In contrast, on 30 June 1978, the two protective custody units, PCUI and PCUII, held 60 percent and 51 percent whites.

50. See: Daniel Lockwood, *Prison Sexual Violence* (New York: Elsevier, 1980), pp. 72-73.

51. Among the most recent contributions to this hypothesis are: Irwin, *Prisons in Turmoil,* pp. 181-213; Carroll, *Hacks, Blacks, and Cons,* pp. 214-217; and Jacobs, "Race Relations and the Prisoner Subculture," pp. 19-24.

52. R.M. Montilla and J.G. Fox, *Pilot Study Report: Soledad* (Sacramento, Calif.: The American Justice Institute, 1978). The interview sample was drawn

primarily from CTF-Central officers. Questionnaire responses (first and second pretest) were obtained from CTF-Central and Folsom officers. While the questionnaire data are reported separately, we have used interview responses from California officers interchangeably.

53. While the Rahway (New Jersey) sample tends to have a slightly disproportionate number of guards within the lower age category (under thirty-one years), the questionnaire responses were not statistically different than other samples that were closer to the official staff profile. According to New Jersey central office statistics, we would have expected to include approximately 66 percent whites in our correctional officer sample at Rahway.

54. Although we did not systematically explore this aspect of correctional officer employment, approximately one-half of the newly hired female guards interviewed at Bedford Hills stated that employment in male institutions was considered essential to being promoted to administrative positions within the Department of Correctional Services.

55. See Jacobs, "Race Relations and the Prisoner Subculture," p. 6.

56. See: ibid., p. 5-6; and Carrol, *Hacks, Blacks, and Cons,* pp. 123-129.

57. See: Joan Potter, "Should Women Guards Work in Prisons for Men?," *Corrections Magazine* 6(October 1980):30-38.

58. For a complete discussion regarding the development of this instrument, see the final report: James G. Fox, *The Organizational Context of the Prison* (Washington, D.C.: The National Institute of Justice, 1980).

59. The item-to-scale correlations included in this and all subsequent COOC scales are presented in appendix B.

60. See: Wynne, *Prison Employee Unionism,* pp. 43-79. Also see: Scott Christianson, "Corrections Law Developments—How Unions Affect Prison Administration," *Criminal Law Bulletin* 15(May-June 1979):238-247; and J. Jacobs and N. Crotty, *Guard Unions and the Future of the Prisons,* Institute of Public Employment, Corenell University, Monograph no. 9 (Ithaca: New York State School of Industrial and Labor Relations, 1978).

61. Each interview excerpt was coded according to site: Oregon (OSP), Soledad (SO), Rahway (NJ), Stillwater (MSP), and Bedford Hills (BH); sample: guards (OF), prisoners (IN), and managers (MGR); and interview sequence number to provide an opportunity for further analysis of respective transcripts.

62. 393 U.S. 483 (1969). The U.S. Supreme Court in this case argued that "it is fundamental that access of prisoners to the courts for the purpose of presenting their complaints may not be denied or obstructed."

63. Even Soledad (CTF-Central), which has a turbulent history of violence toward staff (in the course of the two-year period of 1970 to 1971, nine guards and twenty-four prisoners were killed and over 100 assaults were made against staff), had a relatively low rate of violence. See: Montilla and Fox, *Pilot Study Report,* p. 127.

64. The specific features and activities of prisoner organizations are discussed in chapter 5. While many prison guards have volunteered their time to provide security coverage for prisoner organization activities or offered to

sponsor particular organizations, they, nevertheless, view collective prisoner activities as a potential threat to their personal safety.

65. This was most evident at Stillwater (MSP), where a female officer was soon to be assigned to a newly established Adjustment Center within the Protective Custody Unit. It should be noted that since the period of data collection in 1977-1978, several right-to-privacy suits have substantially reduced the opportunity for women guards to fulfill the promotion requirements for supervisory positions because of requirements of experience in contact posts. Recently, the Oregon Supreme Court upheld a lower court injunction on the use of women officers in contact posts. For the rationale provided by security management see the official transcripts for Sterling, Capps, and Hixon v. Cupp, Murphy, and Bagley, no. 108-452. Circuit Court of the State of Oregon for the County of Marion (27 September 1978), pp. 115-116.

Maximum-Security Prisoners: A Community in Conflict

The nature of prison life and the social structure of the prisoner community has captured the interests of writers, scholars, and lay audiences since the early decades of the present century.[1] Hollywood often cast prisoners as folk heroes of the criminal underground. The popular media's portrayal of male prisoners was of hardened, sometimes desperate and violent men who ran prison rackets, routinely killed stoolies, and silently plotted their escape. Women prisoners were typically cast as molls with blind loyalty to their gangster men.

Ironically, many early prison scholars followed suit, using sociological interpretations to add flavor to stereotyped descriptions of life inside large, walled prisons.[2] Consistent with sex-role stereotypes for women, some scholars focused a disproportionate amount of attention on personal relationships among women in confinement.[3] As a result, much of the early sociological literature on male and female prisoners was based on assumptions, perspectives, and information that was often biased and misguided.

Not only did early academic perspectives tend to perpetuate distorted stereotyped roles, but they often ignored or completely overlooked the obvious presence of racial (or ethnic) minorities and the rigid caste system which systematically divided prisoners by race and ethnicity.[4] While there is an abundance of literature on prisoner social organization, there has been little empirical work that has transcended the theoretical perspectives of early sociological studies.

It has only been within the past decade that attempts were made to examine the nature of social relations among racial groups in confinement.[5] A new sociology of the prison is emerging that attempts to describe structural racism and the nature of racial violence and conflict among prisoners. This growing body of knowledge provides a radical departure from conventional theory and practices in the field of corrections. However, as long as prisoner responses to structural violence and racism are seen as a threat to internal order and control, there can be little productive criticism of prison conditions that foster conflict and racial hatred.

Early Theoretical Views

Early prison research tended to characterize the prisoner community as a holistic association of prisoners having a common cultural origin and sharing common concerns.[6] Prisoners were described as being united in their opposition to the official goals of the prison administration and as evolving specialized (functional) social roles associated with collective efforts to ameliorate the deprivations of prison life. In this framework, prisoners were expected to demonstrate their loyalty to the "convict code" and maintain solidarity when confronted with social controls used by prison officials.

Irwin and Cressey later attempted to demonstrate how different street and criminal (subcultural) experiences, commitments, and identities influence the nature and structure of the prisoner social system.[7] Rather than characterizing prisoners as being primarily organized to offset common deprivations, Irwin and Cressey argued that prisoners "import" a range of specialized adaptive strategies from the outside world and seek common alliances within the context of the prisoner community. Consequently, less emphasis was placed on collective opposition, solidarity, universal conformity to a convict code, and common solutions to prison-related deprivations. In their perspective, stratification of the prisoner social system tended to be related to criminal life styles, skills, and social values acquired prior to imprisonment.

These two major theoretical perspectives, commonly referred to as the *deprivation* and *importation* models, generated a substantial amount of academic interest.[8] Most scholars examining the merits of these models frequently attempted to measure the extent to which prisoners had adopted the normative values of the prisoner community. While a wide range of approaches have been used, most studies viewed the acquisition of special prisoner values as being related to assimilation of the prisoner normative system. Hence, the length of time served in confinement and the degree of adoption of prisoner norms, values, and attitudes were frequently used as indicators of prisonization.[9]

Most of these early studies failed to include the dynamics and influences exerted by other participants within the organizational structure of the prison. For example, the contemporary influences of correctional officer unions, changing program goals, and formal prisoner organizations tend to promote specialized influences and conflicts that affect prisoner adaptation. One of the most frequently overlooked influences was the ever-changing nature of the prisoner community. Most contemporary scholars recognize that the prisoner community is constantly changing in response to external and internal pressures and cannot be viewed as a simplistic, static, prison subculture based on cooperative relationships.[10]

Contemporary Views

Among the major factors contributing to recent changes in the social structure of the prisoner community are shifts in demographic characteristics (particularly increases in the proportion of racial and ethnic minorities in confinement) and severe overcrowding of housing and other fixed institutional resources. As maximum-security-prisoner populations continue to grow, internal and organizational conflict may be expected to intensify and become more highly specialized.

Recent prison literature points to racial conflict as being one of the primary factors in changing the nature of the prisoner social system.[11] Racial conflict, according to Irwin,[12] Carroll,[13] Jacobs,[14] and others has tended to reshape most traditional prisoner roles and social relationships within the prisoner community. Most importantly, racial stratification appears to have altered the system of norms and values governing behavior within the prisoner community. The convict code, especially its proscription against snitching and developing informal relationships with custodians, may not be uniformly held by members of different racial groups. Whites, blacks, Hispanics, and Native Americans may have evolved normative systems that are tailored to their respective cultural and social needs and may place substantially different meanings and emphases on prisoner norms regulating adaptive behavior.

The recent activities of prison gangs and gang-related violence in some prison systems also may have contributed to shifts in prisoner values. Among the values held by contemporary prisoners are a greater acceptance of interracial victimization and predatory violence, a willingness to use collective action for the resolution of problems stemming from racial stratification, and closer relations with prison guards (most frequently among whites and racial independents).[15] Prisoner violence, or acceptance of violence as a means of resolving interpersonal conflict, would appear to be one of the more obvious indicators of such a shift of values. Conventional prisoner values, manifested in stable prisoner communities, inhibit violence or at least restrict its use to personal vendettas and defense of reputation or manhood.

Racial conflict and stratification has not only changed prisoner values, but it has also changed traditional prisoner roles, many of which were developed around white prisoner domination of key prison jobs and hustles. While racial segregation has always existed in our nation's prisons and jails, the degree to which race has become a basis for prisoner social organization (and management decision making) is unprecedented in corrections history. There is some indication that maximum-security prisoners have evolved a new standard of conduct to cope with increased prison pressures. During the field studies, prisoners at all four of the male prisons divided the prisoner community into inmates and convicts. Interviewees described those prisoners who "went along with the program" as *inmates,* and those who adhered to the convict code as *convicts.* While this distinction may have lacked objective criteria, it was widely accepted as a distinguishing feature of prisoner behavior.[16]

Irwin, in his most recent work, argues that earlier prisoner roles have been replaced with a new "convict identity," which no longer reflects the values previously held by most members of the prisoner community:

the respected public prison figure—the "convict" or "hog"—stands ready to kill to protect himself, maintains strong loyalties to some small group of other convicts (invariably of his own race) and will rob and attack or at least tolerate his friends robbing and attacking other "weak" independents or his friend's foes. He openly and subbornly opposes the administration even if this results in harsh punishment. Finally, he is extremely assertive of his masculine sexuality even though he may occasionally make use of the prison homosexuals or less often enter into more permanent sexual alliances with a "kid."

> . . . prisoners who embrace versions of this ideal and who live according to it with varying degrees of exactitude dominate the indigenous life of the large violent prisons. They control contraband distribution systems, prison politics, the public areas of the prison and any pan-prison activities, such as demonstrations and prisoner representative organizations. To circulate in this world—the "convict world"—one must act like a "convict" and with few exceptions have some type of affiliation with a powerful racial gang.[17]

Racial conflict emerging from gang activities in some prisons also may make the use of violence appear to be more commonplace and acceptable to outside observers. In some prisons, violent action may become the only available role for young male prisoners seeking status and recognition from their respective racial groups. However, the organizational structure and the underlying motives of racial violence in prison is not limited to conflict-oriented gangs. While gangs and "super gangs," such as the Mexican Mafia, La Nostra Famila, Disciples, El-Rukns, and Vice Lords, may be found within larger prison systems like California and Illinois, most maximum-security prisons have formally organized racial or cultural organizations. These organizations, particularly those that represent the special interests of racial minorities, appear to reflect an increasing level of specialization, which is relatively new to the prison bureaucracy. In response to this trend, the procedures for obtaining official recognition and approval has become greatly structured and legalistic. Many previously informal prisoner groups have been placed under the authority and supervision of middle prison management staff.

The establishment of formal procedures for authorization of prisoner organizational activities suggests that both management and prisoner interests have been influenced by a larger number of restraints and considerations. The prison bureaucracy appears to be evolving into a more highly complex organization and, consequently, many smaller elements of that organizational structure are more likely to have conflicting interests and objectives. Prisoners, having less real power and influence, appear to be seeking formal solutions to their collective needs and interests through the auspices of legitimate organizations such as Jaycees, Lifer Groups, and a number of racial and cultural organizations. While there is some difference in the composition of such prisoner organizations, most tend to be organized around race or status within the prisoner community.

Together with racial stratification, the formalization of prisoner groups and their relations with management has divided the prisoner community into an aggregation of smaller, specialized, competitive social units organized, primarily, according to race or ethnicity.

Very little literature is available that describes the history, structure, or objectives of prisoner organizations and their relationship to the larger prisoner community. While several works have examined the formation of underground groups and gangs[18] and the emergence of prisoner unions,[19] there has been few systematic studies of formal prisoner organizations in maximum-security prisons in spite of their presence of the past several decades.[20]

Women in Confinement

The literature concerning women in prison departs in essential detail from the male prisoner literature. Throughout, it is implied or stated that the problem of women and their patterns of social interaction differ considerably from those of males.[21] The differences between male and female prisoner adaptive styles has been explained as the product of different patterns of socialization, cultural experiences, and sex roles. For example, Giallombardo argues that several aspects of the larger "culture of women" are brought into the female prisoner community and influence women's primary social relationships during imprisonment.[22] Women are also seen as facing a higher level of uncertainty regarding the care and custody of their children and the stability of their parental roles. As a result, the structure of the female prisoner community often reflects needs and concerns commonly associated with conventional female sex roles. However, the increased interest by women in seeking legal solutions and the expansion of nontraditional vocational training programs in women's prisons appears to have influenced the nature of the female prisoner social system.[23]

Like the literature concerning the male prisoner community, the literature on female prisoners suggests that prisoner communities encompass a wide variety of social roles and life-styles.[24] While it has been widely accepted that the prisoner social system may provide "solutions" for many prison-related deprivations, these adaptive styles or mechanisms are closely tied to cultural backgrounds and experiences in the community.

Conceptual and Methodological Framework

Thus far we have argued that the influx of greater numbers of racial minorities into maximum-security prisons may have influenced social relations among members of different racial groups. Also the coercive features of the prison, as well as the dynamics of racial conflict within the prisoner community, may have promoted specialized social roles and adaptations. However, it is important to bear in mind that not all prisoners may have adopted new convict identities in response to changing organizational influences. Irwin's characterization of the "new convict" based primarily on the California prison system is generally consistent with our observations and findings at Soledad (CTF-Central), but it does not necessarily portray the vast majority of prisoners in other maximum-security prisons included in the study.

As the findings will show, there were substantial differences among maximum-security-prison settings and among racial groups for specialized prisoner social values and attitudes. While an increasing number of prisoners have adopted a hardened posture toward their fellow prisoners and prison officials, many prisoners sought traditional or legitimate solutions to problems of personal and social adjustment in prison.

The following sections of this chapter present the assessment of the relative strength and importance of prisoner social values for each of the research sites. These values were measured on a forty-seven-item Prisoner Social Values Scale that was organized into five related dimensions: prisonization, criminalization, radicalism, collective action, and racism-sexism.[25] Several of the prisonization and criminalization items were taken from an earlier study of maximum-security prisoners in Pennsylvania.[26] Many of the radicalism items were drawn from Faine and Bohlander's study of prisoner attitudes toward the justice system.[27] Each of the remaining scales were constructed from items corresponding to themes, concerns, and attitudes expressed during the pilot study at Soledad (CTF-Central) and are intended to reflect contemporary prisoner perspectives.

As indicated in chapter 1, the conceptual framework of this study viewed prisoners as participants of the larger organization and as being involved to some extent in the daily management and routine of the prison. In this perspective, the prison cannot function effectively (except for short-term situations) without the cooperation of all of its members. It is essential that the basic values and concerns of each organizational participant are understood before we can realistically assess their organizational role and potential for increased involvement in organizational decisions.

An organization in which members share common goals and values may be expected to develop and maintain working relationships to a greater extent than within coercive organizations.[28] Prisons, under conventional management, do not operate with these principles in mind. Rather than having common organizational goals, participants more often reveal diversity in interest and conflict in goals. In addition, the coercive features of the prison may actually perpetuate conflict through competition for power and control over limited opportunities and resources.

As prisoners comprise the largest group of participants (but have the least amount of legitimate power), their social values may play a crucial role in shaping organizational dynamics and influencing management policy. For example, a prisoner community that places an emphasis on the use of personal violence to resolve conflict will certainly stimulate management responses that express concern for control and the personal safety of staff.

Table 4-1 presents the sample size and proportion of population sampled at each of the maximum-security prisons. As shown, we obtained a total of 757 completed questionnaires and 125 interviews from prisoners at the five research sites. We intentionally sampled a slightly greater number of female prisoners (Bedford Hills) to give us a larger data base for possible male-female comparisons.

Prisoner-Demographic Characteristics

Complete descriptions of demographic and social background characteristics for each of the prisoner samples are presented in table 4-2. These data indicate that Bedford Hills prisoners had a slightly lower median age (28.2 years) than any of the male samples. These data also reveal that the Soledad (CTF-South) sample was slightly older (31.9 years) than the remaining male prisoner samples. When these data were organized into three major racial categories, ignoring site and sex differences, we found that blacks tended to be slightly younger than either all other racial groups or whites.[29] For example, nearly one-half of all whites and 44 percent of all other minorities (Hispanics, Native Americans, and Orientals), compared to 37 percent of all blacks were over the age of 31 years.

As shown in table 4-2, Rahway and Bedford Hills reflected the highest proportion of racial minority prisoners, 78.6 and 79.3 percent, respectively. While Stillwater and Oregon (OSP) prisoners had very similar racial and ethnic characteristics, they contrasted sharply to all other samples. For example, Stillwater and OSP each had a low proportion of blacks, 18.3 and 10.6 percent, respectively. However, both sites had larger Native American prisoner populations than

Table 4-1
Distribution of Prisoner Samples at Five Research Sites

	Questionnaire Sample	Defined Population[a]	Percentage of Population Sampled[b]	Interview Sample
Soledad (CTF-South)	45	349	12.9	16
Stillwater	186	952	19.5	10
Rahway	146	1,070	13.6	39
Oregon (OSP)	189	1,473	12.8	28
Bedford Hills	191	412	46.4	32
Total	757	4,256	(17.8)	125

[a]The official count on the first day of sampling is the figure used for population.

[b]The percentage given is the percent of the population sampled for questionnaire administration.

Table 4-2
Prisoner Demographic and Social Background Characteristics

	Soledad (CTF-South) (N = 45)		Stillwater (N = 186)		Rahway (N = 146)		OSP (N = 189)		Bedford Hills (N = 191)	
	N	Percent	N	Percent	N	Percent	N	Percent	N	Percent
Age										
25 and younger	5	11.6	34	18.6	35	25.4	46	25.3	64	34.8
26 to 30 years	11	25.6	60	32.8	42	30.4	51	28.0	54	29.3
31 and older	27	62.8	89	48.6	61	44.2	85	46.7	66	35.9
Total	43	100.0	183	100.0	138	100.0	182	100.0	184	100.0
Median age	31.9 years		30.2 years		29.9 years		29.6 years		28.2 years	
Race										
White	18	41.9	137	73.7	31	21.4	156	83.0	39	20.7
Black	13	30.2	34	18.3	96	66.2	20	10.6	111	59.0
Hispanic	11	25.6	5	2.6	14	9.6	2	1.1	36	19.1
Native American	1	2.3	10	5.4	4	2.7	10	5.3	2	1.1
Total	43	100.0	186	100.0	145	99.9[a]	189	100.0	188	99.9[a]
Education										
Less than 12 years	18	40.9	54	29.5	71	50.4	48	25.9	102	55.4
12 or 13 years	21	47.7	101	55.2	55	39.0	95	51.4	64	34.8
14 or 15 years	4	9.1	21	11.5	13	9.2	32	17.3	15	8.2
16 or more years	1	2.3	7	3.8	2	1.4	10	5.4	3	1.5
Total	44	100.0	183	100.0	141	100.0	185	100.0	184	99.9[a]
Median education	11.7 years		11.9 years		11.5 years		12.2 years		11.3 years	
Marital Status										
Single	11	25.0	70	37.8	74	51.0	66	35.1	93	48.7
Married	21	47.7	51	27.6	44	30.3	59	31.4	50	26.2
Split family	12	27.3	64	34.6	27	18.6	63	33.5	48	25.1
Total	44	100.0	185	100.0	145	99.9[a]	188	100.0	191	100.0

	N	%	N	%	N	%	N	%	N	%
Dependent children[b]										
None	9	25.0	71	41.5	46	35.4	90	49.2	56	32.7
1 or 2	20	55.6	65	38.0	64	49.3	78	42.6	77	45.0
3 or more	7	19.4	35	20.5	20	15.3	15	8.1	38	22.2
Total	36	100.0	171	100.0	130	100.0	183	99.9[a]	171	99.9[a]
Current Offense										
Violent personal[c]	12	29.3	92	51.1	75	55.1	109	58.9	68	36.8
Property	15	36.5	50	27.8	27	14.9	58	31.3	57	30.8
Drug	9	22.0	7	3.9	19	14.0	10	5.4	48	25.9
Other	5	12.2	31	17.2	15	11.0	8	4.3	12	6.5
Total	41	100.0	180	100.0	136	100.0	185	99.9[a]	185	100.0
Age at First Arrest										
17 and younger	10	24.4	87	47.3	70	52.6	103	56.3	39	22.0
18 to 25 years	18	43.9	64	34.8	38	28.6	50	27.3	82	46.4
26 and older	13	31.7	32	17.9	25	18.8	30	16.4	56	31.6
Total	41	100.0	183	100.0	133	100.0	183	100.0	177	100.0
Median age	20.3 years		17.8 years		17.0 years		17.0 years		22.0 years	
Prior Felony Convictions										
None	15	38.5	56	30.6	36	27.5	47	26.3	92	52.9
1 or 2	16	41.0	48	26.2	45	34.4	56	31.3	72	41.4
3 to 5	7	17.9	58	31.7	33	25.2	61	34.1	7	4.0
6 or more	1	2.6	21	11.5	17	12.9	15	8.3	3	1.7
Total	39	100.0	183	100.0	131	100.0	179	100.0	174	100.0
Median number of convictions	1.0		1.9		1.9		1.8		.45	

Table 4-2 continued

	Soledad (CTF-South) (N = 45)		Stillwater (N = 186)		Rahway (N = 146)		OSP (N = 189)		Bedford Hills (N = 191)	
	N	Percent	N	Percent	N	Percent	N	Percent	N	Percent
Time to Be Served on Current Sentence(s)										
Less than 6 months	5	11.4	39	21.2	15	10.6	29	15.8	27	14.7
6 to 12 months	10	22.7	37	20.1	27	19.0	26	14.1	40	21.9
13 to 24 months	14	31.8	30	16.3	25	17.6	38	20.7	61	33.3
25 to 48 months	6	13.6	38	20.6	48	33.8	59	32.1	41	22.5
More than 48 months	9	20.5	40	21.8	27	19.0	32	17.3	14	7.6
Total	44	100.0	184	100.0	142	100.0	184	100.0	183	100.0
Time Served (lifetime)										
Less than 1 year	7	16.3	21	11.4	11	7.9	18	9.7	49	28.0
1 to 2 years	3	7.0	28	15.2	9	6.5	20	10.9	59	33.7
3 ot 5 years	12	27.9	33	17.9	34	24.5	52	28.3	40	22.9
6 to 10 years	12	27.9	55	29.9	47	33.8	55	29.9	21	12.0
More than 10 years	9	20.9	47	25.5	38	27.3	39	21.2	6	3.4
Total	43	100.0	184	99.9	139	100.0	184	100.0	175	100.0
Time Remaining on Current Sentence(s)										
Less than 6 months	5	11.9	19	10.5	10	7.3	11	6.0	18	9.9
6 or 12 months	2	4.8	30	16.6	7	5.1	12	6.6	19	10.4
13 to 24 months	11	26.2	31	17.1	15	10.9	26	14.2	41	22.5
25 to 48 months	15	35.7	48	26.5	46	33.6	43	23.5	57	31.3
More than 48 months	9	21.4	53	29.3	59	43.1	91	49.7	47	25.8
Total	42	100.0	181	100.0	137	100.0	183	100.0	182	99.9a
Total of Visits (past 30 days)										
None	19	48.7	65	36.1	37	28.0	81	46.0	41	23.4
1 or 2	16	41.0	50	27.8	30	22.7	53	30.1	63	36.0
3 or more	4	10.3	65	36.1	65	49.3	42	23.9	71	40.6
Total	39	100.0	180	100.0	132	100.0	176	100.0	175	100.0

Most Frequent Visitor										
Spouse only	9	27.3	10	6.4	6	4.6	24	17.1	7	4.0
Spouse and children	6	18.2	20	12.8	21	16.0	12	8.6	9	5.2
Children only	1	3.0	4	2.6	3	2.3	5	3.5	14	8.1
Family members	9	27.3	37	23.7	44	33.6	33	23.6	93	54.1
Friends	8	24.2	85	54.4	57	43.5	66	47.2	49	28.6
Total	33	100.0	156	99.9[a]	131	100.0	140	100.0	172	100.0
Number of Close Friends in Prison										
None	14	35.0	40	22.1	43	30.9	52	27.8	26	14.1
1 to 3	17	42.5	58	32.0	65	46.8	75	40.1	115	62.5
4 or more	9	22.5	83	45.9	31	22.3	62	32.1	43	23.4
Total	40	100.0	181	100.0	139	100.0	189	100.0	184	100.0

[a] Percentages do not total 100.0 due to rounding.
[b] Under 16 years of age.
[c] Includes forcible rape (Bedford Hills not included).

any of the remaining prisons. Compared to their representation within their larger respective state populations, racial minorities were disproportionately represented at each research site. For example, in 1975, blacks comprised only 1.3 percent of the Oregon state population and 1.0 percent of the Minnesota state population.[30] While New York and New Jersey state populations contained a larger proportion of blacks (13.2 and 11.9 percent, respectively), blacks remained disproportionately represented at Rahway and Bedford Hills.

The median educational achievement levels were surprisingly similar for each site, although Rahway, Bedford Hills, and Soledad (CTF-South) prisoners has a higher proportion of prisoner having terminated their education prior to completion of high school. For example, the median education achievement for all sites ranged from 11.3 years (Bedford Hills) to 12.2 years (OSP). However, the data also revealed that over 50 percent of the Bedford Hills and Rahway prisoners and 42 percent of the Soledad prisoners had not completed high school. This finding may be attributed to the greater proportion of blacks and other minorities within these prisoner populations. When race was examined separately, we found that a greater proportion of blacks and other racial minorities had terminated their education prior to the completion of high school requirements. For example, 52 percent of all blacks and 51 percent of all other racial minorities, compared to only 28 percent of all whites, had completed less than twelve years of education.

Several differences were indicated between the samples for current offense. For example, Stillwater, Rahway, and OSP prisoners revealed a greater proportion of crimes against the person (51 percent, 55 percent, and 59 percent, respectively). Conversely, Soledad and Bedford Hills reflected substantially fewer violent personal offenders.[31] The data also revealed that the Bedford Hills and Soledad samples had a greater proportion (26 percent and 22 percent, respectively) of drug offenders. The relatively greater proportion of drug offenders within the Bedford Hills population may be attributed to New York's stringent drug legislation (now repealed) commonly known as the Rockefeller Drug Law.

The data revealed several interesting differences among samples for age at first arrest and number of prior felony convictions. For example, at the time of the first arrests, all male samples had median ages that were substantially lower than those of the female sample, indicating that male prisoners have earlier criminal involvement than women prisoners. The data also indicated that Bedford Hills prisoners had substantially fewer prior felony convictions than any male sample. For example, 43 percent of the Stillwater prisoners, 42 percent of the OSP prisoners, 38 percent of the Rahway prisoners, and 21 percent of the Soledad prisoners had three or more prior felony convictions, compared to only 6 percent of the Bedford Hills prisoners. Furthermore, 53 percent of the Bedford Hills prisoners were first offenders, a finding that seriously challenges the commonly held belief that "only women with heavy criminal involvement are sent to prison.

Of the four male samples, Rahway and OSP prisoners revealed the earliest criminal involvement. The data indicated that 53 percent of the Rahway prisoners and 56 percent of the OSP prisoners were arrested prior to the age of eighteen years. In contrast, only 22 percent of the Bedford Hills prisoners were first arrested before their eighteenth birthdays.

Several interesting findings were revealed when we examined racial differences. For example, whites, rather than blacks or other racial minorities, comprised a slightly greater proportion of those convicted of violent or property crimes. Conversely, blacks and all other racial minorities comprised the greater proportion of all those convicted of drug offenses. Furthermore, a greater proportion of whites than blacks or other racial groups had three or more prior convictions, suggesting that the popular belief that blacks represent the more violent and persistent offenders is open to serious debate. Whites also tended to be arrested at a slightly earlier age than either blacks or other racial minorities. For example, 47 percent of all whites, compared to 42 percent of all blacks and 32 percent of all other minorities, were arrested for the first time before the age of eighteen years.

As expected, differences were revealed between prisoner samples for the total amount of time served in correctional institutions. The data indicated that women had served substantially less time in correctional institutions than men. As shown in table 4-2, 26 percent of the Stillwater prisoners, 27 percent of the Rahway prisoners, and 21 percent of the OSP and Soledad prisoners had been confined ten or more years, compared to only 3.4 percent of the Bedford Hills prisoners. However, when we examined racial differences, we found virtually no difference between the three racial categories for length of time served in correctional institutions.

The data indicated much greater differences between males and female samples than between racial groups for demographic and social background characteristics. These findings are likely to stem from sex roles, differential access to criminal opportunities, and a number of additional influences that are associated with sex differences. With the exception of age at the onset of criminal involvement and number of prior convictions, the differences between racial groups tended to be consistent with demographic data (for example, education) for racial groups within urban communities.

In addition to demographic characteristics, we also found major distinctions between male and female prisoner social systems. The female prisoner social system is organized around experiences, needs, and interests not widely shared or held by male prisoners. Rather than having a social system based on competitive relationships and power, women prisoners often rely on a kinship structure to promote cooperative and supportive relationships.

The data revealed that 27 percent of the Bedford Hills sample had current affiliation with the *kinship system* (pseudofamily structure). Of these, 35 percent assumed the role of mother; 27 percent, the daughter, 6 percent, the father;

13 percent, the son; and the remaining 19 percent, ancillary roles such as aunt or in-laws. Furthermore, approximately one-fourth of the Bedford Hills prisoners were currently involved in a close personal relationship with another prisoner, suggesting that interpersonal relationships (and a social structure that is supportive of interpersonal needs) are more important to women during periods of incarceration than they are to men. According to our observations, the male prisoner social systems generally supported impersonal rather interpersonal relationships, and the primary social units were more likely to be gangs, cliques, or *homies* (hometown members) organized around racial or ethnic identity.

Prisoner Social Values

The following findings are organized by descending rank order to allow the reader to quickly identify those scale items or scale dimensions that statistically reflect the salient values of each prisoner sample. It should be noted that the instrument was developed from themes taken from interviews with male prisoners. Consequently, while the scale items were modified to reflect gender for the Bedford Hills sample, there remains the risk that they do not accurately portray the special values and experiences of women prisoners. However, few studies of prisoner perspectives have compared male and female responses to the same instrument. It is hoped that the findings presented here will at least offer theoretical and empirical support for further comparative research efforts.

Prisonization

Prisonization has traditionally been defined as the process by which prison inmates are assimilated into the normative culture of the prisoner social system. While there are a number of approaches that may be used to measure prisonization, the focus here is on attitudes and values that characterize commitment to the normative structure of the prisoner community. Our interests centered on the degree of adoption rather than on the process by which they were adopted. We recognized that values manifested at any one maximum-security prison change over time, as internal and external influences affect prisoner adaptation to the prison organizational environment. We also anticipated considerable variation among the samples in the relative strength and order of importance of any particular set of social values. In this framework, the task was to assess the extent to which these attitudes and values were adopted by any particular prisoner group at each of the research sites.

We defined *prisonization* as a configuration of specialized social values, attitudes, and normative role expectations differentially held by various elements of a prisoner population which illustrate their acceptance of a value system intended to promote the common interests, needs, and concerns of the prisoner community.

The scale items were as follows:

Prisonization Scale Items

5   When an inmate talks to a guard, he'd (she'd) better talk loud or he's (she's) likely to be seen as a snitch.[a]

10 If someone steals from you in this prison, you are expected to go up the side of his (her) head.

15 You have to go along with the program they set up for you in here if you're going to do easy time.

20 I don't hang with anyone in prison that I can't identify with.

25 Nobody will bother you in this joint as long as you don't mess with their business.

30[b] I don't mind snitches as long as they don't drop a dime on me.

35[b] Today it's no longer important to stand behind your manhood (womanhood) to survive in prison.

40 The staff won't listen to anything you have to say around here.

44 I nearly always have someone watch my back when I move around in this joint because you never know what might jump off.

47 There isn't any convict code anymore; people around here will snitch on anybody about anything.

[a]Items reflecting gender were adjusted to correspond to male and female prisons.
[b]Polarity of scale was reversed during analysis.

Table 4-3 presents the rank-order mean and standard deviation values for each of the ten prisonization scale items. A number of similar responses emerged from these data. For example, prisoners at each site expressed strong rejection of snitches (item 30), one of the most traditional prisoner normative values. However, the maintenance of social distance between prisoners and guards (item 5) was not strongly supported by the prisoner samples. Somewhat surprisingly, prisoners did not view other prisoners' personal communication with guards in a suspicious manner, suggesting that while snitches remain outcasts of the prisoner community, their rejection does not impede the development of informal communications between guards and prisoners. This appeared to be a departure from the observations of earlier studies that identified proscriptions of limited contact between prisoners and custodial personnel.

Prisoners at each site also perceived prisoner solidarity being eroded by flagrant abuses of the convict code (item 47), although Stillwater prisoners tended to be somewhat less concerned about these abuses than all other samples. While these data may illustrate strong support for the convict code, they also suggest that many prisoners question the conduct of their peers. Consequently, a climate of distrust and a lack of solidarity was evident at each prison setting observed. This was most evident between black and white males, who viewed each other as a threat to racial solidarity and as a hinderance to institutional stability.

Table 4-3
Prisonization Scores Rank-Ordered by Item Means

	Soledad			Stillwater			Rahway			OSP			Bedford Hills		
Item No.	$\overline{X}$	S.D.	Item No.	$\overline{X}$	S.D.	Item No.	$\overline{X}$	S.D.	Item No.	$\overline{X}$	S.D.	Item No.	$\overline{X}$	S.D.
30	4.42	1.06	30	4.33	1.16	30	4.49	1.13	30	4.34	1.10	30	4.38	1.23
35	4.18	1.25	35	3.98	1.16	47	4.41	1.12	35	3.89	1.34	47	3.98	1.31
25	3.95	1.28	10	3.65	1.43	35	3.86	1.54	15	3.69	1.38	15	3.95	1.29
47	3.77	1.42	25	3.62	1.32	25	3.71	1.40	20	3.68	1.30	25	3.76	1.47
15	3.46	1.39	15	3.42	1.33	15	3.59	1.45	47	3.68	1.32	20	3.59	1.58
20	3.25	1.61	20	3.29	1.43	40	3.46	1.37	10	3.57	1.43	35	3.53	1.59
10	3.21	1.47	47	3.24	1.31	10	3.41	1.60	40	3.62	1.22	40	3.48	1.33
40	2.85	1.42	40	3.07	1.27	20	3.37	1.60	25	3.59	1.28	5	2.94	1.54
5	2.42	1.24	5	3.00	1.27	5	3.03	1.53	5	3.31	1.40	10	2.86	1.55
44	2.42	1.60	44	2.10	1.27	44	2.26	1.39	44	2.06	1.23	44	2.73	1.31
Mean scale score	3.43	.59		3.37	.50		3.56	.58		3.56	.53		3.50	.53

Note: $\overline{X}$ = Arithmetic mean.
         S.D. = Standard deviation of the mean.

The interviewees suggested that this phenomena stemmed from management's attempts to undermine and discourage large-scale prisoner solidarity. Hence, prisoners tended to perceive more fragmentation, disloyalty, and racial friction that may have actually existed.

An OSP prisoner who had served over three years on his current sentence told us that OSP management unequivocally did not tolerate prisoner solidarity unless it served organizational goals:

> They feel that they have to control us. They feel that the more they harass us and keep us unsettled and wondering, the better control they have on us. And it's a fact, there hasn't been any kind of prisoner unity. Because up front, the warden has said that if you organize against me, I'll throw you in the hole. If he couldn't control it or wouldn't have the ability to manipulate it, he doesn't want it. The only things that they allow in here are things that they can control or manipulate. (OSP-IN-13)

Another Oregon prisoner who had served sentences in other prison systems, provided a similar perspective. He told us that during a recent work strike the prison administration was able to further undermine prisoner unity by the use of coercive tactics during routine investigations:

> They got a bunch of people in there and they told them, "Listen, we know you were a part of this, and if it happens again we'll throw you in the hole, and you'll never get back out again. We've already got five of your buddies in the hole, do you want to follow them?" So they got a lot of people who were on the borderline of this thing who said, "Well, wait a minute, I don't want to go to the end of the block for a year on a trumped-up charge." And the prisoner workers in here aren't going to stand up. You've got a bunch of cowards trying to stand up against a well-armed imposing enemy, and there's no way of beating them. (OSP-IN-17)

The data also revealed that prisoners at all sites except OSP adhered to the do-your-own-time tenet of the inmate code. (item 25). While all prisoner samples were not concerned about having personal protection from predatory or assaultive prisoners (item 44), most prisoners held fairly strong views regarding the perceived requirement for the use of personal violence to settle (or prevent) disputes arising from theft of personal property (item 10). This perspective appeared to carry greater emphasis among Stillwater prisoners, particularly whites who saw blacks as being the primary source of cell burglary. Our interviews with Stillwater prisoners and guards indicated that cell "rip offs" were becoming commonplace and that "rip-off artists" were protected by their respective racial groups.

Marked differences between male and female prisoners were found for attitudes and values related to prison survival, particularly the "manly man" posture of male prisoners, which was uniformily valued by white, black, and other racial minorities. Prisoners at each male prison tended to place substantial emphasis on the projection of their "manhood," a mannerism that was intended to demonstrate their ability to withstand physical and sexual harassment.

One of the most commonly expressed concerns of male prisoners, particularly younger prisoners who lacked street culture experience and who were sometimes seen as being physically attractive, was the constant pressure stemming from sexual aggression (some of which was in the form of disguised horseplay), sexual harassment, and predatory sexual violence. This reaction appeared to be derived from several facets of the macho image, including an emphasis on physical strength,[32] the use of force or violence to resolve (or avoid) interpersonal conflict, and a conscious avoidance of conduct, speech, or social relationships that may imply a tendency toward homosexuality. These forms of prisoner conduct were commonly associated with the way a prisoner carried himself within the prisoner community. Our observations indicated that recognition and status within the prisoner community were gained through strict adherence to these values, whereas social rejection often resulted from backing down or being a punk by not retaliating for economic or sexual victimization.

According to the interviews and observations at Bedford Hills, women prisoners placed less emphasis on the achievement of status or recognition within the prisoner community and were less likely to impose as severe restrictions on the sexual (or emotional) conduct of other members. Rather, they tended to view womanhood as a personalized virtue arising from individual taste in dress, appearance, and social relations. These traits and preferences were portrayed as analogous to self-respect and feminine pride rather than to the male self-concept based on strength or status within the male peer group.

The data in table 4-3 indicate that women prisoners viewed some need to protect their womanhood during imprisonment, but the concepts of manhood and womanhood are not derived from the same set of social values and, therefore, may not provide a useful comparison of male and female prisoners to this item (item 35).

The findings appeared to be highly related to differences between male and female prisoner social systems. The kinship system was the primary unit of female prisoner social organization, although membership was not universal and at times was short-lived. This social system appeared to be primarily structured around dyadic and small-group relationships with an emphasis on helping and sharing of resources.

One of the Bedford Hills interviewees told us that her prison family served as a mechanism for prison adjustment and as a collective for sharing and problem solving:

> The families sort of try to look out for their own. Like, I have a family
> here. ——— , she's kind of old and she has high blood pressure, and a lot

of other things wrong with her, so she's my mother. And if she thinks that I'm getting into something that she doesn't like, then we talk about it. I also have a brother, I have a sister, and we all sit and talk. But all the families aren't the same. Our is sort of calm. —— believes that we shouldn't get charge sheets, and if one of us gets a charge sheet, it's really something because we normally don't have any. So we try to stay on the cool side. When any of us gets a visit, we all cook together. When we go to the commissary, we put our sheets together and we buy food. (BH-IN-17)

The *family* is an extended primary social unit consisting of both maternal and paternal roles with maternal roles being the central figures within the family. The maternal roles consisted of mother, daughter, and sister, with the mother-daughter dyad being the most frequent dyadic pattern within the kinship system. While dyadic marital relationships appeared to evolve within the context of the family, they most frequently were brought into a family unit after a close personal relationship had been established.

Another Bedford Hills interviewee provided an elaborate explanation of the complexity of the mother-daughter relationship. She also told us that mutually satisfying prison family roles overcome racial barriers:

I have a jailhouse daughter, she just left Wednesday, and it hurt me when she left, it hurt me badly. I was glad that she was going home, but it hurt. There's a lot of us with a maternal thing, motherly instincts. So a kid may latch on to me, especially a kid like my jailhouse daughter. She was a very big woman, about 185 pounds and seventeen years old. And I took a liking to her, because everybody thought that she was mean. We got along very well, she would curse a white woman out in a minute, and then she would turn around and say, "Not you, Mom." And I'd say, "Well, it's all right." It's like some people need guidance and special care or special love. And like you have a brother or sister or whatever, you know, things like that. Because some people don't have a family at all, or their family may be down South or whatever, and they can't see them. And if you've got those kinds of instincts, you look for that kind of outlet or friendship. (BH-IN-10)

In addition, she told us how informal relationships between the prisoner community and the official world of the prison staff break down under conventional custody-oriented policies and procedures:

The officers, they don't really like the family at all. But then again, there was a time that the officer called me to get my daughter off of another officer. Because they had her caged up in a corner one time and the officer called me immediately. I said, "What the hell is going on? You'd better get away from her before she knocks you down." And she had just tore out the bubble, just literally punched out the bubble and all the glass shattered. Just completely fell apart. She was strong as an

ox. And I told them, "You all don't understand." Instead of hitting an
officer, she hit the bubble. At that moment, I had more control than
the officers because they were scared of her. Another time, she tore up
her room. The officers were scared to go down there and talk with her.
So they came down to my room and said, "—— is tearing up her
room, will you please go down there and talk to her?" Which is a violation of the rules, you're not allowed to go from corridor to corridor. So
I went down there and I stayed the whole night in her room. They
asked me to break the rules because they were scared of what could
happen. (BH-IN-10)[33]

The paternal figures (father, son, brother, and uncle) operated in ancillary
roles accomodated by the family in exchange for occasional protection from
predatory (unaffiliated) prisoners, stability, and surrogate (stereotypical) male
roles which served to remind family members (and other observers) of the absence of men. Paternal family members generally had substantially less community contact and occupied a role within the family consistent with their
down-and-out social image.

The maternal members (mother, sister, daughter, aunt, and "gran") were the
dominant roles. They made most of the decisions, provided most of the resources, and determined the appropriate course of action during moments of
crisis. Observations indicated that prison families shared their resources with few
conditions except loyalty to the norms established within each family unit. This
pattern of social organization was in sharp contrast to the male prisoner community, which emphasized autonomy, self-sufficiency, and the ability to cope
with one's own problems (except those occurring from racial conflict). Sharing
among male prisoners tended to be limited to short-term or conditional economic assistance (most frequently through the assistance of a prison loan shark),
cooperative efforts among homies or *crime partners*, gifts given to *kids* in exchange for sexual favors, or exchange of goods and services among members of a
racial minority. Male prisoner sharing rarely crossed racial or ethnic boundries,
whereas female prisoners were more likely to share limited resources without
conditions or self-interest across all racial groups. The only exception was that
female Hispanic prisoners tended to form families around the common use of
their language, although families with black, Hispanic, and white members were
common within the prisoner community.

We combined the prisonization scale items into an aggregate score representing the total amount of agreement to the ten items included in the scale.
This was accomplished by recoding the *strongly agree* and *mostly agree* responses and including them into an agreement score ranging from zero to ten.
These values were then categorized into *low agreement* (agreement with less than
three items), *moderate agreement* (agreement with three to six items), and *high
agreement* (agreement with more than six items).

Table 4-4 presents the distribution of aggregated prisonization scores for
four of the five prisoner samples.[34] As shown, each of the male samples revealed

Table 4-4
Distribution of Aggregated Prisonization Scores

	Stillwater		Rahway		OSP		Bedford Hills	
	N	Percent	N	Percent	N	Percent	N	Percent
Low (0-2)	15	8.7	1	.9	12	7.1	22	14.9
Moderate (3-5)	74	43.0	46	40.7	57	33.7	78	52.7
High (6-10)	83	48.3	66	58.9	100	59.2	48	32.4
Total	172	100.0	113	100.0	169	100.0	148	100.0

Note: N = Number of cases.

substantially higher agreement scores than female prisoners. For example, the data indicate that only 32 percent of the Bedford Hills prisoners, compared to 48 percent of the Stillwater prisoners, 59 percent of the Rahway prisoners, and 59 percent of the OSP prisoners, revealed high agreement with the prisonization items. These findings suggest that male prisoners placed a greater amount of importance on those normative values than their female counterparts.

Radicalism

Within the past decade or so prisoners, particularly those of racial minorities, have become increasingly outspoken on issues pertaining to social and distributive justice. A number of factors, including increases in the proportion of racial minorities in confinement, overcrowding, greater prisoner involvement in civil-rights litigation, shifts in public attitudes toward crime and its correction, and the popularization of contemporary political prisoner status may have contributed to the development of radicalized prisoner perspectives.

While the development of radical political attitudes and perspectives among prisoners has been of some concern to corrections administrators, particularly after the early stages of the Muslim movement, the events of George Jackson and the Soledad Brothers, and the tragedy of Attica, there has been comparatively little empirical investigation of the radicalization of prisoners. The process of radicalization has been the least studied aspect of prison adjustment.[35]

We viewed radicalism as the manifestation of values and attitudes rejecting the legitimate political, legal, and economic powers of larger society. Our application of this concept differed somewhat from previous studies in that we intended only to measure the *relative strength* (mean values) and *importance* (mean rank order) of maximum-security-prisoner radical perspectives. In our judgment, radical attitudes and values (if held by a substantial proportion of the prisoner community) may impede the development of cooperative relationships between prisoners and representatives of prison management and may result in the further use of oppositional strategies and collective action.

We defined *radicalism* as a configuration of specialized social values, attitudes, and normative role expectations held by some members of the prisoner community which illustrate their rejection of the predominant political and economic structure.

The radicalism scale items were:

Radicalism Scale Items

2 The solution to the problem of crime is to tear down prisons and rebuild the whole society that forces people into crime.

7 Most inmates are nothing more than the victims of an oppressive society.

12 People who have money or power almost never wind up in prison.

17[a] The police were only doing their job when they arrested me.

22[a] The way I see it, I'm more of a common criminal than I am a political prisoner.

27 The ruling class has no right to imprison the poor when all they've done is try to survive in an unjust system.

32 The laws in this country mainly protect the interests of the rich and the powerful.

37 Most of the real criminals in this society wear business suits to work.

[a]Polarity of scale was reversed during analysis.

Table 4-5 presents the mean and standard deviation values for the radicalism scale items. Nearly all prisoner samples revealed strong views (mean values ranging from 4.47 to 3.88) asserting that the rich and powerful do not experience the same consequences for their criminal acts (items 12, 32). Prisoners also expressed firm viewpoints that the real criminals are found in conventional dress and occupations (item 37). Each of these attitudes appeared to reflect a sense of injustice resulting from disparity in criminal-justice sanctions. They also represented prisoners' perception of the type and extent of criminal involvement by members holding secure positions and roles within the legitimate opportunity system.

One of the Rahway interviewees expressed this point vividly. He saw the criminal-justice system as serving the interests of those with political and economic power. He also told us that judges appear to respect the behavior of white-collar criminals while giving much heavier penalties to less serious street crimes:

> I feel that you have to deal with the whole aspect of the entire criminal-justice system as it relates to this country. And it's my personal opinion

Table 4-5
Radicalism Scores Rank-Orderd by Item Means

	Soledad			Stillwater			Rahway			OSP			Bedford Hills		
	Item No.	$\overline{X}$	S.D.	Item No.	$\overline{X}$	S.D.	Item No.	$\overline{X}$	S.D.	Item No.	$\overline{X}$	S.D.	Item No.	$\overline{X}$	S.D.
	37	4.03	1.25	12	3.98	1.12	32	4.47	1.03	12	4.37	.91	32	4.37	1.17
	32	3.92	1.44	32	3.88	1.09	12	4.20	1.13	32	4.17	1.10	37	4.09	1.24
	12	3.78	1.46	37	3.48	1.32	37	4.00	1.31	37	3.81	1.16	12	4.04	1.44
	27	3.23	1.41	22	2.75	1.47	27	3.69	1.40	27	3.31	1.26	27	3.65	1.32
	22	3.03	1.57	27	2.68	1.21	7	3.36	1.48	22	2.94	1.57	7	3.43	1.51
	7	2.89	1.48	7	2.51	1.36	22	3.25	1.55	7	2.87	1.44	22	2.90	1.58
	17	2.58	1.57	2	2.42	1.33	2	2.87	1.65	2	2.76	1.56	2	2.89	1.62
	2	2.34	1.54	17	2.38	1.50	17	2.51	1.62	17	2.31	1.50	17	2.72	1.63
Mean scale score	3.22	.81		2.99	.72		3.51	.72		3.33	.74		3.54	.73

Note: $\overline{X}$ = Arithmetic mean.
S.D. = Standard deviation of the mean.

that the laws, and the criminal-justice system, the police, their primary
concern is to protect the power structure, the people who control the
money. See, it's the money. Like they talk about us ripping off the taxpayers. The criminal, the guy who sticks up or breaks in a store, snatch-
es a pocketbook, whatever crime, he's seen as ripping off the taxpayers.
Well, they're ripping them off too. They're ripping them off more than
I am. And then white-collar criminals get caught what do they get?
Nothing. Three months, six months, or a fine. I can understand them
not getting that much time because it goes back to the power structure,
O.K.? It seems like judges or whoever they deal with, when they sentence them, they respect the fact that it wasn't petty. They like guys
ripping off big money, so consequently they give them a small amount
of time because the guy was thinking big. But another guy goes in there
and pulls the nickle and dime stuff, and they hide him forever. So it
keeps going back to money. (NJ-IN-25)

Another Rahway prisoner told us that many of those given power and
authority over prisoners' lives commit illegal acts but are not apprehended for
their crimes:

As far as I'm concerned, what I see and what I know is that the entire
criminal-justice system here is just as crooked as we are. They talk
about the guys in prison, there are a lot of criminals out there who
haven't been caught. There are people who work right in these systems
and they're criminally oriented just like we are. They use the system.
Misappropriation of money and everything. Maybe the illiterates can't
see it but the guys who have a little common sense, who've been here
for awhile, they see a lot of things that go on. And it doesn't make you
feel any better. It makes you hostile and gives you a lot of animosity
because you say, look at these people, they've got me in here for fifteen
to thirty years, and they're stealing hundreds of thousands of dollars
and nothing happens to them. It makes the guys bitter and angry, and
most guys want revenge. (NJ-IN-34)

These perspectives were more representative of Rahway prisoners than of
the remaining prisoner samples. Overall, the data indicated that prisoner attitudes toward criminal-justice authority (items 2, 7, 17) were not strongly oppositional, suggesting that most prisoners accept the legitimacy of authority used
in their apprehension, conviction, and incarceration. However, these views were
not uniformily held by members of different racial or ethnic groups. Blacks and,
to a slightly lesser degree, other racial groups, expressed stronger opposition to
the legitimacy of criminal-justice authority. Many black prisoners saw the
criminal-justice system as an extension of white dominance in political power
structures. In addition, blacks frequently pointed to the disproportionate number of black prisoners in controlled housing areas, such as isolation and segregation units.
    While there were only slight differences among the male prisoner samples
for the relative importance of radicalism items, substantial differences were

found for relative strength. For example, Stillwater prisoners revealed somewhat lower radicalism scores than the remaining male prisoner samples. Surprisingly, we found that Bedford Hills prisoners reflected the highest radicalism scores of all prisoner samples. This appeared to be linked to a growing political awareness by women prisoners, possibly influenced by the actions of a number of feminist organizations that have provided support and legal services to Bedford Hills prisoners.

It may be argued that many otherwise conforming members of society also hold radicalized attitudes and values. Our intention was not to suggest that prisoners hold exclusive rights to radical perspectives and a sense of injustice, since many disadvantaged societal members hold similar views. However, prisoners experience a substantially greater amount of coercive control over their lives and are subjected to a greater amount of discretionary judgments than most members of the "free world." Consequently, the nature, object, and extent of radical views are important factors in understanding their response to imprisonment.

Our observations and interviews indicated that many prisoners' radical attitudes were the result of excessive controls exerted by prison management. That is, prisoner hostility and dissatisfaction appeared to be related to the extent of administrative control maintained over the prisoner's life in confinement. The interviewees more frequently expressed anger and hostility toward prison management than toward the larger criminal-justice system.

Table 4-6 presents the aggregated radicalism scores. These data indicate that women prisoners held higher agreement to radicalism items than males. For example, nearly 92 percent of the Bedford Hills prisoners revealed moderate or high agreement, compared to only 67 percent of the Stillwater prisoners, 86 percent of the Rahway prisoners, and 80 percent of the OSP prisoners. As stated earlier, Stillwater prisoners revealed the lowest radicalism scores.

We have viewed radicalism as being only one indicator of prisoner alienation and oppositional values. According to Etzioni, alienated members are involved in the organization, but in an oppositional manner.[36] Hence, radical prisoner attitudes may partially indicate the nature of their relationship within the prison organization. We have also viewed radicalism as a salient but insignificant concern that does not present a major threat unless it is accompanied with a strong commitment to translate radical perspectives into collection action.

Collective Action

The translation of prisoner attitudes into action is of much greater significance to prison management than the attitudes themselves. Prisoner feelings of powerlessness, frustration, or hostility directed toward management have the potential of disrupting the institutional routine and may stimulate the need for even

Table 4-6
Distribution of Aggregated Radicalism Scores

	Stillwater		Rahway		OSP		Bedford Hills	
	N	Percent	N	Percent	N	Percent	N	Percent
Low (0-2)	57	32.8	16	14.0	33	19.5	12	8.2
Moderate (3-5)	97	55.7	58	50.9	94	55.6	78	53.4
High (6-10)	20	11.5	50	35.1	42	24.9	56	38.4
Total	174	100.0	114	100.0	169	100.0	146	100.0

Note: N = Number of cases.

greater coercive control. While individual expressions of hostility (often called *special incidents*) are regular occurrences in maximum-security prisons, collective disturbances are less frequent and present a more serious threat. Collective action of prisoners (such as strikes, work stoppages, demonstrations, and other forms of collective expression) frequently represents the inability (or unwillingness) of prison management to effectively resolve organizational problems, particularly those that directly affect the quality of life for prisoners.

The application of this concept was intended to assess attitudes and values that indicated a willingness to seek collective solutions to organizational problems. We assumed that most collective-action strategies would lie outside the range of acceptable involvement opportunities established by prison management, such as inmate liaison committees, advisory councils, and outside-sponsored organizations. In this regard, the collective-action scale reflects a broad range of strategies (and their underlying concerns) which are based on prisoners' rejection of conventional opportunities for participation in organizational decisions.

We defined *collective action* as a configuration of specialized social values, attitudes, and normative role expectations held by some members of the prisoner community which illustrates their rejection of conventional and/or individualized methods of bringing about fundamental change within the institution.

The items in the scale were as follows:

Collective-Action Scale Items

1[a] Prisoners will always have the same basic conditions even if they have a strong organization to bargain with management.

6 To survive in this prison, it's almost essential to belong to a group or gang.

11 Most prisons would be better places if prisoners were allowed more decision-making power.

16 We will never get anywhere in this prison because the administration is op-
    posed to any kind of inmate organizations.
21 Certain inmate groups make life inside more dangerous.
26[a] In this prison, most correctional officers are in favor of establishing legi-
    timate inmate organizations.
31 Conditions will never change in here because prisoners can't stick together
    for their rights.
36 If it weren't for the dope, money, and power games in here, inmates would
    have a better chance of sticking together.
41 The snitches in here make it dangerous for inmates to organize.
45 The main reason the guards have so much power is that they are well
    organized.

[a]Polarity of scales were reversed during analysis.

Table 4-7 presents the mean and standard deviation values for the collective-
action scale items. Slight differences were revealed for the order of importance
and strength of prisoner responses. For example, Rahway and OSP prisoners,
consistent with their prisonization responses, viewed snitches as a major obstacle
to prisoner organization (item 41). Stillwater and Bedford Hills, with slightly
different concerns, saw prison conditions remaining essentially the same because
prisoners are unable to stick together for their rights (item 31). Soledad prisoners, reflecting a basic concern of nearly all California prisoners, pointed to
certain groups (or gangs) making prison life more dangerous (item 21).

The findings pertaining to racial differences were a slight surprise. While
blacks and other racial minorities may have held more radicalized attitudes and
values, they were no more likely than whites to pursue collection-action strategies intended to gain more power and influence within the prison organization.
That is, few differences were found between the three racial categories for
collective-action scores.

It was also somewhat surprising to observe that those items describing
conditions underlying a need for collective action were scored more highly than
items directly related to prisoner empowerment. This suggests that prisoners are
sensitive to conditions within the prisoner community but accept conditions
imposed on them by prison management, possibly because they have greater
ability to influence those events within their community than within the prison
organization.

The responses to collective-action items were generally consistent with the
observations and interviews at each site. For example, OSP prisoners, particularly, were sensitive to the warden's policy of grooming informers by offering
token rewards for their betrayal. As a result, OSP prisoners saw "rats" as the
major inhibitor of organized opposition to prison management. Similarly,
Bedford Hills prisoners most frequently stated that dissension, rivalry, and

Table 4-7
Collective-Action Scores Rank-Orderd by Item Means

	Soledad			Stillwater			Rahway			OSP			Bedford Hills	
Item No.	$\overline{X}$	S.D.	Item No.	$\overline{X}$	S.D.	Item No.	$\overline{X}$	S.D.	Item No.	$\overline{X}$	S.D.	Item No.	$\overline{X}$	S.D.
21	4.05	1.13	31	3.93	1.07	41	4.26	1.18	41	4.01	1.21	31	4.41	1.09
11	3.44	1.36	11	3.59	1.36	31	4.18	1.42	31	3.93	1.25	11	4.01	1.30
31	3.25	1.43	21	3.57	1.06	26	3.86	1.26	11	3.89	1.30	41	3.79	1.30
41	3.24	1.53	26	3.44	1.05	11	3.60	1.49	26	3.65	1.16	16	3.63	1.39
16	3.21	1.30	36	3.42	1.45	45	3.42	1.49	16	3.62	1.30	26	3.51	1.27
45	3.18	1.62	41	3.34	1.19	16	3.34	1.31	21	3.26	1.40	21	3.45	1.53
26	3.13	1.07	16	3.21	1.18	36	3.33	1.55	45	3.21	1.34	45	3.10	1.51
1	2.89	1.45	45	3.11	1.39	1	2.95	1.54	1	2.97	1.47	36	2.79	1.51
36	2.79	1.60	1	2.99	1.45	21	2.94	1.55	36	2.67	1.42	1	2.70	1.45
6	1.78	1.18	6	1.99	1.03	6	1.62	1.20	6	1.65	1.06	6	1.83	1.32
Mean scale score	3.14	.52		3.26	.54		3.35	.53		3.30	.47		3.31	.52

Note: $\overline{X}$ = Arithmetic mean.
S.D. = Standard deviation of the mean.

contrasting styles of prison adjustment made it nearly impossible to present a collective point of view to prison management.

A black prisoner at Bedford Hills, active in several prisoner organizations, told us that informants have divided the prisoner community:

> You have a group of snitches, they tell every little thing that you're trying to do to make this a better place. They go and tell it before it even happens, so there's nothing that can ever be accomplished in here. It separates us. There are all kinds here, and none of them have ever accomplished anything, because none of them have gone home, none of them are getting a reward for this, all they're getting is a reputation. (BH-IN-05)

She also told us that many prisoners' efforts to make their peers more aware of the underlying conditions of management policies and institutional practices have resulted in being seen as a troublemaker:

> The administration tends to see me as a manipulator, as a political prisoner, militant, and a leader. So when you get a reputation like that, they don't want you to mingle with too many women. They're afraid I'm a threat, because if I were to wake up these women and tell them, "Look this is what you are in here for, this is what this is about, the system is like this," then maybe we could form some unity. And if we did, then we could beat the administration on what they're doing. But we can't form this unity as long as the administration keeps us apart. We'll never accomplish anything. Anytime that you try to fight against this bullshit, you're seen as rebellious, militant, and all that. As long as you're not following them, you're fighting them. That's what it is all about. (BH-IN-05)

This perspective was also supported by several previous members of the Inmate Liaison Committee who were removed from their positions officially because of "disciplinary charges," but from the prisoners' point of view, because they took too strong of a stand against prison management. This type of limitation on prisoner empowerment was also easily observed at OSP where the warden would not permit any form of prisoner representation. Consequently, Oregon prisoners tended to consider alternative forms of opposition.

One OSP prisoner argued for the establishment of a prisoner's union and a prison newspaper to convey prisoner perspectives to the general public. He also told us that prisoner empowerment ultimately lies in their ability to express the reality of imprisonment and prison conditions:

> The things that this institution needs, I think, are more of a form of prisoner's union. They need a newspaper, they need a way to air out their inside turmoil here within the institution to the people out on the streets, so that people can find out the real gist of what's happening in

here. Not what the warden and his associates are putting in the media. And with a prisoner's union you would have some sort of rebuttal, you would have some input into the system. That isn't saying that your demands would have to be met, but they would have to listen to them. That gives prisoners the power to be assertive. I think the power is being able to let people on the streets understand what's happening in here. (OSP-IN-17)

Table 4-8 presents the aggregated collective-action scores for each sample. Only minor differences were found among prisoners for agreement with collective-action items. That is, each prisoner sample tended to reveal substantially high agreement, ranging from 32 percent of the Stillwater prisoners to nearly 46 percent of the Rahway prisoners. These findings suggest that the majority of prisoners support concerns for greater collective roles within the prison organization, especially in sharing decision-making powers with management.

Racism and Sexism

Existing sociological theory of prisoner social organization does not adequately consider the impact of racial and ethnic influences. Nor does it address the underlying attitudes and values held by different participants of the larger prison organization; that is, correctional officers and management.

Many significant changes in the social structure of maximum-security-prisoner communities have resulted from racial violence and conflict. While racial attitudes have historically divided the prisoner community, contemporary racial stratification more closely resembles an arena of multiracial conflict. Attitudes and values underlying racism and sexism are among the most salient but least studied aspects of prison adjustment. An area that has been almost completely ignored is the relationship between structural (or institutional)

Table 4-8
Distribution of Aggregated Collective-Action Scores

	Stillwater		Rahway		OSP		Bedford Hills	
	N	Percent	N	Percent	N	Percent	N	Percent
Low (0-2)	26	15.3	13	11.6	26	15.7	14	9.7
Moderate (3-5)	90	52.9	48	42.9	71	42.8	77	53.5
High (6-10)	54	31.8	51	45.9	69	41.5	53	36.8
Total	170	100.0	112	100.0	166	100.0	144	100.0

Note: N = Number of cases.

racism and prisoner racial conflict. While these concerns are of crucial importance, many lie outside the scope of this book. However, the data presented in this section partially illustrates the extent to which racism and sexism has shaped the attitudes and values of the prisoner community.

Our assessment of prisoner social values related to racial and sexual differences was aimed at understanding the nature and extent of attitudes toward members of different racial groups and determining the degree of support (or rejection) of women correctional officers. While prisoner attitudes and values concerning female guards may have less theoretical appeal, they nevertheless reflect social values currently under examination in larger society. Male prisoners' values and attitudes related to social relationships with women have not been seen as being related to their prison adjustments or postprison experiences.

Our application of these concepts within the context of social values was intended to assess the extent to which racist and sexist attitudes influenced the nature of prisoner social organization. We were equally interested in understanding how prisoner attitudes affected their relationship with female correctional officers and managers.

Racism-sexism was defined as a configuration of specialized values, attitudes, and normative role expectations held by members of the prisoner community which illustrate their rejection of other racial, ethnic, or sex groups (particularly when their own achievements and/or opportunities are seen as being threatened by one or more of these groups).

The items in the scale were:

Racism-Sexism Scale Items

3 A prisoner's race is more important than anything else in determining who hangs together in the joint.

8 When it comes to making money on the street, you have to put your hustle above the feelings of your woman (man).[a]

13 Black correctional officers tend to do more for black inmates than they do for other inmates.

18 It's OK to be friendly toward a prisoner of another race, but in here you stick to your own kind.

23 The use of female (male) guards in male (female) prisons just puts more pressure on the inmates.

28[b] If I know that a dude (woman) is OK, it doesn't matter to me whether he's (she's) black, white, or brown.

33 Female (male) officers are easier to get over on because women (men) are more (less) emotional than men (women).

38 Around here it seems like most decisions are made by the standard, "If you're white, you're right."

42[b] The better jobs for inmates are hardly ever decided by the racial preferences of the administration in this prison.

46   The prisoners here will never be able to get themselves together because of
the racial conflict that exists.

[a]Items reflecting gender were adjusted to correspond to male and female prisons.
[b]Polarity of scale was reversed during analysis.

Table 4-9 presents the mean and standard-deviation values for the racism-sexism
scale items. These data revealed several different patterns of racial attitudes. For
example, Stillwater and Bedford Hills prisoners, two markedly different populations in terms of race and sex, each saw racial conflict as being an impediment to
prisoner solidarity (item 46). Soledad prisoners expressed the strongest concern
about the use of racial bias favoring whites in organizational decisions (item 38),
while Rahway prisoners viewed the prison administration as using racial preferences to award the better jobs (item 42).

One black Rahway prisoner told us that racial conflict among prisoners was
minimal, but pointed instead to the racist attitudes of guards as being the major
source of racial tension:

> Between the inmates, as far as racial discrimination, it's not like it used
> to be. It's always going to be there to some extent because of the men-
> tality of certain people, but both black and white agree that in order to
> get along, in order to survive, they have to get along. You understand,
> fighting in here is only fighting a losing battle because both sides are
> going to lose. So if both sides lose, what is the sense of fighting? We're
> all prisoners, and we're locked up, and we all want to be free. Now the
> racial problems between the inmates and the correctional officers is
> something different. Because you have some people who keep the same
> kind of racial mentality, like blacks should be here and whites should
> be there. And they feel that many of the organizations in here are run
> by blacks. They feel that blacks have too much power. And as long as
> they have that kind of mentality there's always going to be racial con-
> flict. They've got this thing, it's an old fable, "If you're white, you're
> right." And this is the thing with the cops, they feel they're right. The
> inmates are not supposed to be smart. I guess because we came to jail,
> we're dumb, and we have to remain dumb. (NJ-IN-29)

Another black prisoner at Stillwater told us that systematic stereotyping of
blacks on television and the lack of experience with black culture contributes
to racial conflict between prisoners and guards:

> You have a lot of guards in here who never had any communication
> with black people until they started working here. See, when a white
> man from up north never had any communication with a black man in
> his whole life, and he is put in this environment where he's with blacks,
> and all he's read in history all his life is that the black man was a slave
> and he was the master, it's a terrible thing. He sees this all the time on
> TV. A lot of white people are brainwashed, and the black people are

Table 4-9
Racism–Sexism Scores Rank Ordered by Item Means

	Soledad			Stillwater			Rahway			OSP			Bedford Hills		
	Item No.	$\overline{X}$	S.D.	Item No.	$\overline{X}$	S.D.	Item No.	$\overline{X}$	S.D.	Item No.	$\overline{X}$	S.D.	Item No.	$\overline{X}$	S.D.
	38	4.03	1.28	46	3.29	1.98	42	3.24	1.38	23	3.38	1.57	46	3.12	1.53
	3	3.57	1.32	3	3.24	1.36	23	3.02	1.53	13	3.29	1.32	42	3.02	1.44
	46	3.10	1.37	23	3.11	1.43	46	2.76	1.48	3	3.10	1.47	38	2.97	1.54
	42	3.08	1.34	13	3.08	1.17	38	2.74	1.56	18	3.00	1.39	23	2.83	1.62
	18	2.98	1.39	42	3.07	1.21	3	2.73	1.53	42	2.98	1.15	33	2.79	1.43
	23	2.81	1.69	18	2.74	1.38	18	2.26	1.34	38	2.42	1.21	3	2.49	1.47
	13	2.73	1.45	33	2.43	1.06	8	2.24	1.47	33	2.38	1.16	8	2.31	1.50
	8	2.45	1.55	38	2.15	1.25	13	2.07	1.36	46	2.32	1.14	13	2.05	1.32
	33	2.38	1.46	8	2.12	1.42	33	2.02	1.24	8	2.10	1.46	18	1.97	1.34
	28	1.68	1.03	28	1.68	.94	28	1.34	.82	28	1.94	1.27	28	1.24	.73
Mean scale score	2.74	.53		2.69	.57		2.42	.61		2.70	.59		2.48	.59

Note: $\overline{X}$ = Arithmetic mean.
S.D. = Standard deviation of the mean.

brainwashed too. You take Tarzen, he's white, and Jane's white, and they live in the jungle and rule the whole jungle and all of the African tribes. You see Wonder Woman on TV, she's a white woman, so naturally the kids feel a complex about themselves. And all the things we portray on TV, like Starsky and Hutch, where blacks are either dope dealers or snitches. (MSP-IN-04)

Soledad, Stillwater, and OSP prisoners tended to view racial identity as being more important than anything else in determining social relationships within the prisoner community (item 3), a view that was not shared by Rahway and Bedford Hills prisoners. However, all prisoner samples saw trust as being more important than racial or ethnic identity when forming primary relationships. This may seem to be a contradictory finding, but it appeared to be more of a matter of establishing priorities. While prisoners perceived racial self-segregation to be the predominant pattern in the formation of most social relationships, the need for trust within the prisoner (and criminal) subculture generally made race a secondary consideration.

Substantial differences among prisoner samples were found for attitudes toward black correctional officers. For example, OSP prisoners, a predominantly white population, generally viewed black guards as favoring black prisoners (item 13). The only other prisoner sample with a similar perspective was at Stillwater, which also had a high proportion of white prisoners. These findings suggest that the smaller the size of the black prisoner population, the greater the tendency for white prisoners to adopt a blacks-help-blacks attitude. Such a perspective was not shown by Soledad, Rahway, or Bedford Hills prisoners who had substantially more experience with black guards. Furthermore, a sizable number of black prisoners told us that black guards were actually harder on blacks than on other racial or ethnic groups. For example, a black prisoner at Bedford Hills told us that social awareness and cultural familarity did not necessarily result in sensitivity and understanding:

There are some white officers in here who brought along their prejudice and racism, but you're going to find that anywhere. Most of the officers here are black or Puerto Rican. We have a few whites, and I feel like some of the whites are prejudiced, but not that some of the blacks aren't. Some of the Puerto Ricans are prejudiced against their own kind, too. So it's just oppressed people on top of oppressed people. You get poor people from the ghettos and you put them in here to work over poor people from the same ghettos, and you know what happens. I'm poor and you're poor, and somebody gives you a little bit more authority than me, and then you have that type of conflict, like you're superior and I'm inferior. So that's where it comes from, it's not really where I could blame the white officers. That would be easier, but I can't even say it's just them, because I've seen blacks being prejudiced over their own people when it comes time for them to put their foot in our stomach or on our head. You will find that you're own kind will write you up more than a white officer. You'll find those black officers who know where you came from, and they know how you feel, and they will write you up quicker and get nastier and will harass you more than the white officer. (BH-IN-05)

According to observations and interviews with Stillwater and OSP prisoners, Native Americans in confinement face a different form of racial discrimination and prejudice than blacks or Hispanics. Since they comprised only a small proportion of the prisoner population at each prison we studied, their interests were often seen as secondary to the interests of the larger prisoner community. For example, most prison management responses to Native American requests were routinely considered in light of the possible reaction of other racial or ethnic groups. The vast majority of Native American requests were linked to their desire to follow traditional spiritual and cultural practices. However, most of these customs and practices were not clearly understood by the predominantly white front-line custodial staff. Native American prisoner frustration in seeking spiritual and cultural expression frequently established greater solidarity and unity among Native Americans and, in some instances, served to further divide the prisoner community into competitive racial groups.

Where prison management had acted responsibly and appropriately to Native American interests, such as allowing the use of sweet grass, traditional pipes, drums, sweat lodges, and other cultural practices, there has been substantial conflict emerging from line-staff ignorance and intolerance to these Native American customs. Much of the conflict appeared to stem from line custodial staff who were either unfamiliar with the culture or were prejudiced in their views. One of the Native American group leaders at OSP told us that guards' ignorance and prejudice was the most frustrating experience during imprisonment:

Like our spiritual worship, our pipe ceremony, they don't consider it to be a religion. We are told that we have to have a certain amount of supervision and a certain amount of this and that, whereas, any other religious domonination in here, all they do is call it over the microphone, and they go right up to the services. In the first place, the Indian religion, the word *religion* really is a misconception with Indians. It's not a religion, it's a way of life. It's something that is done every day, it's with you all the time. There are many ways of practicing it, not just with the pipe or the sweat lodge or peyote ceremonies, it's something that you live. An Indian believes that we're related to everything, everything alive has meaning, it has something to say. With the sweat lodge, there are Indians who don't sweat, they don't have a sweat lodge. There are some who don't smoke the pipe. In here, we're all in the same position, you can't live you're religion in here the way it's supposed to be lived anyway. If I could, I would go up on the mountain every week and pray. You can't do that in here, so I go to the sweat lodge, or I go to the pipe ceremony, one of the two. The materials that are used are no different than the wine that's used in the Catholic church. In fact, it's less, but we had a hell of a time getting the sweet grass for our ceremony. The sweet grass is used for purification, it's our sacred tobacco. But, before we can get it, it's got to be sent downtown and be analyzed to make sure that it's not a narcotic. This is a sad thing, I think that they ought to worry more about the jug of wine that they keep in the chapel. These people make a mockery of our religion. They refuse to recognize it as a religion. I hear officers all the time, like on Saturday morning when we're going up to the pipe ceremony, "Well, it's time for that Indian shit." Stuff like that, it angers me. It hurts me inside and it makes me feel bad. I don't disrespect their religion, but they don't even recognize ours as a religion. (OSP-IN-12)

Overall, the data indicated that blacks and other racial minorities in prison held greater concern about racism than whites. However, whites expressed substantial concern about racial conflict and racial violence, particularly when they viewed themselves as the target of a "pay back."

The findings pertaining to prisoner attitudes toward women correctional officers crossed racial lines. For example, OSP prisoners, regardless of racial identity, expressed the strongest opposition to women officers. At the time of the data collection in Oregon, there were only six female correctional officers, none of whom were working inside the main areas of the institution as a result of prisoner initiated right-to-privacy litigation.[37]

One Oregon prisoner told us that women officers' "emotional make-up" is different than men's and that he strongly objected to being "skin searched" by women:

I got shook down by one of the women officers out in the yard, going to work. She shook me down just like the men do. I haven't run into a situation of having a woman stand by and watch me take a shower, and I don't know what my on-the-spot reaction would be. My reaction right now is that I don't particularly like the idea. I don't like women in a penitentiary because a woman's emotional make-up is such that—I don't know how to exactly say this—guards, male guards, can be friendly to convicts and he's still a guard. A female guard could be friendly to convicts and suddenly she becomes a woman. A woman's way is to be nice to men, to try to get the vibes from them. And you put her in a prison and she's going to be dying to get those vibes. If it comes to the point where a women wanted to skin search me, I'm afraid that I'd have to refuse. Now a man is bad enough, but I'm not going to have a woman look up my ass, that's all there is to it. (OSP-IN-09)

With the exception of OSP, prisoners at all of the research sites expressed mixed feelings about women correctional officers.[38] Some, perhaps a small majority, saw women officers as having the potential to normalize the prison environment and as providing a new source of interpersonal contact. Others, divided into a numerous perspectives, saw women officers as a new (or different) threat to established routines of the institution and proven relationships within the prisoner community. For many of these prisoners, women were a new element of uncertainty in a desire for a stable and structured environment. These views were more frequently expressed by prisoners who had already spent a considerable period of time in correctional institutions.

There was a tendency for some male prisoners to emphasize situations highly unlikely to occur. For example, the common scenario was a collective disturbance in which women officers were taken hostage and sexually assaulted. It is interesting to note that this was also a commonly expressed concern of male officers, suggesting that male prisoners' perspectives may be influenced, in part, by male officers. A small number of male prisoners also expressed concern for a loss of their personal privacy, which was assumed to be respected by male officers. These prisoners frequently pointed to the possibility of being directly supervised during their use of the shower or toilet facilities. Our observations indicated that female officers were rarely given assignments that would have made this situation possible. The only possible exception was at Soledad, where officers apparently are assigned to posts with consideration given only to experience and seniority.

Female prisoners expressed similar concerns about the presence of male correctional officers at Bedford Hills, but the proportion of women opposed was substantially lower than the proportion of male prisoners opposed to female officers. Several women raised the issue of personal privacy, an issue that was also being litigated during the period of data collection at Bedford Hills. The issue arose from allegations of male officers intentionally viewing women in various states of undress during showering or during the evening hours while prisoners were asleep. A court injunction ordered the removal of male officers from housing areas until the court completed an adequate review of the complaints.[39]

A small number of women raised a much different concern. Namely, they felt that male officers represented a greater amount of force to be used at the discretion of management or supervisors during minor skirmishes involving prisoners and line officers. Given the increased use of physical violence against line staff during the past four years and the corresponding increase in the use of force by staff, this concern appeared to have substantial merit. The interviewees told us that staff tolerance to prisoner complaints was decreasing and the threat to "call the men" was frequently used in an attempt to stop situational conflict or verbal harassment. While many prisoner complaints about unnecessary restriction on their freedom of movement or about the pace at which program staff responded to their requests appeared to be legitimate, these issues typically remained outside of the discretionary powers of custodial personnel. In these instances, prison guards (whose role and authority were limited to control) were perceived by female prisoners as being unresponsive to their personal needs.

These conflicting perceptions evolved from past practices where line workers frequently resolved minor grievances at their own discretion in an attempt to reduce friction and play helping roles. Consequently, prisoners began to anticipate line-staff intervention in minor problems and demanded a level of responsiveness that was generally unavailable to many situations. As the level of dispute intensified, female guards developed an increased dependency on the intervention of male officers to control situations of escalating conflict and hostility. The increased reliance on male officers may have encouraged as much conflict as it was intended to resolve, particularly because conflict resolution was being made at higher rather than lower staff levels.

One Bedford Hills prisoner told us that a judgment error by the floor officer concerning the number of women in a shower stall triggered an escalated conflict that resulted in her serious injury:

> It was a holiday, we didn't have our regular officers on the floor, we had the evening officers and there was no lieutenant on duty. So when I got up in the morning and went out, they were rushing us to get dressed and get out of the cells. Women were bitching right and left, saying, "It's a holiday, leave the doors open." There were a whole bunch of people in there, some were showering, others were waiting and goofing, typical female bullshit. So anyway, the officer walked into the shower and says, "Who's in the shower?" So the curtains were drawn to the side and we stepped out. There was no one in there except the three individuals in the three stalls. So this upset the women and they started cursing her. When we finished with our showers I walked down the corridor to put my stuff away and when I reached my room, the officer says, "Step inside, I'm locking you up." So I said, "For what? I want to know what you're locking me up for, and on who's orders." She says, "Well, I'm writing you up for having a woman in the shower with you." I tried to talk to her and she says, "Well, I suspect !" So I got into this type of bickering with her, because I feel if a person is wrong, I'll argue and argue and argue. So I kept on and this went on from 10:30 to 2:30 that afternoon. I was not allowed to see the sergeant or the lieutenant. So this thing went on and I wasn't allowed to go to lunch, I was confined to the floor. At this point she got on the phone and talked to someone in the main building and she said, "Yes, the lieutenant is coming." So I went into the rec room and sat down. All of a sudden, I saw about seven officers. Now I'm starting to get leary because it's not the first time it had happened. So I saw the lieutenant, and she said, "You're going to seg." And she turned around and said, "Ladies, lock in." So I told them, "It's cool." And I said, "Why don't you sit down and talk to me?" So as I'm sitting, talking to her, there are twelve officers of the search team, all mostly men. The place was swarming with cops with night sticks. They're coming toward me, right? So, I'm backing off. I haven't hurt anybody. So I said, "OK, I'll go to seg." Then one of the officers came up and hit me with his night stick on my wrist, and I double over. So when I doubled over, I came back and started lashing out and everything. Because it was like me against the

world. I got kicked in the head, they stepped on my neck. They scratched up my face. They ripped my clothes off my back. They twisted my arm back and snapped it. My legs were twisted. And somebody kicked me under the armpit. I thought I was gone. I couldn't believe it. They took me to seg. They didn't want me to see a doctor. I was in pain and I was starting to swell up. The sergeant came in and I'm crying and I showed her my arm which was starting to swell. And she went back and called the nurse. The nurse came and said that I had to go out on emergency. So they dressed me and took me out to the hospital. I had a hairline fracture, and torn ligaments and stuff like that. (BH-IN-03)

Female prisoners' concern regarding the use of male guards to control "disturbances" should be viewed as more substantive than their male counterparts' fear that women correctional officers may violate their personal privacy rights. Certainly, both male and female prisoners' concerns were legitimate, but the consequences were potentially disproportionately harsh for women. In addition, women prisoners faced both the potential for privacy invasion by male guards and the impact of superior strength during confrontations with male custodial personnel. The double-victim role frequently reserved for women was not shared by most male prisoners. That is, women guards, realistically, cannot both intrude into the realm of male prisoner's personal privacy and represent a new threat of physical force.

Table 4-10 presents the aggregated racism-sexism scores. As indicated, Bedford Hills prisoners revealed slightly higher agreement, although Stillwater and OSP prisoners (with predominently white prisoner populations) revealed similar scores. For example, nearly 56 percent of the Stillwater and OSP prisoners revealed high or moderate agreement, compared to only 46 percent of the Rahway prisoners. In contrast, over 69 percent of the Bedford Hills prisoners revealed high or moderate agreement.

Table 4-10
Distribution of Aggregated Racism-Sexism Scores

	Stillwater		Rahway		OSP		Bedford Hills	
	N	Percent	N	Percent	N	Percent	N	Percent
Low (0-2)	76	44.7	59	53.6	73	44.5	45	30.6
Moderate (3-5)	76	44.7	45	40.9	77	47.0	84	57.2
High (6-10)	18	10.6	6	5.5	14	8.5	18	12.2
Total	170	100.0	110	100.0	164	100.0	147	100.0

Note: N = Number of cases.

Criminalization

Many researchers have used the concept of criminalization to denote a process of assimilation into a criminal subculture or life-style, as well as the acquisition of values and attitudes through criminal associations.[40] Our primary focus was to assess the extent to which maximum-security prisoners held antinormative values and attitudes. Among such values were those that positively sanction the use of violence to achieve criminal objectives, the rejection of conventional life-styles (and the concomitant postponement of personal gratification), and the acceptance of the victimization of those having greater economic or social resources. Values and attitudes indicative of a criminal-normative system may influence many aspects of participation in formal and informal organizations within the prisoner community. *Antinormative* (or criminal) values may also influence the nature of prisoner involvement in prisoner representative bodies, such as advisory councils or inmate liaison committees. Quite expectedly, management would be unwilling to extend greater autonomy and participatory powers to prisoners who indicated a tendency to pursue individual goals at the expense of the interests of the larger prisoner community. Hence, measurement of the extent and nature of antinormative values and attitudes appeared to be useful in evaluating the ramifications of prisoner involvement.

The criminalization scale items were developed with the sole purpose of examining the extent to which members of the five prisoner communities held traditional criminal values and attitudes.

Criminalization Scale Items

 4 Good thieves are not much different from straight folks because they work hard for what they get.
 9 If someone gets in your way during a gig, you have no choice but to take him out.
14 When you're down-and-out, its OK to plot and scheme to outsmart people who have money.
19 Sometimes the use of force or violence is the only way to get what you're after.
24 I usually respect junkies and street hustlers, even if they rob and steal from their friends.
29[a] I rarely get off on the excitement of crime and the satisfaction of knowing that I got over on somebody.
34 Only a fool would work if he (she) could skim it off the top.[b]
39 In order to survive, everybody has to have some kind of a hustle.
43[a] Even though I am in prison, I really don't consider myself to be a "criminal."

[a]Polarity of scale was reversed during analysis.
[b]Items reflecting gender were adjusted to correspond to male and female prisons.

Table 4-11 presents the mean and standard-deviation values for each of the five prisoner samples. As indicated, there were few substantial differences among samples. The criminalization means ranged from a low of 2.36 (OSP) to 2.65 (Soledad), suggesting that the prisoner samples did not hold highly developed criminal values and attitudes. Furthermore, several similar responses were revealed. For example, each prisoner sample saw the necessity of having a hustle to survive in contemporary society (item 39). While many conforming and conventional members of society may also agree with this statement, the term *hustle* has special meanings that differ from one socioeconomic stratum to another. Generally, criminal actors considered hustles to be money-making schemes that lie outside of the realm of legitimate and lawful economic behavior.[41] Among these activities were gambling, fencing, swindling (and other con games), pimping, and wheeling and dealing.

According to table 4-11, all male samples placed substantial importance on the use of physical force or violence to achieve criminal objectives (item 19). However, some minor variation among these samples was identified. For example, Soledad prisoners placed slightly greater emphasis on the use of force than either OSP, Stillwater, or Rahway prisoners, which was somewhat surprising considering that Soledad prisoners had the lowest proportion (29 percent) of violent offenders among male prisoners.

Bedford Hills prisoners tended to place greater emphasis on values supporting skilled criminal activity (item 4) than on those supporting the use of force or violence (item 19), a finding consistent with research on sex differences in aggression.[42] Few remaining differences were found between male and female prisoners. For example, many prisoners acknowledged that personal satisfaction was derived from successful criminal conduct (item 29), a value shared equally by male and female prisoners. Socialization into sex roles may have affected the formation of antinormative values, but once criminal conduct was performed, male and female responses to the amount of satisfaction obtained from criminal behavior were markedly similar.

When we examined racial differences in antinormative values and attitudes, we found that while all three racial groups had relatively low criminalization scores, blacks and other racial minorities consistently scored higher than whites. The only exception to this pattern was the combined racial minority category at Rahway, which revealed the lowest criminalization scores of all three racial groups. The higher criminalization scores of blacks and other minorities were likely to be related to their specialized adaptation to the prison community. For example, values supporting the use of force to resolve disputes may be more common among racial minorities who may have to demonstrate their ability or willingness to stand up to white domination and control. In addition, other antinormative values may stem from a perceived need to hustle because of restricted legitimate opportunities for gaining income and status.

Table 4-12 illustrates the distribution of aggregated criminalization scores. As shown, female prisoners reflected slightly stronger agreement with criminal

Table 4-11
Criminalization Scores Rank Ordered by Item Means

	Soledad			Stillwater			Rahway			OSP			Bedford Hills		
Item No.	$\overline{X}$	S.D.	Item No.	$\overline{X}$	S.D.	Item No.	$\overline{X}$	S.D.	Item No.	$\overline{X}$	S.D.	Item No.	$\overline{X}$	S.D.
39	3.51	1.57	39	2.93	1.44	39	3.27	1.57	39	3.10	1.49	39	3.25	1.55
19	3.18	1.58	29	2.81	1.39	29	3.10	1.62	19	2.78	1.49	29	3.18	1.69
29	3.14	1.55	19	2.71	1.52	19	2.62	1.47	29	2.61	1.49	4	3.07	1.57
9	2.81	1.51	4	2.56	1.43	4	2.50	1.58	14	2.47	1.36	19	2.43	1.47
4	2.46	1.52	43	2.42	1.39	14	2.46	1.47	4	2.35	1.33	9	2.36	1.40
14	2.42	1.40	14	2.30	1.31	34	2.11	1.39	43	2.27	1.35	14	2.21	1.30
43	2.23	1.50	9	2.02	1.10	9	2.03	1.32	9	2.15	1.37	34	2.12	1.43
34	2.07	1.44	34	2.02	1.13	43	1.99	1.36	34	2.11	1.27	24	2.03	1.36
24	1.79	1.23	24	1.59	1.04	24	1.98	1.34	24	1.51	.90	43	1.58	1.14
Mean scale score	2.65	.76		2.39	.72		2.50	.70		2.36	.75		2.48	.67

Note: $\overline{X}$ = Arithmetic mean.
S.D. = Standard deviation of the mean.

Table 4-12
Distribution of Aggregated Criminalization Scores

	Stillwater		Rahway		OSP		Bedford Hills	
	N	Percent	N	Percent	N	Percent	N	Percent
Low (0-2)	115	67.6	64	58.2	117	68.8	64	44.7
Moderate (3-5)	45	26.5	40	36.3	42	24.7	65	45.5
High (6-10)	10	5.9	6	5.5	11	6.5	14	9.8
Total	170	100.0	110	100.0	170	100.0	143	100.0

Note: N = Number of cases.

attitudes and values than male prisoners. For example, nearly 68 percent of the Stillwater prisoners, 69 percent of the OSP prisoners, and 58 percent of the Rahway prisoners had low agreement, compared to only 45 percent of the Bedford Hills prisoners. Hence, a slightly greater proportion of female prisoners revealed high or moderate agreement.

Thus far we have examined different emphases within scale dimensions for each of the prisoner samples. These data have revealed the predominant attitudes and values of members of the prisoner communities studied. Table 4-13 presents a summary of each scale value, listed in descending rank order to illustrate the prevalence of the attitudes and values comprising each scale. We are cognizant of the methodological limitations on comparing mean scale values with each other, as each scale independently represents a pool of arbitrarily selected items. While the items were derived from themes drawn from prisoner interviews and were included with statistical criteria, they nevertheless remain arbitrary. Hence, conventional methodological standards limit the comparison to different respondent groups with the same scales. However, as the scale-to-scale correlations (appendix B) revealed strong interscale relationships for most samples, we have attempted to provide some limited interpretation of the differences among prisoners' social values.

As indicated, prisoners' attitudes and values supporting radicalism and collective action ranked second and third, respectively, to prisonization. While the relatively high prisonization scores were anticipated, we were somewhat surprised to observe radicalism and collective action scores of nearly equal value. Most theoretical perspectives on prisoners' social values would have suggested that the strongest scores would have been shown for prisonization and criminalization, a relationship consistent with the importation model of prisoner social organization.

The scale-to-scale correlations provided an additional perspective on these findings. For example, the most closely associated pair of social values were

Table 4–13
Summary of Prisoner Social Values Scale Scores
$(\bar{x})$

Scale Dimension	Soledad	Stillwater	Rahway	OSP	Bedford Hills
Prisonization	3.43	3.37	3.56	3.56	3.50
Radicalism	3.22	2.99	3.51	3.33	3.54
Collective action	3.14	3.26	3.35	3.30	3.31
Racism-sexism	2.74	2.69	2.42	2.70	2.48
Criminalization	2.65	2.39	2.50	2.36	2.48

Note: $\bar{X}$ = Arithmetic mean.

prisonization and collective action, with correlation coefficients ranging from
.34 (OSP) to .67 (Soledad).

A similar pattern emerged from the relationship between radicalism and
collective action. However, Bedford Hills and OSP prisoners revealed slightly
weaker relationships (.11 and .19, respectively) than all other prisoner samples
(ranging from .40 to .61). Generally, the relationships between prisonization,
radicalism, and collective action were strong, with the association between
prisonization and collective action being the weaker of the three combinations
of relationships. A part of this weaker relationship may be explained by race
and ethnicity, as OSP and Stillwater (both of which have predominantly white
prisoner populations) revealed weaker relationships (.15 and .19, respectively)
than the remaining samples which has substantially greater proportions of racial
minorities. This suggests that there may be a relationship between race and
radicalism. As indicated earlier in this chapter, blacks and other racial minorities
tended to reveal slightly higher radicalism scale scores.

The relationship between prisonization and criminalization was moderately
and consistently strong for all prisoner samples, with Bedford Hills and Rahway
(each with predominantly black and Hispanic populations) having the weaker
associations (.33 and .34, respectively) and all remaining samples having moderate associations (.41).

The findings suggest that restricted opportunities for meaningful input into
the prison organization and limited autonomy and self-determination of prisoners have played a role in the formation of antinormative and oppositional attitudes and values, particularly those that were critical of the abuse of official
power and social control.

In spite of the relatively strong association between prisonization and
criminalization scores, we were surprised by the low criminalization scale mean
values revealed by all samples. If we were to follow the impressions given by
many prison administrators, we would be led to conclude that today's prisoners
are becoming more highly criminalized. Possibly prison management has mis-
taken the evolution of critical and oppositional values as criminal values. Our

data did not support the commonly held impression that maximum-security prisoners represented highly criminalized populations. As shown in table 4-13, only 7 percent of all prisoners sampled revealed high agreement to the criminalization scale items.

The findings suggest that contemporary prisoner communities held strong concerns about issues of social justice and racial discrimination and that these concerns are reflected in social values markedly different than those described in many early studies. Furthermore, findings suggest that as long as the prisoner community remains divided along racial and ethnic lines, many of the adjustments made by prisoners will reflect specialized adaptations to racial conflict. As illustrated, prisoners have little ability to reduce racism and conflict generated by the control and power interests of prison management and line custodial personnel. It is more likely that structural racism and conflict will be reduced by extending greater participatory rights and privileges to prisoners and front-line staff who have the greatest stake in a stable and cooperative organizational climate. Of course, this would require an organizational approach that takes into consideration prisoner skills, interests, and values and ultimately requires the cooperation of front-line staff.

Notes

1. For example see: Victor Nelson, *Prison Days and Nights* (Boston: Little, Brown and Company, 1933); Thomas Gaddis, *The Birdman of Alcatraz* (New York: Random House, 1955); Kenneth Lamott, *Chronicles of San Quentin: The Biography of a Prison* (New York: David McKay Company, 1961); Claude Brown, *Manchild in a Promised Land* (New York: Macmillan and Company, 1965); Malcolm Braly, *On the Yard* (Boston: Little, Brown and Company, 1967). A recent article examining the tragic circumstances surrounding the popularity of Jack Henry Abbott's, *In the Belly of the Beast,* points to the intellectual community's fascination with prison writers who are frequently accorded the (temporary) status of folk hero. See: Michiko Kakutani, "The Strange Case of the Writer and the Criminal," *The New York Times Book Review,* 20 September 1981, pp. 1-39.

2. Among the early scholarly works are: Donald Clemmer, *The Prison Community* (Boston: Christopher Publishing Company, 1940); Clarence Schrag, "Social Role Types in a Prison Community." M.A. thesis, University of Washington, 1944; N. Hayer and E. Ash, "The Prison Community as a Social Group," *American Sociological Review* 4(1939):362-369; N. Hayer and E. Ash, "The Prison as a Community," *American Sociological Review* 5(1940):577-583; Gresham Sykes, "The Corruption of Authority and Rehabilitation," *Social Forces* 34(1956):257-262; Gresham Sykes, *The Society of Captives: A Study of a Maximum Security Prison* (Princeton: Princeton University Press, 1958);

G. Sykes and S. Messinger, "Inmate Social System," *Theoretical Studies in Social Organization of the Prison,* ed. Richard Cloward, in Pamphlet no. 15 (New York: Social Science Research Council, March 1960), pp. 5-19; For some of the best historical works describing early American prisons, see: Blake Mc-Kelvey, *American Prisons: A Study in American Social History Prior to 1915* (Montclair, N.J.: Patterson Smith, 1972); Harry Barnes, *The Evolution of Penology in Pennsylvania* (Indianapolis: Bobbs-Merrill, 1927); Gustave de Beaumont and Alexis de Tocqueville, *On the Penitentiary System* (Carbondale, Ill.: Southern Illinois University Press, 1964); and David Rothman, *The Discovery of the Asylum* (Boston: Little, Brown and Company, 1971).

   3. For example, see: D. Ward and G. Kassebaum, *Women's Prison: Sex and Social Structure* (Chicago: Aldine Publishing Company, 1965); D. Ward and G. Kassebaum, "Lesbian Liaisons," *Trans-action*, vol. 1, no. 2 (1964):28-32; Theodora Abel, "Negro-White Interpersonal Relationships Among Institutionalized Girls," *American Journal of Mental Deficiency* 46(January 1942):325-339; J. Ball and N. Logan, "Early Sexual Behavior of Lower-Class Delinquent Girls," *Journal of Criminal Law and Criminology* 51(1960-1961):209-214; Anne Bingham, "Determinants of Sex Delinquency in Adolescent Girls Based on Intensive Studies of 500 Cases," *Journal of Criminal Law and Criminology* 13(February 1923):494-586; J. Gagnon and W. Simon, "The Social Meaning of Prison Homosexuality," *Federal Probation* 32(March 1968):23-29; S. Halleck and M. Herstso, "Homosexual Behavior in a Correctional Institution for Adolescent Girls," *American Journal of Orthopsychiatry* , vol. 32, no. 5 (1963):911-917; Max Hammer, "Hypersexuality in Reformatory Women," *Corrective Psychiatry and Journal of Social Therapy* 15(Winter 1969):20-26.

   4. Nearly all male maximum-security prisons have been informally divided by race, but it was only recently that courts have declared official policies of racial segregation to be unconstitutional. See: Gates v. Collier, 349 F. Supp. 881 (N.D. Miss. 1972), McClelland v. Sigler, 327 F. Supp. 829 (D. Neb. 1971); Battle v. Anderson, 376 F. Supp. 402 (E.D. Okla. 1974). Many maximum-security prisons in the South maintained racially divided operations well into the 1960s in defiance of the Civil Rights Movement. For example, Kentucky State Penitentiary (Eddyville) ran black and white mess hall and movie lines and maintained segregated shops throughout the period from 1958 to 1967. In spite of blacks averaging approximately 40 percent of the prisoner population, there were never any black guards or prison employees hired during this period. In addition, guards would frequently write up prisoners on petty beefs when racial barriers were crossed, particularly when there was a substantial age difference.

   5. Among the recent works that have included race or culture in analyses of prisoner behavior and social organization are: Lee Bowker, *Prison Victimization* (New York: Elsevier, 1980); Leo Carroll, *Hacks, Blacks, and Cons: Race Relations in a Maximum Security Prison* (Lexington, Mass.: Lexington Books, D.C. Heath, 1974); R. Theodore Davidson, *Chicano Prisoners: The Key to San*

Quentin (New York: Holt, Rinehart and Winston, 1974); James Jacobs, *Stateville: The penitentiary in Mass Society* (Chicago: University of Chicago Press, 1977); James Jacobs and Lawrence Kraft, "Integrating the Keepers: A Comparison of Black and White Prison Guards in Illinois," *Social Problesm* 25(1978): 304-318; John Irwin, *Prisons in Turmoil* (Boston: Little, Brown, and Company, 1980); and Robert Johnson, *Culture and Crisis in Confinement* (Lexington, Mass.: Lexington Books, D.C. Heath, 1976).

6. See: Schrag, "Social Role Types in a Prison Community," M.A. thesis, University of Washington, 1944; Clemmer, *The Prison Community* (Boston: Christopher Publishing Company, 1940); Sykes, *The Society of Captives*; Sykes and Messinger, *Theoretical Studies in Social Organization of the Prison,* pp. 5-19.

7. John Irwin and Donald Cressey, "Thieves, Convicts, and the Inmate Culture," *Social Problems* 10(Fall 1962):142-155.

8. See the review of these studies in Lee Bowker, *Prison Subcultures* (Lexington, Mass.: Lexington Books, D.C. Heath, 1977); and Charles Thomas and David Petersen, *Prison Organization and Inmate Subcultures* (Indianapolis: The Bobbs-Merrill Company, 1977).

9. See: Charles Thomas, "Prisonization or Resocialization? A Study of External Factors Associated with the Impact of Imprisonment," *Journal of Research in Crime and Delinquency* 10(January 1973):13-21; Charles Thomas, "Theoretical Perspectives on Alienation in the Prison Society: An Empirical Test," *Pacific Sociological Review* 18(October 1974):483-499; Charles Thomas, "Theoretical Perspectives on Prisonization: A Comparison of the Importation and Deprivation Models," *Journal of Criminal Law and Criminology,* vol. 68, no. 1 (1977); Charles Thomas and Samuel Foster, Prisonization in the Inmate Contraculture," *Social Problems* 20(Fall 1972):229-239; Charles Thomas and Samuel Foster, "Importation Model Perspective on Inmate Social Roles: An Empirical Test," *Sociological Quarterly* 14(Spring 1973):226-234; Charles Wellford, "Factors Associated with Adoption of the Inmate Code: A Study of Normative Socialization," *Journal of Criminal Law, Criminology, and Police Science* 58(April 1967):197-203; and Stanton Wheeler, "Socialization in Correctional Communities," *American Sociological Review* 26(1961):697-712.

10. This perspective is advanced by a number of scholars, including: Thomas and Peterson, *Prison Organization and Inmate Subcultures,* pp. 17-29; James Jacobs and Norma Crotty, *Guard Unions and the Future of Prisons,* Institute of Public Employment, Monograph no. 9 (Ithaca: Cornell University, August 1978); Irwin, *Prisons in Turmoil*; Carroll, *Hacks, Blacks, and Cons*; Davidson, *The Key To San Quentin.*

11. Davidson, *The Key to San Quentin,* Irwin, *Prisons in Turmoil,* James Jacobs, "Race Relations and the Prisoner Subculture," *Crime and Justice: An Annual Review of Research,* ed. Norval Morris and Michael Tonry, vol. 1 (Chicago: The University of Chicago Press, 1979).

12. Irwin, *Prisons in Turmoil*, pp. 72-76.

13. Carroll, *Hacks, Blacks, and Cons*, pp. 197-198.

14. Jacobs, *Stateville*, pp. 144-174.

15. See: Irwin, *Prisons in Turmoil*, pp. 195-196. During the field studies we observed that many white prisoners who had served lengthy terms in prison, developed close relationships with guards. These prisoners tended to rely on these relationships to obtain personal safety and avoid the stress of life on the *mainline* by seeking job assignments that offered protective environments.

16. Many of the front-line custody staff also made such a distinction. They told us that a "new breed of inmate" was entering the prison, who didn't care about other prisoners' property and who would steal anything to purchase drugs in the prisoner community. These guards felt that the "old style convicts" were better prisoners, because they maintained loyalties and were "trustworthy."

17. Irwin, *Prisons in Turmoil*, p. 195.

18. See: Jacobs, *Stateville* pp. 138-174; James Jacobs, "Street Gangs Behind Bars," *Social Problems* 21(1974):395-411; Davidson, *The Key to San Quentin*, pp. 80-100; Kevin Krajick, "The Menace of the Supergangs," *Corrections Magazine* 6(June 1980):11-14.

19. See: C. Ron Huff, "Unionization Behind the Walls," *Criminology*, 12(August 1974):175-193; C. Ron Huff, "Prisoners' Union: A Challenge for State Corrections," *State Government* 48(Summer 1975):145-149; C. Ron Huff, J. Scott, and S. Dinitz, "Prisoners' Unions: A Cross-National Investigation of Public Acceptance," *International Journal of Criminology and Penology* 4(November 1976):331-347.

20. This aspect of prisoner organization has been overlooked in most prison studies. Many researchers may have underestimated the role and impact of formal organizations and focused their attention on informal and primary associations. When it became obvious that many of the violent racial and ethnic gangs were highly structured, interest increased in the area of prisoner organization. See the final report to the National Institute of Justice for the Prisoner Organization Research Project: James G. Fox, *The Organizational Context of the Prison* (Sacramento, Calif.: The American Justice Institute, 1979).

21. Among the most widely recognized studies of the female prisoner social system are: Ward and Kassebaum, *Women's Prison: Sex and Social Structure*; Rose Giallonbardo, *Society of Women: A Study of a Women's Prison* (New York: John Wiley and Sons, 1966); Esther Heffernan, *Making It in Prison: The Square, The Cool, and The Life* (New York: John Wiley and Sons, 1972). Also see: Ida Harper, "The Role of the 'Fringer' in a State Prison for Women," *Social Forces* 31(October 1952):53-60; G. Jensen and D. Jones, "Perspectives on Inmate Culture," *Social Forces* 54(1976):590-603; T. Hartnagel and M. Gillan, "Female Prisoners and the Inmate Code," *Pacific Sociological Review*, 23, no. 1 (January 1980):85-104; and Thomas Foster, Make-Believe Families:

A Response of Women and Girls to the Deprivations of Imprisonment," *International Journal of Criminology and Penology* 3(1975):71-78. For the best literary work describing the difficulties facing women in prison, see: Kathryn Burkhart, *Women in Prison* (New York: Doubleday, 1973).

22. Giallombardo, *Society of Women*, p. 16.

23. I have had the opportunity to observe and gather quantitative and qualitative data at Bedford Hills on three different research projects during the periods from 1972-1974 and 1977-1978. The earliest study focused on personal crisis (see: James G. Fox, "Women in Crisis," in *Men in Crisis: Human Breakdowns in Prison*, in Hans Toch [Chicago: Aldine Publishing Company, 1975], pp. 193-203) and self-injury of female prisoners. During that study period, approximately two-thirds of the Bedford Hills prisoner population self-reported current involvement in the kinship system. By 1978 that proportion had dropped to approximately one-fourth of the population.

24. Ward and Kassebaum, *Women's Prison: Sex and Social Structure*; Giallombardo, *Society of Women*; Heffernan, *Making It in Prison*; Rose Giallombardo, *The Social World of Imprisoned Girls* (New York: John Wiley and Sons, 1974).

25. The item-to-item and scale-to-scale correlations are presented in appendix B. For a complete discussion of the procedures used in developing this instrument, see: Fox, *The Organizational Context of the Prison*; and R.M. Montilla and James G. Fox, *Pilot Study Report: Soledad* (Sacramento, Calif.: The American Justice Institute, 1978).

26. James G. Fox, Brenda A. Miller, and Bruce Bullington, "A Study of the Drug and Alcohol Abuse Problems in Pennsylvania's Criminal Justice System," Commonwealth of Pennsylvania, Governor's Council on Drug and Alcohol Abuse, 1977.

27. J. Faine and E. Bohlander, "The Genesis of Disorder: Oppression, Confinement, and Prisoner Politicization," in *Contemporary Corrections: Social Control and Conflict*, ed. C. Ron Huff (Beverly Hills, Calif.: Sage Publications, 1977), pp. 54-77. Also see: Erika Fairchild, "Politicization of the Criminal Offender: Prisoner Perceptions of Crime and Politics," *Criminology* 15(November 1977):287-318.

28. This perspective has been set forth in several works examining the social psychology of the work organization and the nature of complex organizations. See, for example: Amitai Etzioni, *A Comparative Analysis of Complex Organizations*, 2d ed. (New York: The Free Press, 1975); Amitai Etzioni, ed., *A Sociological Reader on Complex Organizations*, 2d ed. (New York: Holt, Rinehart, and Winston, 1969).

29. Our category, *other racial minorities*, combined all remaining racial and ethnic groups at each site. At Stillwater, this included only 10 percent of the total prisoner population. An even smaller porportion of other minorities was

found at OSP, where they comprised only 6.4 percent of the prisoner popula-tion. In addition, this category tended to represent different racial minorities at each prison. For example, the *other* group was predominantly Hispanic at Sole-dad and Bedford Hills, while Native Americans represented the largest pro-portion of this group at OSP and Stillwater.

30. U.S., Bureau of the Census, *Statistical Abstracts of the U.S.*, 99th ed., (Washington, D.C., 1978) table no. 35.

31. It should be noted that forcible rape was included as a violent offense for all of the male samples. If we were to compare male and female prisoners on all other violent crimes, the relative differences would be slightly reduced.

32. Many male prisoners, particularly the younger, less street smart, spend an inordinate amount of time on the "weight pile" developing their arm and upper body muscles in an effort to impress fellow prisoners with their "strength" and to make their bodies less "appealing" to sexual aggressors.

33. According to our interviews with female guards and prisoners, the reliance of custodial personnel on the helping network of kinship members, and partners in personal relationships, is a common occurrence at Bedford Hills. In several instances, guards told us that some violation of custody regulations was necessary in women's prisons to protect larger security interests.

34. The smaller size (*n* = 45) of the CTF-South (Soledad) sample did not permit the use of this technique. However, a cursory examination of the CTF-South data did not reveal any major differences among male prisoner samples on prisoner-social-value scale dimensions.

35. Only a handful of studies have been reported in the literature. For representative empirical and theoretical works see: J. Faine and E. Bohlander, "The Genesis of Disorder"; Erika Fairchild, "The Politicization of the Criminal Offender"; Daniel Glaser, "Politicalization of Prisoners: A New Challenge to American Penology," *American Journal of Corrections* 33(November-December 1971):6-9; J. Pallas and R. Barber, "From Riot to Revolution," in *The Politics of Punishment: A Critical Analysis of Prisons in America,* ed. Erik O. Wright (New York: Harper Colophon Books, 1973), pp. 237-261; and G. Alpert and D. Hicks, "Prisoner's Attitudes Toward Components of the Legal and Judicial Systems," *Criminology* 14(February 1977):461-482.

36. Etzioni, *A Sociological Reader on Complex Organizations*, p. 65.

37. Sterling, Capps, and Hixon v. Cupp, Murphy, and Bagley, no. 108-452, The Circuit Court of the State of Oregon for the County of Marion (27 Septem-ber 1978). There was a growing debate as to whether this litigation was "en-couraged" or "suggested" by J.C. Keeney, Assistant Superintendent at OSP. David Sterling, one of the prisoners who initiated the court action, told the *Eugene Register Guard* that "Keeney called me down to his office and told me. When Keeney asked me to do it, I did it." "State Inmates Offer Opinions About Women As Prison Guards," *Eugene Register Guard,* 25 March 1979. The motive to provide this statement, according to a number of prisoners who associated

with Sterling, was that Keeney failed to fulfill a promise to assign Sterling to the prison law library as clerk.

38. OSP prisoners, as we have indicated, were aware of the controversy surrounding the litigation aimed at restricting female officers to noncontact posts. Some prisoners told us that their wives and mothers were opposed to female officers conducting "strip searches," which were required after visits.

39. See: Forts v. Ward, 471 F. Supp. 1095 (1978).

40. See: Albert Cohen, *Delinquent Boys* (New York: The Free Press, 1955); Kai Erickson, "Notes on the Sociology of Deviance," *Social Problems* 9(Spring 1962):307-314; Walter B. Miller, "Lower Class Cultures as a Generating Milieu of Gang Delinquency," *Journal of Social Issues* 14(1958):5-19; Edwin Lemert, *Social Pathology* (New York: McGraw-Hill, 1951); M. Wolfgang and F. Ferracuti, *The Subculture of Violence* (London: Tavistock Publishers, 1967).

41. See: Howard Becker, *Outsiders: Studies in the Sociology of Deviance* (New York: The Free Press, 1963); John Irwin, *The Felon* (Englewood Cliffs, N.J.: Prentice Hall, 1970); Ned Polsky, *Hustlers, Beats, and Others* (Chicago: Aldine Publishing Company, 1967).

42. The principle that males have a greater tendency toward aggression is accepted as a universal phenomena in most of the animal world. For a review of the biosocial theories and research findings, see: J. Williams, *Psychology of Women: Behavior in a Biosocial Context* (New York: Norton, 1977); M. Fietlebaum, ed., *Sex Differences* (New York: Double Day, 1976); E. Maccoby and C. Jacklin, *The Psychology of Sex Differences* (Stanford, Calif.: Stanford University Press, 1974).

Prisoner Organizations: United We Stand, Divided We Fall

One of the most significant developments within maximum-security prisons during the past two decades has been the formation of formal organizations representing diverse prisoner interests. While the entry of formal organizations began some time ago, it has been only recently that their activities have caught the attention of prison scholars.[1] Some scholarly interest was directed toward the evolution of the prisoner movement,[2] radical political protest,[3] self-governance,[4] prisoner gangs,[5] and prisoner unions.[6] However, little more than brief mention has been made of specialized organizations seeking legitimate solutions to diverse prisoner needs and interests. In addition, prison management in most state prison systems were unprepared for the surge of legitimate prisoner collective activity.[7] Consequently, the early stages of many prisoner organizations reflect substantial bureaucratic regulation, cooptation, and manipulation by management.

The Evolution of a Pluralist Prisoner Community

The political, legal, and social influences underlying the formation of contemporary prisoner organizations have their roots in the 1960s. Most contemporary prison scholars agree that the period following the major prison riots of the 1950s had profound and lingering effects on prisoner rights and empowerment.[8] For example, the Civil Rights Movement gave rise to black political consciousness and cultural awareness, and served to strengthen Muslim prisoner efforts to gain religious and ideological freedoms. In addition, prisoner-rights groups, largely supported by liberal and New Left activists, attempted to define the limitations of state power through litigation of internal issues. Furthermore, predominantly white, middle-class, antiwar groups, many radicalized by the overreaction of police in Chicago, Detroit, Washington, D.C., and other major cities, began to include the inhumane treatment of prisoners within their political and economic criticism. The foundation was being laid for what was to become known as the prisoner movement.[9]

Many prisoners, particularly blacks and other racial minorities, saw the opportunity for a new alliance with radical and liberal community groups and a chance to achieve new reforms and individual rights. The initial thrust of this alliance was borne, primarily, by blacks who had the most readily accessible and broadest based community support. A number of prisoner organizations with linkage to established community organizations began to emerge in nearly every maximum-security prison in the nation. Some were authorized by prison management to pursue specific objectives. Others remained as underground political and support groups in defiance of disciplinary sanctions.[10] Nearly all prisoner organizations formed during the height of political and racial turmoil were organized around race or ethnicity.[11] Whites tended to control the leadership of conventional organizations, such as the Jaycees, while blacks formed Afro-American cultural and educational groups and bid for positions on prisoner representative organizations. Blacks also sought increased collective power through a number of informal and formal organizations emphasizing cultural and revolutionary nationalism.[12] Whites, lacking a means of cultural expression, frequently sought refuge within self-help groups (spawned during the emphasis on rehabilitation) or formed loose alliances with underground, extremist organizations such as the Aryan Brotherhood, Klu Klux Klan, Nazis, or Hell's Angels.[13] Predictably, racial conflict intensified with new forms of black militancy and challenge to white domination.

Jacobs argues that much of the impetus of black political expression at Stateville during the 1970s was linked to four Chicago street gangs who brought their organizational structure, ideologies, and *symbol systems* into the prison:

> The young gang members had assimilated a justificatory vocabulary as well as a set of rising expectations as they were growing up in the Chicago ghettos during the 1960s. The old prison reward system, which promised better jobs and the opportunity to score for 'hooch,' coffee, and extra food, was no longer compelling. Unlike the Muslims, the gang members had no specific issues or concrete agenda. They brought to the prison diffuse goals and a general attitude of lawlessness and rebelliousness. The small minority of whites left at Stateville found themselves in grave danger, as did those blacks who were not affiliated with one of the gangs.[14]

In many California prisons, Mexican-Americans also formed cultural awareness and education organizations, as well as underground groups intended to insure protection of Chicano interests within the larger prisoner community. While there is some disagreement among observers as to the specific sequence of events leading up to their formation, these informal Chicano groups eventually evolved into powerful ethnic gangs, competing for control of the subterranean prisoner economy.[15]

Shortly after the shooting of George Jackson at San Quentin and the Attica tragedy, the prisoner movement was at its highest level. However, both internal and external support and solidarity reached their peak about the time the Vietman War was unwinding in 1975.[16] What had been accomplished, from the perspective of many prisoners, was an unprecedented surge of community awareness and support, substantial gains in procedural safeguards for the imposition of disciplinary sanctions and other social controls, and the creation of a pluralist group structure within the prisoner community.[17] Furthermore, racial consciousness and the evolution of formal prisoner organizations altered both the social structure of the prisoner community and the nature of prisoner-management relations.

Management Reaction

To the greater extent, the evolution and expansion of formal organizations has resulted from three major factors. First, prison management has shown a greater willingness to provide productive outlets for many prisoner interests. The motives for this policy appear to be multifaceted. Certainly, constructive group activities serve the limited rehabilitative goals of corrections, as idle time is seen as being detrimental to both prisoner and management interests. However, a less obvious motive appears to have played a substantial role in stimulating management support. Namely, supervised (nearly all authorized groups are required to have a sponsor approved by management) group activities allow management to establish a more extensive and elaborate system of social control through regulation, cooptation, and division of prisoner interests. Management's social controls are enhanced by the creation of a pluralist group structure, competitively seeking authorized goals and activities. As prisoner interests are translated into formal organizational structures, management can prevent collective opposition by manipulating administrative policy controlling both the utilization of limited resources and the degree to which any organization may pursue its specialized objectives.

Berkman argues that this is often accomplished by maintaining a balance of control over organizational activities:

> Group policy must be administered with a degree of equilibrium. The group structure must be afforded a degree of legitimacy and credence to encourage prisoners to participate—demonstrating that participation in this type of activity can produce some results.
>
> If the administration pulls the reins of a group too lightly, the constituency sees the whole group as a puppet. The result is that the administration loses touch with, or alienates, the faction it is trying to promote.
>
> On the other hand, if the administration allows the group too much latitude, it feels the group will move toward insurrection and hence be taken over by a militant faction. Group activity was designed to avoid this very occurrence. Consequently, the administration must fashion a policy that will give groups a degree of legitimacy and prevent them from engaging in any form of radical politics.[18]

Second, there has been a proliferation of special interests among prisoners, sparked by racial and political awareness and the accomplishments of the prisoner movement. The number and type of formal organizations has increased substantially during the past two decades. Carroll found a range of "inmate voluntary associations" at ECI in 1971, including a prison chapter of the Junior Chamber of Commerce (Jaycees), the Afro-American Society, the Beacon (a prison newspaper group), a Yoga Society, a Lifer's Association, an art club, a drama club, and Alcoholics Anonymous.[19] Likewise, Berkman reported that one-fifth of the prisoners actively participated in one or more of the fourteen different organizations at West Prison.[20]

While much prisoner organizational activity is intended to promote racial and ethnic solidarity, there is also substantial involvement in social and legal reform efforts through specialized legal and legislative study groups and service programs, such as the Juvenile Awareness Project sponsored by the Lifers at Rahway. On the one hand, it may be asserted that the proliferation of diverse special-interest groups provides an opportunity for prisoners to develop leadership, problem-solving, and human relations skills. On the other hand, it may be argued that the further division of the prisoner community undermines collective interests and increases competition among groups for community volunteers, staff sponsors, prisoner talent, and meeting space and other institutional resources. According to Berkman:

> The process of acquiring resources also breeds a considerable amount of hostility among the groups. Since resources within the prison are very scarce, the competition for acquiring resources should be keen. It should be expected that when scarce resources are being sought by many competing groups, divisiveness rather than unity will emerge as the dominant political characteristic.[21]

In this situation management, as well as prisoner interests may be undermined by organizational competition. If hostility manifests itself in the form of confrontation and force, custody and control issues may arise. Likewise, intense competition for limited resources may serve to alienate prisoners and foster a view that management is pursuing a policy of divide and conquer.

Third, the further bureaucratization of the prison organization has resulted in the formalization of many previously informal prisoner groups and activities. The creation of bureaucratic rules and regulations governing prisoner organizations, including formal procedures for obtaining official approval (for example, submission of a charter and statement of objectives), formal request procedures for special programs (for example, guest speakers, banquets), and organizational sponsorship (subject to approval by management), has greatly increased management's control and influence over prisoner activities. While the associate superintendent for programs has traditionally supervised many prisoner (self-help) groups, the expansion of special interests has pulled executive and security management into a more direct relationship with organizational members. This has resulted, in part, because of the nature of many organizational objectives.

Security routinely becomes involved when outside guests are included in group activities; not only for initial screening, but for supervision and security during group meetings, banquets, and special programs. Executive management occasionally enters the picture when the activities of any given organization present a threat to administrative policy and guidelines. Frequently, executive management may meet with organizational representatives to review formal requests and insure that their activities conform to their charter. Failure to follow specific guidelines may result in disbandment or, in some instances, disciplinary action against leadership.

The bureaucratization of prisoner activities has also resulted in many informal groups being required to conform to administrative procedures and guidelines. For example, Alcoholics Anonymous groups were typically structured around informal relationships, with an outside or staff sponsor, and remained a relatively autonomous group within the prison organizational bureaucracy. Currently, Alcoholics Anonymous and other self-help groups are required to conform to the same guidelines as other organizations. In addition, the formalization of relationships between organizational leaders and management has established a new form of communication. In spite of prohibitions against cooperating with prison officials, many prisoner-organization leaders attempt to negotiate a mutually satisfactory deal with management. To the extent that their efforts are viewed as being successful by their membership (and unaffiliated prisoners), such meetings are not considered to be suspect. However, if an organization fails to win any concessions from management, elected leaders (and their respective organizations) may lose credibility within the prisoner community. Custodial personnel may also view some organization leaders as wielding an inappropriate and inordinate amount of power and influence. Hence, many traditional norms governing cooperation with prison officials have been altered with the growth and development of formal prisoner organizations.

Conceptual and Methodological Framework

As stated in chapter 1, we viewed formal prisoner organizations as occupying an important stratum within the prison organizational hierarchy. We also argued that while prisoner participation may be coopted or subverted by management (and underground groups), some mechanism must be established for meaningful prisoner input into many aspects of the management decision-making process. The specific nature of this involvement would be determined by a number of factors including organizational structure, social climate, and extent of management and prisoner experience with participatory methods.

Formal involvement in decisions essential to the goals of the prison organization, under contemporary management approaches, tends to be limited to advisory roles. Prisoners are rarely seen as participants whom management involves in decisions. Instead, they are more often viewed as persons to be controlled and regulated according to the current needs and interests of prison security. However, prisoners in nearly all maximum-security prisons are informally involved in many aspects of daily prison operations, such as work assignments (particularly those requiring skilled labor), food service, and health care. At Stillwater, prisoners assigned to prison industries were organized into a Worker's Council and provided regular input into design, cost, safety, and production decisions.

While the role and effectiveness of prisoner participation in self-governance, grievance procedures, and representative organizations has been examined, little attention has been focused on the role of formal organizations pursuing diverse interests. It was our judgment that these organizations provided an underused, innovative organizational resource that could serve both prisoner and management interests.

Our research objectives were to determine the number of authorized organizations at each site, the size and composition of their membership, and line custodial staff, management, and prisoner perspectives on their goals and activities. We also attempted to determine the extent to which formal organizations provided meaningful opportunities for prisoner self-determination, empowerment, and input into policy and decision-making structures. We did not attempt to systematically gather information on the occurrence (or activities) of informal groups such as gangs or other unauthorized groups, although we made an effort to determine the extent to which they influenced the activities of authorized organizations. The primary analysis was based on information pertaining to organizations formally sanctioned by prison or departmental management.

The methods of data collection departed only slightly from the procedures used to gather questionnaire and interview data from other components of our research design. First, we obtained an official list of prisoner organizations and their respective membership from management. Too often it was discovered that this list was inaccurate or was not systematically updated. However, we were able to identify the present leadership of active organizations by talking with staff and prisoners involved with organizational activities. Next, we conducted structured and semistructured interviews with all elected (or appointed) organization leaders, including those who were recently removed from their positions as a result of disciplinary charges or for pursuing objectives seen as a threat by prison management. These interviews focused on the structure of their respective organizations, the procedures for selecting leaders, past and current activities, and their relationship with correctional officers and prison management.

We also interviewed sponsors of these organizations who, in many instances, were correctional officers with an active interest in the respective organization's goals or purpose. Quite often, line custodial staff would offer their off-duty time to assist the organizations by providing supervision and guidance. In some instances, sponsors were appointed (or approved) by prison management for reasons other than providing a service or supervisory function. That is, management frequently assigned guards with demonstrated loyalty to institutional policies to supervise some organizations, particularly those that promoted prisoner solidarity and/or were organized along racial or ethnic lines. In spite of strong management interest in the choice of sponsors, we found that most prisoner organizations played a significant role in the selection of their sponsors.

Characteristics of Organizational Members

The data revealed that 59 percent of the Stillwater prisoners, 49 percent of the Oregon prisoners, 44 percent of the Bedford Hills prisoners, and 24 percent of the Rahway prisoners held active membership in at least one prisoner organization at the time of the data collection. Only 9 percent of the Soledad sample reported membership in an organization, and nearly all of these were affiliated with Friends Outside, Alcoholics Anonymous, or the Men's Advisory Council (MAC). As stated in the *Pilot Study Report*, the California Department of Corrections policy regarding prisoner organizations did not permit a wide range of organizations, and groups organized by race or ethnicity were prohibited at Soledad.[22]

A comparison between affiliated and nonaffiliated prisoners indicated that blacks, Hispanics, and Native Americans were more likely to hold membership in prisoner organizations than whites. This pattern was most evident at Stillwater and OSP, where these racial and ethnic groups were a small minority within the prisoner community as well as within their respective state populations. While age differences were not marked, the data suggested that younger (under twenty-six) prisoner were less likely than older prisoners to hold membership in formal prisoner organizations. Data pertaining to the amount of time served and time remaining in confinement revealed that members of organizations tended to be serving longer prison terms than those who were not affiliated. For example, 51 percent of all affiliated prisoners had served more than forty-two months at their respective prisons, compared to only 37 percent of those without membership.

Types of Prisoner Organizations

Table 5-1 illustrates the total number of formal prisoner organizations at each of the five research sites. It should be noted that a substantial proportion (26 to 41 percent) of those affiliated held membership in more than one organization.

These memberships were organized into four major types of organizations (ethnic, religious, self-help, and special interest) to facilitate an examination of the relationships between type of organizational membership and demographic

Table 5-1
Self-Reported Memberships by Organization and Site

Soledad (CTF-Central)	Stillwater	Rahway	OSP	Bedford Hills
Alcoholics Anonymous	Advisory Council	Alcoholics Anonymous	Alcoholics Anonymous	Al-Anon
Aryan Brotherhood[a]	Afro-American Culture Education, Inc.	Forum	Bible Club	Alcoholics Anonymous
Black Guerilla Family[a]	Alcoholics Anonymous	Lifers Group, Inc.	Car Club (Racing)	Committee Against Life for Drugs
Crypts[a]	Asklepieion	Muslims	Gavel Club	Hispanic Committee
Friends Outside	Atlantis	NAACP	Jaycees	Inmate Liaison Council
Hell's Angels[a]	Aztlan (Hispanics)		Keen Club	Lifers
Inmate Committee on Higher Education (ICHE)	Insight		Lakota (Native American)	New Directions
Men's Advisory Council	Jaycees		Lifeline	Parent Awareness
Mexican Mafia[a]	Muslims		Lifers	Reality House
Muslims	Native American Culture Education, Inc.		Master Men (Chess Club)	South Forty Program
Nuestra Familia[a]	Sounds Incarcerated, Inc.		Motorcycle Club	Violence Alternative
	Worker's Council		Muslims	
			Seventh Club	
			Slot Car Club	
			Toastmasters	
			Uhuru (Black Culture)	

[a]Self-reported membership in unauthorized organizations.

and social background characteristics. The proportion of prisoners holding membership in each of these four types of organizations is shown in table 5-2.

Ethnic and Cultural Awareness Organizations

The classification of *ethnic* organizations included racial or ethnic organizations that placed a primary focus on cultural awareness and education. For example, this category included several different types of black prisoner organizations (except Muslims), which were solely concerned with the needs and interests of blacks. Similarly, cultural awareness organizations representing the interests of Hispanics and Native Americans were placed into this category. The latter were most frequently intertribal organizations, intended to meet needs and interests common to Native Americans regardless of their tribal affiliation.

As indicated in table 5-2, membership in ethnic organizations accounted for 19 percent of all male prisoner organizations.[23] The data revealed substantial differences in the proportion of prisoners affiliated with ethnic organizations among sites. For example, 31 percent of the affiliated Stillwater prisoners, compared to only 13 percent of the affiliated OSP prisoners, held active membership in one or more ethnic organizations. In contrast, Rahway, which had a substantial proportion of blacks and Hispanics within the prisoner community, had only 5 percent of all memberships in ethnic organizations. The greater proportion of Stillwater prisoners holding membership in ethnic organizations suggests that they held stronger interests in cultural awareness and education. This was supported, in part, by the level of activity observed among the three major Stillwater ethnic organizations: Aztlan (Hispanics), Afro-American Group, and the Native American Culture Education group. Together, these

Table 5-2
Distribution of Formal Organization Memberships

	Stillwater		Rahway		OSP		Bedford Hills		Total	
	N	Percent	N	Percent	N	Percent	N	Percent	N	Percent
Ethnic	45	31.5	2	4.9	23	13.3	20	15.5	90	18.5
Religious	23	16.1	9	22.0	27	15.6	8	6.2	67	13.8
Self-help	37	25.9	11	26.8	30	17.3	55	42.6	133	27.4
Special interest	38	26.5	19	46.3	93	53.8	46	35.7	196	40.3
Total[a]	143	100.0	41	100.0	173	100.0	129	100.0	486	100.0

[a]Several authorized organizations appearing on the official list (maintained by prison management) do not appear in table 5-1. Either our sampling design failed to include these members or they did not report their membership in those organizations.

three organizations comprise nearly 32 percent of all prisoner-organization memberships at Stillwater.

It was found also that members of ethnic organizations tended to be slightly younger than members of other types of organizations. In addition, we discovered that the proportion of each minority represented in ethnic organizations was inversely related to the extent to which they were represented in the larger prisoner community. That is, the smaller the racial or ethnic minority, the greater the likelihood that they held membership in an ethnic organization. For example, 60 percent of the blacks (who represented 18 percent of the Stillwater prisoners), compared to 90 percent of the Native Americans (who represented only 5.4 percent of the prisoners) and 82 percent of the Hispanics (who represented only 2.7 percent of the prisoners), were members of Stillwater ethnic organizations. A similar pattern was found for the remaining sites.

It is possible that the greater proportion of Hispanics and Native Americans holding membership in ethnic organizations reflects their specialized cultural needs and interests. For example, blacks appeared to have a much greater range of interests and, consequently, held membership in more diversified types of organizations. Only 36 percent of all affiliated blacks, compared to 50 percent of the Hispanics and over 68 percent of the Native Americans, were ethnic-organization members. In a similar vein, blacks represented over 37 percent of the membership in special-interest organizations, while Hispanics (15 percent) and Native Americans (23 percent) represented substantially smaller special-interest membership.

There were also slight differences in educational achievement. For example, members of ethnic organizations completed less formal education than members of other organizations. The data indicated that 31 percent of the members of ethnic organizations, compared to 24 percent of the members of religious organizations, 24 percent of the members of self-help organizations, and 14 percent of the members of special-interest organizations had completed less than twelve years of education. No substantial differences were observed for any of the remaining variables examined.

Ethnic organizations were frequently the principal target of correctional officer concern about prisoner organizations. A substantial number of guards at each site viewed the formal structure of ethnic organizations as facilitating illicit activities and contraband traffic. Others pointed to the potential for power struggles and argued for more control over the development of ethnic and racial solidarity. Compared to line custodial staff at all research sites except Soledad, Stillwater officers tended to be the most reluctant to support ethnic organizations. One Stillwater officer, representative of many day-shift guards, told us that prisoner organizations could serve an important function but most organizations do not adhere to their stated objectives:

I think that prisoner organizations could help the correctional officer's job and I think it would be good for the inmates to have those organizations, but I don't think they are being run right because if you read the charters for the organizations, it's nice. But I believe that the inmates feel that's merely a front and they don't, by and large, use the organization for what it's been set up for. They use it as a vehicle for other motives, mainly contraband and female companionship. (MSP-OF-36)

The same officer told us that predatory and exploitative actions of some prisoners were shielded by ethnic solidarity. He saw few instances where white prisoners were able to stand up to blacks or Native Americans and felt that the few white groups wielding power at Stillwater were "rip off artists" who respected racial boundries. In this victim–victimizer dyad, whites were characterized as being more vulnerable to extortion by racial groups:

You can go into a cell hall and watch, and where you see a group of four or five blacks go up to a certain cell, you can almost bet that man is going to pay off. He's gonna—they're gonna take his TV set, or whatever. And there's little confrontation with the inmates in the Afro-American Group, they pretty well run things here. I can't think of a time when the whites stood up to the blacks as a group. There are a lot more whites here than blacks, but the blacks have the power. Three of four blacks can go up to a cell and say, "Pay off or the Afro-American Group is going to get you." He gives in or he ends up in PC [protective custody]. You see very few blacks go into protective custody, they don't have to. The same with the Indians, you don't see a lot of Indians worried about PC. There are some white groups, bikers, rip-off groups, and they're left alone by the blacks and Indians as long as they don't tread on them. (MSP-OF-36)

Officers at Rahway and OSP tended to be much more supportive of prisoner organizations than those at Soledad and Stillwater and provided a sharper perspective on the internal dynamics of the various active organizations. For example, one Rahway officer, representing the views of the majority of the guards, saw the organizations as a positive element that allowed a greater amount of activity time and provided an opportunity for prisoners to pursue their interests and gain self-respect. He also told us that when any particular organization begins to create a problem for line staff or management, they are "shut down" until a determination can be made regarding the potential for disruption or conflict:

I would say that the organizations work. They've been around for awhile now. This is not really new here. It's been around and they seem to work. And when an organization doesn't work or when it's abused in any way, we just shut it down. Not necessarily permanently, we just shut it down until we can investigate and find out what's going on and what should be done. And lots of times it's allowed to reorganize and reform under different leadership. (NJ-OF-39A)

Correctional officer perspectives and attitudes toward ethnic organizations tended to be shaped by their experiences within the prison and to some extent by their experiences with racial minorities in the community. At prisons where ethnic organizations provided stability and predictability within the prisoner community, guards held a more positive and supportive perspective. However, at locations where racial conflict or violence emerged periodically, guards stressed a need for greater control and a concern for personal safety.

According to our observations, prisoners were more likely than guards to experience the impact of racial or ethnic conflict. We found that whites and older or unaffiliated blacks were more frequently the target of racial conflict and criminal activity. This usually resulted from a lack of support (or protection) from their respective racial groups. To combat occasional victimization, many of these prisoners formed loosely structured cliques comprised of members of the same (or nearby) communities or sought job assignments such as porters, hospital or staff mess clerks, or other jobs that offered ameliorative or protective environments.

Black prisoners appeared to have more experience in working out an organizational strategy for pursuing their needs and interests than any other racial or ethnic minority. The history of black social organization in American prisons suggests that one outcome of early black struggle has been a new sense of legitimacy in cultural awareness organizations. In contrast, Hispanics and Native Americans appeared to be only developing the sense of collective struggle and determination shown by blacks.

The emerging cultural and religious interests of Native American prisoners, denied in most prisons prior to religious-freedom court decisions, also played a key role in promoting ethnic division within the prisoner community. Most Native Americans told us that their cultural "gains" frequently carried the price of constant harrassment from racist guards and prisoners. In many instances, their religion was the primary target of guard cynicism, ridicule, and distrust.

One Stillwater guard, admittedly unfamiliar with the cultural and religious cermonies practiced by Native Americans, saw their requests as capitalizing on the absence of religious precedent and as having secondary motives:

A lot of this pow-wow stuff is under the direction of religious activities, saying that it's a part of their culture, part of their religion, and that stuff. I was talking with some of the Native Americans that I know and work with, and they say, "Yes, they get involved with this type of stuff here, but on the outside, no, they seldom do." You know, the drums and the pow-wow. I think there's a lack of knowledge about their religion in general. You see, they can bluff a lot with that. At one time the peace pipe was coming in, and no white man could touch the pipe or look at it. Well, I don't know what's a part of their religion or not—who knows? And the same thing with the drums, and it can go on and on, you see. It's not like other religious groups that we know something about, and we can say, "Well, you're bluffing." (MSP-OF-42)

It should be noted that both Stillwater and OSP, which had the greatest proportion of Native American prisoners within their respective populations, had policies authorizing Native American cultural awareness, including the use of ceremonial pipes and sweet grass. Furthermore, Stillwater management permitted Native Americans to have their drums in their housing areas, while OSP management authorized the construction of the first Sweat Lodge on prison grounds.

Religious Organizations

As shown in table 5-2, religious organizations accounted for only 14 percent of all memberships. The proportion of male prisoners involved in religious organizations was similar at each prison, but substantially fewer Bedford Hills prisoners held membership in religious organizations. The data indicated that members of religious organizations were predominantly white (70 percent) and had served lengthy periods of time in confinement.

The classification of religious organizations included formal organizations, organized apart from regularly scheduled religious programs, for Christian, Islamic, Hebrew, and Moslem faiths. While Native American spiritual worship may be characterized as being within this category, the failure of prison staff to view their worship as a bona fide religious practice and their emphasis on cultural education, convinced us that Native American organizations would be best understood within the context of ethnic organizations.

Interviews with correctional officers, sponsors, and religious organization leaders suggested that prison guards were much more supportive of religious organizations than any other type of prisoner organization. Furthermore, guards' views were generally consistent across all research sites and were not influenced by racial or ethnic differences in membership. That is, black religious organizations (for example, the Muslims), were seen as equally beneficial and non-threatening as organizations that were predominantly white or Hispanic.

One Muslim prisoner at Rahway told us that over a ten-year period the Nation of Islam has been able to gain the respect of prison officials because of their emphasis on personal discipline and a strong commitment to the Islamic faith:

Ten years ago when the administration felt a need to repress what they termed, Black Muslims or the Nation of Islam, they found out something about the Nation of Islam. They found that they were trustworthy and honest, courteous, clean, dependable, and an organized group of individuals. Their word was as good as law. They have had less trouble from them, in term of anti-social behavior, than they did from all those who were not religious or a part of a religious organization. As the years progressed, the administration found a tremendous degree of success in working with the members and followers of Elijah Muhammed. Today we have established that type of relationship. So the administration finds themselves relaxed in dealing with us because we are coming from a more modern, updated, rational perspective in terms of religion. (NJ–IN–02)

Self-Help Organizations

As illustrated in table 5-2, membership in self-help organizations accounted for 27 percent of all prisoner organization memberships. Self-help organization members represented the greatest proportion of whites (81 percent), were more frequently arrested for the first time between the ages of eighteen and twenty-five years, and were more likely to have prior felony convictions than members of any other type of prisoner organization.

The data revealed substantial differences between male and female prisoner involvement in self-help organizations. For example, over 43 percent of all Bedford Hills affiliated prisoners held membership in one or more self-help organizations, suggesting that either the opportunity for participation in self-help programs was substantially greater at Bedford Hills or that female prisoners were more likely than males to view self-help organizations as being a legitimate means of fulfilling personal needs and interests. Interviews with program management and staff suggested that male and female differences in participation may have been influenced by both factors. That is, the opportunities for male prisoner involvement in self-help organizations tended to be more limited (due to a greater emphasis on security and control) and, consequently, many male prisoners did not pursue the formation of self-help organizations. Furthermore, male prisoner participation tended to be influenced more directly by their peer culture and social relationships within the prisoner community.

Our observations revealed that male prisoners had a greater range of status-conferring opportunities within the context of the prisoner social system and the prison-organization hierarchy. They could more readily obtain assignments which, from their perspective, provided satisfaction of personal needs, for example, income from prison industry work, a hustle, or special clerical jobs. Underlying these influences is the marked differences in penal philosophy for male and female corrections. In spite of a limited New York State Department of Correctional Services budget during the study period, the correctional approach of Bedford Hills was more closely associated with the rehabilitation philosophy than any of the male prisons included in the study. In this vein, female prisoners may have received more official support and recognition for their participation in treatment-oriented programs and activities.

It was sometimes difficult to determine the difference between prisoner self-help organizations and institutional treatment programs. In some instances, both management and line staff referred to these two types of activity interchangeably. Alcoholics Anonymous, for example, was frequently seen as an official institutional program—in spite of their long-standing policy of voluntary membership.

In one state, this resulted in conflict between the official goals of the Mutual Agreement Program (MAP) and Alcoholics Anonymous (AA) policy. We were told that the institutional policy of assigning prisoners with a history of alcoholism to AA under the MAP concept tended to undermine the philosophy of Alcoholics Anonymous. While this conflict was subsequently resolved in policy revisions, it serves to illustrate the interface problems between prisoner self-help organizations and institutional programs. Many self-help organizations resembled therapeutic communities (Atlantis, Asklepion, Narcotics Anonymous), but their organizational structure provided a substantial amount of prisoner self-determination and self-governance. Furthermore, self-help members tended to view themselves more as participants of an organization than as clients of a treatment program. Thus, while the major goals of self-help organizations were therapeutic in nature, the organizational dynamics and structure resembled more conventional prisoner organizations.

Special-Interest Organizations

Special-interest organizations reflected a greater amount of diversity in their organizational activities than any of the three remaining types of prisoner organizations. For example, organizations at OSP (referred to as *clubs*) were involved in activities ranging from maintaining a stock car on the Pacific Northwest racing circuit to lobbying for improvements in prison conditions before the Oregon legislature. At other sites, the Jaycees operated fund-raising projects within the prisoner community, such as popcorn sales and visitor picture programs, to provide a range of community services. At Soledad, the Jaycees cleaned and maintained the trailers for prisoner family visits. Other special-interest organizations pursued more specialized goals, but together they reflected a wide range of prisoner interests and organizational activities. Membership in organizations intended to provide limited prisoner participation may be viewed as representative organizations, but the relatively small numbers of members and the parallel efforts of other prisoner organizations involved in quality-of-life issues seemed to justify their inclusion in the special-interest category.

According to table 5-2, special-interest members comprised over 40 percent of all prisoner memberships. The greatest proportion of special-interest membership was found at OSP (54 percent), although all sites except Stillwater (26.5 percent) had substantially large memberships. We found that special-interest-organization members tended to be slightly older, were more likely to have been arrested for the first time under the age of eighteen years, had completed more formal education, had served longer periods of time in correctional institutions, and had a slightly longer amount of time to be served on their current sentences than members of all other organizations. In addition, special-interest organizations attracted a greater proportion of blacks than self-help or religious organizations.

Our observations and interviews with organization leadership, sponsors, and prison management suggested that the framework and objectives of special-interest organizations provides a vehicle for greater prisoner involvement in many facets of prison operations. For example, several special-interest organizations were structured primarily for prisoner input (for example, Men's Advisory Council, Inmate Liaison Committee at Bedford Hills, Worker's Council at Stillwater), but, with few exceptions, prisoners were not offered an opportunity for involvement in policy development or decisions that could change the conditions of their imprisonment.

One Soledad prisoner told us limitations on the potential for the Men's Advisory Council stems from staff reluctance to seriously consider MAC requests:

> Any type of small problem that comes up in the institution, MAC is supposed to try to handle it to the best of their ability. But they're powerless because whatever the staff tells them they're going to do, that's what they do. There's nothing that they can do about it. So it's up to the staff to weigh it out and see if they're going to let them have it or whatever. Like a lot of times it's just a refusal. (SO–IN–05)

Another Soledad prisoner with a lengthy period of incarceration in the California Department of Corrections, felt that the MAC is caught in a paper production game intended to keep the important issues at a distance:

> They allow the MAC to negotiate, and they let them out when we get locked down, and all that. They allow them to get into conversation with the upper level administration, sure, and they have meetings with them. But it really doesn't mean anything because the administration doesn't respond to anything. Anytime you want to talk to them about something, they want it in writing. And listen, I used to turn out bales of that shit. I can turn it out in my sleep, and if you turn it out in writing, itemized, comprehensive, logical, and everything, it just gets shelved. (SO–IN–21)

Prisoners at other institutions saw the failure of advisory groups as stemming from a lack of support from both prisoners and staff. The lack of trust and the suspicion of advisory group members being coopted by management tended to work against the effort to develop these organizations into an effective mechanism for participation and involvement. Often the issues to be resolved were simple problems that could have been dealt with by line-staff levels.

Members and sponsors of special-interest organizations, for different reasons, argued that greater involvement is essential for the success of existing organizations. While prisoners advocated a greater opportunity for autonomy, self-determination, and a wider scope of organizational activities, sponsors pointed to responsible shared decision making, planning, and recognition for the organizations' service to the institution.

A guard who sponsored the Jaycees at Stillwater told us that support from the administration for special activities and the responsible conduct of the membership were two key factors in the continued success of prisoner organizations:

> I would think first, that the administration would have to be supportive of prisoner organizations for it to be successful. I think that without their support, there is no way it could really get going on an up and up basis. You'll always have underground groups in a prison, but I think the fact that this administration supports prisoner organizations and makes room for their meetings, and makes an officer available for the meetings, and pays overtime for sponsors to supervise the meetings, and pays overtime for the banquets, and allows bands to come in and play, that's probably the things that makes the groups go, the fact that the administration is in support of it. And also the fact that the inmates are responsible enough to participate in a group event in an orderly, mannerly, fashion that they do. We haven't had any problems at any of these major events for a long time. (MSP-OF-48)

Line officers (with little direct experience with prisoner organizations) nearly always rejected the possibility of an extension of prisoner participation, asserting that it would compromise their ability to control the population. Even those officers who saw prisoner organizations in a positive light tended to stress the need for more control over their activities.

One Rahway officer told us that prisoner organizations, such as the Lifer's Group, were a meaningful activity for prisoners during their imprisonment, but that changing dynamics within the organizations and changes in leadership required constant intelligence on their activities. He told us that groups are very difficult to control because prisoners attempt to alter the rules and regulations governing their objectives:

> I think organizations are hard to control because inmates are people, and people always seem to go around the rules and regulations to suit their own benefit. They require manpower, they require expertise, and they require experience because you have to work with these various groups. So you have to know who you are dealing with and what the

rules are. You can't say the organizations are a big problem, but you
can't say there isn't any problem either. It's like anything else, it has
to be regulated. We have a Lifer's Group, which is a very popular thing
here. Okay, what are the rules for the Lifer's? Are they allowed to go
back and forth to their office? What are they allowed to have in their
office? And the rules have evolved out of experience, dealing with the
Lifers as the thing grew. (NJ–OF–39A)

Management appeared to be more willing to explore the potential for
increased prisoner involvement but limited their acceptance to "proven" relationships, which were most often linked to specific control and information
interests. The central issue or obstacle in the way of greater prisoner participatory powers was the fear of abuse of power and influence. Maximum-security-
prison management is geared toward minimizing decision-making risks, common
to many organizations. Prisoner empowerment is one of the risks commonly
ascribed to internal security and control concerns. However, without positive
precedents, there is little way in which to demonstrate the positive applications
of empowerment. At one point, the superintendent of OSP considered the
prospects for a President's Club, an organization made up of elected top officers
of each prisoner organization. The stated intention was to better coordinate
prisoner requests and use of limited resources. However, when it became
apparent that representatives of the new and innovative organizational body
wanted to address more basic quality-of-life issues, it was quickly disbanded
(before it officially began). With prisoner populations increasing and internal
conflict likely to intensify, prisoner organizations may become viewed as a
means to "cool out" hostility and discontent. The temptation of cooptation
will likely increase once management senses a diminishing return on control
strategies. However, few prisoner-organization leaders could maintain respect
within the prisoner community for responding to such untimely gestures
of conciliation.

Departmental management held similar perspectives on the current role
of prisoner organizations. For example, one of the New Jersey Department
of Corrections central office management staff expressed reserved support
but recognized the potential benefits for management:

Although I've been out of direct contact with the control of Rahway
for the past two years, I would have to say that inmate groups can be
beneficial. There's no question about it, they can be helpful to the
administration. My feeling is that the department is trying to make
an effort to develop a positive response to inmate organizations. I
think that there are elements within these organizations that not only
benefit the inmate population, but benefit prison management. At
the same time, I am not the type of individual who would go on record
as saying that every inmate organization has a positive influence. Some
of them can be very threatening. I think that New Jersey's policy would

try to eliminate them or reduce their influence, basically policy decisions, hoping, of course, that you can do this without "going to war" with certain inmate groups. (NJ–MGR–46)

We found that special-interest organizations received a greater amount of official support from management than any other type of prisoner organization. They also attracted the most talented and highly motivated leaders, primarily because they offered the greatest potential for prisoner self-determination, autonomy, and empowerment. However, the reluctance (or ambivalance) of management to embark on a plan intended to extend their contributions to the prisoner community appeared to limit and dampen their broad achievements inside and outside of the prison walls. The organizations that prospered were incorporated (typically as not-for-profit corporations) and affiliated with well-established community organizations. In this instance, the voices of outside members carried substantially more influence than the collective voice of any individual prisoner-organization leader.

Regulation and Control

The development of formal procedures for granting recognition and sponsorship of prisoner organizations has tended to follow their proliferation and expansion within the prisoner community. These trends suggest that management and prisoner interests have become subjected to a larger number of organizational restraints and considerations and that the prison is evolving into a more highly complex organization. As a result, many smaller elements of the prison organizational structure may be expected to stimulate conflicting interests.

Prison management is faced with a relatively new role—managing conflict among competing, legitimate interests. Until recently, prison management has faced conflict arising primarily from prisoner attempts to offset or undermine official prison goals. Today management must respond to conflict resulting from competition among legitimate prisoner organizations for limited prison resources. This is not to say that traditional challenges to control goals have been replaced by intergroup competition. Prisoner opposition to structural imbalances in power and control remain—and may have increased. Rather, prison management is confronted with the additional burden of regulating the legitimate activities of prisoner organizations while maintaining control over internal conflict within the larger prisoner community.

Lacking much of the experience, knowledge, and orientation that management has evolved in the private sector, prison management has tended to follow along the path of traditional coercive control. Consequently, most prisoner organizations have been viewed as carrying the potential for collective opposition to official policies and goals or as being a vehicle for distribution of illicit

goods and services. Our observations suggest that coercive or restrictive management approaches do not necessarily reduce the level of undesirable activity
within prisoner organizations. While control strategies may have some short-
term value in inhibiting practices deemed unacceptable by management, in a
long-range perspective, excessive restriction tends to move prisoner collective
activity back into the arena of informal group networks, which are likely to
gain wider support from underground organizations. It is not mere coincidence
that the growth of underground ethnic gangs at Soledad and other California
prisons corresponded with the disbandment and reduction of formal organizations. It would appear to be in management's interest to keep prisoner-organization activity on a formal level and develop policies that provide a broad range
of legitimate opportunities for prisoner involvement.

We found little evidence that the granting of expanded opportunities for
prisoner involvement, empowerment, or self-determination was directly linked
to security problems. In fact, there was substantial evidence to the contrary.
For example, Rahway's management policies allowed prisoner-organization
leadership to maintain private offices, unrestricted use of telephones, and a
substantial amount of autonomy in conducting their activities. Consequently,
Rahway prisoner-organization members appeared to be relatively satisfied
with their relationship with management and viewed their opportunity in a
positive light. Two notable products of this policy were the Juvenile Awareness
Project of the Lifer's that was featured in the television film, "Scared Straight,"
and James Scott, a light heavyweight contender who made boxing at Rahway
a "vocational training" opportunity through profit-sharing from his professional
boxing proceeds. We found little evidence that Rahway prisoner organizations
were involved in illicit activities centered around power struggles or subterranean
economic goals. We assumed that this was related to the availability of legitimate
opportunities and strong management support.

It is our conclusion that the pluralist structure found within most maximum-security prisons provides a unique opportunity to channel prisoner talent
and productivity into meaningful and beneficial directions. However, this can
be accomplished only with policies that are supportive of prisoner self-determination and empowerment. Unless management is willing to view prisoners
as productive, adult human beings capable of making decisions in their own
behalf, there can be no meaningful discussion regarding their participation in
prison-organization affairs. Furthermore, structural conflict cannot be reduced
until a joint effort is made by prisoners and management to identify and seek
objectives and strategies that serve mutual interests.

Notes

1. See: Ronald Berkman, *Opening the Gates: The Rise of the Prisoners Movement* (Lexington, Mass.: Lexington Books, D.C. Heath, 1979), pp. 113-157;

Leo Carroll, *Hacks, Blacks, and Cons: Race Relations in A Maximum Security Prison* (Lexington, Mass.: Lexington Books, D.C. Heath, 1974), pp. 32-33.

2. See: John Irwin, *Prisons in Turmoil* (Boston: Little, Brown and Company, 1980), pp. 62-122; Berkman, *Opening the Gates*. For an example of official governmental reactions to the activities of militant prison reform organizations, see: U.S., Congress, House Committee on Internal Security, *Revolutionary Target: The American Prison System*, H. Rept. 93-738 (Washington, D.C.: U.S. Government Printing Office, 1973).

3. See: John Pallas and Robert Barber, "From Riot to Revolution," in *The Politics of Punishment: A Critical Analysis of Prisons in America*, ed. Erik O. Wright (New York: Harper Colophen Books, 1973), pp. 237-261. Also see: Malcolm Little, *The Autobiography of Malcolm X* (New York: Grove Press, 1965); George Jackson, *Soledad Brothers: The Prison Letters of George Jackson* (New York: Coward-McCann, 1970); U.S., Congress, *Revolutionary Target: The American Prison*.

4. See: J.E. Baker, *The Right to Participate: Inmate Involvement in Prison Administration* (Meuchen, N.J.: Scarecrow Press, 1974); Tom Murton, "Inmate Self-Government," *University of San Francisco Law Review* 6(October 1971):87-101; Gabrielle Trynauer, "What Went Wrong at Walla Walla?," *Corrections Magazine* 7(June 1981):37-41; Tom Murton and Phillis Jo Baunach, *Shared Decision-Making As A Treatment Technique in Prison Management* (Minneapolis: Murton Foundation for Criminal Justice, 1975).

5. James Jacobs, *Stateville: The Penitentiary in Mass Society* (Chicago: The University of Chicago Press, 1977), pp. 138-174; James Jacobs, "Street Gangs Behind Bars," *Social Problems* 21(1974):395-411; R. Theodore Davidson, *Chicano Prisoners: The Key To San Quentin* (New York: Holt, Rinehart, and Winston, 1974), pp. 80-100; Kevin Krajick, "The Menace of the Supergangs," *Corrections Magazine* 6(June 1980):11-14.

6. See: C. Ron Huff, "Unionization Behind the Walls," *Criminology* 12(August 1974):175-193; C. Ron Huff, "Prisoner's Union: A Challenge for State Corrections," *State Government* 48(Summer 1975)145-149; C. Ron Huff and S. Dinitz, "Prisoner's Unions: A Cross-National Investigation of Public Acceptance," *International Journal of Criminology and Penology* 4 (November 1976):331-347.

7. During our personal contacts with prison officials at conferences and meetings, we were informed that many states were just developing official policy and guidelines for prisoner organizations. During a survey of incorporated organizations in state prisons, we found that only one-third of the twenty-eight states responding maintained accurate records on the number and type of formal prisoner organizations operating within their correctional institutions.

8. Irwin, *Prisons in Turmoil*, pp. 24-26; Pallas and Barber, *Politics of Punishment*, pp. 237-261.

9. See: Irwin, *Prisons in Turmoil*, pp. 102-122; Berkman, *Opening the Gates*.

10. See: Min Y. Yee, *The Melancholy History of Soledad Prison* (New York: Harper's Magazine Press, 1973); Jacobs, *Stateville.*

11. Carroll, *Hacks, Blacks, and Cons,* pp. 63-113; Jacobs, *Stateville,* pp. 138-174.

12. Carroll, *Hacks, Blacks, and Cons,* pp. 95-97.

13. These white extremist groups were most prevasive in California during the period of racial violence and confrontation. Some remain in several prisons as a means of providing protection to whites who have become the new minority in many state prison systems. See: Jacobs, *Stateville,* p. 159.

14. Jacobs, *Stateville,* p. 207.

15. Davidson, *The Key to San Quentin,* pp. 101-147.

16. Irwin, *Prisons in Turmoil,* pp. 112-113.

17. Berkman, *Opening the Gates,* pp. 113-157.

18. Ibid., p. 117.

19. Carroll, *Hacks, Blacks, and Cons,* pp. 32-33.

20. Berkman, *Opening the Gates,* pp. 114-115.

21. Ibid., p. 120.

22. R.M. Montilla and James G. Fox, *Pilot Study Report: Soledad* (Sacramento, Calif.: American Justice Institute, 1978).

23. Male and female memberships were computed separately to facilitate a more precise analysis of the relationships between type of membership and individual characteristics.

6

Where from Here: Conflict or Concensus?

This final chapter assesses the likelihood of organizational change in light of the major findings. Rather than presenting a summary apart from an analysis of the issues related to the change process, they are considered part of one general discussion.

Change is a nebulous concept that carries many different meanings and connotations to organizational members who may be affected by the change. For example, prison management may perceive change in terms of obtaining more staff, a larger budget, and broader discretion in making difficult organizational decisions. Likewise, prison guards may view the acquisition of more control over prisoners and more direct influence over their work as desirable change. In contrast, prisoners may see change as being a higher standard of institutional living and more opportunities to influence decisions that directly affect their lives during confinement.

While all these perceptions of change have some merit, they generally reflect the specialized interests held by each group of organizational members. Our findings have demonstrated that the interests held by different members of the prison organization are centered around basic organizational goals: management and custodial workers desired more order and restraint; prisoners desired more self-determination and participatory powers. Given the nature (and extent) of conflict within the organizational structure of maximum-security prisons, members are unlikely to support changes that oppose their specialized needs and interests. Stated more directly, organizational members most often view change in a positive light when it squarely addresses their most basic concerns and interests.

As indicated earlier, organizational structure, specific organizational problems, and availability of resources are also crucial factors in determining the likelihood and directions of change. But the essential issue underlying meaningful change in maximum-security prisons is whether proposed changes are likely to foster greater conflict or cooperation among members of the prison organization. The long-range success of meaningful change ultimately depends not only on the cooperation of those most affected by the change, but also on the theoretical and philosophical principles on which the change is based. Without a willingness to modify rigid, control-oriented strategies, there is little reason to believe that management can formulate organizational change goals that will reduce (or limit) intraorganizational conflict.

Summary of the Major Findings and Implications for Change

Prison Management

This study has characterized the prison as an organization in conflict. Correctional officers' interests were frequently in conflict with both management and prisoners, and their collective powers were aimed typically at resolving perceived imbalances in power and influence. By the same token, a substantial proportion of prisoners (and their formal organizations) often sought greater opportunities for self-determination and empowerment. We also saw that competition for power among members of the prison organization frequently stimulated the development of specialized strategies aimed at undermining long-range management interests. Consequently, management was often placed in the tenuous position of attempting to address all organizational interests without establishing a precarious imbalance of power.

Many scholars agree that sound prison management not only carries the responsibility of security, safety, and control but also the burden of directing effective organizational change.[1] "Keeping the lid on" is not only incompatible with contemporary management principles, but it may actually induce a greater amount of stress within the organizational structure. While many prison administrators may disagree, the blending of organizational members' interests produces extremely complex problems that cannot be addressed solely with "security" or "custody" intervention strategies. Management effectiveness requires that power relationships be visible and recognized as major organizational dynamics. In the broader sense, this has been accomplished through the formalization of prisoner organizations and by the establishment of labor-management meetings with correctional officers. However, substantially greater opportunities for meaningful involvement and participation need to be developed before attempts at reducing intraorganizational conflict can be successful.

Management attitudes were largely incompatible with flexible organizational change strategies. For example, manager responses to two organizational change scales indicated that they were generally inflexible to both structural and participatory change. When we examined the change scales separately, we found that structural changes (which have only secondary implications for altering the prison organization) were accepted somewhat more readily than participatory changes (which tend to increase the level of involvement of organizational members). However, substantial differences were observed between executive and security management for resistance to change. For instance, security managers were much less willing to support organizational change initiatives than executive managers, particularly change initiatives that include prisoner empowerment. A large proportion of these differences appeared to be related to educational background, socialization into work roles, and security management's closer ties to line staff. The chances of obtaining security management support for prisoner participation in organizational decisions would appear to be linked to opportunities for custodial staff to influence policies and procedures governing prisoner empowerment.

One approach to this situation would be to identify the specific areas of agreement and compatibility between prisoner and correctional officer interests, as well as the identification of specific areas of conflict. In this approach, management would play a much different role in the regulation of internal conflict. Special emphasis would have to be given to utilizing and directing conflict in a positive and productive manner. There are several precedents for this approach in the literature. For example, Dahrendorf has argued that conflicts are never completely resolved but are regulated by controlling power and authority.[2] In addition, he asserts that such regulation is most effective when each group in conflict is able to recognize the social reality and dynamics of the conflict and when they are organized to pursue special interests.[3] This approach allows agreement on formal procedures for seeking solutions to most conflict issues.

These principles of conflict management would appear to be readily applicable to the organizational structure and internal conflict of the prison, where structural conflict stems from opposition to control and restraint goals. It seems reasonable to assume that a coordinated opportunity structure that incorporates prisoner and guard participation in the establishment of cooperative relationships may reduce conflict stemming from opposing interests. If security management can play an important role in formulating conflict reduction strategies, their resistance to participatory change may be substantially reduced and their views may resemble more closely those of executive management.

The focus on prison management revealed several *pro forma* criteria for selecting management personnel. For example, the vast majority of maximum-security management staff had been employed in institutional corrections for over ten years, and most had obtained their present management position as a result of demonstrated performance in line-security assignments within their respective facilities. According to interviews with management personnel, their assignments and promotions were made primarily on the basis of their ability to maintain control over the prisoner community and their commitment to official policies. Together these criteria will inhibit innovative organizational change and will serve to create a climate of unnecessary uniformity and conformity.[4] In the contemporary prison organizational climate, these traditional work roles have limited value. Certainly, they are supportive of the paramilitary structure supporting internal control and security. But it is doubtful that these criteria represent the perspectives held by younger officers or members of racial or ethnic minorities (or women) who are entering the prison work environment in increasing numbers. Indeed, one factor underlying the relatively short tenure and slow progress of racial and social minorities within the prison opportunity structure has been the attitudes of rejection and emphasis on traditional control strategies held by security management.

Correctional Officers

The assessment of correctional officer work-related concerns revealed consistent findings across all five sites. For example, prison guards at each site were most concerned about power (ability to influence correctional policy and management decisions), control (ability to maintain control over prisoners within an increasingly legalistic social climate), and safety (ability to insure personal safety in a perceived hostile setting). The communications and support dimension (ability to communicate effectively with supervisors and management) yielded the most varied responses. The majority of officers at each site pointed to a gradual reduction of their authority, which they saw as stemming from the introduction of standardized disciplinary procedures (which have shifted discretionary powers to an impartial tribunal). Most frequently, officer concerns regarding communications and support was linked to the morale of the work force and the degree of stability within the prisoner community.

Formal correctional officer relationships with management were largely uncoordinated with long-range goals. In part, this has evolved from the introduction of labor-management relations and the increasingly adversary and political posture taken by correctional officer unions. Officers with the backing of their unions are relatively free to pick and choose which management initiatives they will support or reject. Compliance relationships under these conditions are highly unpredictable and management's ability to take more proactive positions in approaching organizational problems is seriously impaired.

One of the most salient concerns expressed by male officers was the impact of affirmative action programs, resulting in the employment of women in security posts. While this concern was not strongly illustrated in the racism-sexism scale scores (because of the combined effects of scale items), the interviews clearly conveyed the intensity of male feelings and attitudes toward female officers. Nearly all male officers, particularly those who had worked in institutional corrections for four years or more, strongly objected to the practice (or plan) of women holding security assignments in housing, work, or recreational areas of the prison. Among the male concerns were a fear that women officers would create an additional security burden, a doubt that women could "carry their weight" during confrontations with assaultive prisoners, and a basic distrust of their performance due to a perceived "susceptibility" to male prisoner sexual ploys.

Blacks and other racial minorities in the four male prisons also reported experiencing prejudice, social rejections, and insensitivity to their cultural background, but their position within the social hierarchy of line officers tended to be substantially higher than that of women officers. While women have been employed less time in male facilities than racial minorities, much of their lower status tended to be linked to the sexual attitudes and prejudices of the male work force, rather than seniority or experience.

The issues arising from conflict within officer ranks does not appear to be an insurmountable obstacle to organizational change. For example, the salience of male officer resistance to affirmative action is likely to be reduced as women's roles in security operations, representation in supervisory and administrative positions, and leadership in union activities are expanded and as the prison organization gains more experience with their performance and job expectations. To be effective, women officers must be viewed as a part of a larger scheme to normalize social relationships within the prison. In the long-term perspective, changes in the physical design of the prison may be required to protect the privacy rights of prisoners and insure that the safety of women officers is not substantially at risk.

Conflict between officers and prisoners was primarily a structural phenomena. For example, line officers and security management manipulated conflict among prisoners to insure larger control interests. In most instances, this was a tacit acceptance of racial conflict—as long as the level of conflict did not directly threaten their personal safety.

Correctional officers were collectively opposed to organizational change initiatives that reflected an endorsement of greater prisoner participation in institutional affairs. The prevailing attitudes among prison guards were that imprisonment is intended as punishment, restraint, and social isolation. In this context, it is unlikely that management can easily gain wide support for changes that are perceived as threatening or undermining custodial worker's concern for power and control.

Prisoners

The greatest differences between the five prisoner communities were predictably between male and female prisoners. Women prisoners had substantially fewer prior convictions and had served substantially less time than their male counterparts. In addition, women prisoners tended to be younger and were more often black or Hispanic.

Most of the differences in demographic characteristics among the four male prisoner communities appeared to be related to the proportion of racial minorities and the priorities of the criminal-justice system in their respective states. For example, Minnesota had a very low (per capita) rate of incarceration, a well-developed community corrections program, and a relatively low proportion of racial and ethnic minorities (26 percent) among maximum-security prisoners. Consequently, the Stillwater prisoner population was markedly different than that of Rahway, which was predominantly black (66 percent) and had a large proportion of the population (43 percent) serving lengthy sentences.

The five-scale instrument measuring prisoner social values produced findings indicative of contemporary prisoner perspectives. For example, the prisonization scale revealed that the majority of prisoners at each site shared traditional *inmate-code* values, but substantial differences were revealed between male and female prisoners and among different racial and ethnic groups in the extent to which the values were supported.

Racial stratification appears to have altered the system of norms governing adaptive behavior within the prisoner community. The inmate code, especially its norms proscribing the establishment of informal social relationships with custodial staff, was not uniformly adopted by members of different racial groups. Instead, whites, blacks, Hispanics, and Native Americans appear to have evolved normative system tailored to their respective cultural and social needs and they place substantially different meanings and emphases on norms regulating prison survival. For example, where victimization previously carried peer expectations of retribution, current patterns of victimization and retaliation are predominantly interracial events, and assailants are most often protected by the collective powers of organized racial or ethnic groups. The prisoner community can no longer be described as a holistic association of common needs and interests. Rather, it is best understood as an aggregate of smaller, specialized, social units organized primarily according to race and ethnicity.

Contrary to popular impressions that maximum-security prisoners hold strong commitments to criminal values and life-styles, it was found that less than 10 percent of the prisoners at each site held highly criminalized attitudes and values.

Also, many prisoners held strongly critical perspectives of their treatment during confinement, particularly at prisons with large black-prisoner populations. For example, both Bedford Hills and Rahway prisoners revealed higher radicalism scores than all other prisoners, and female prisoners tended to be slightly more critical of the criminal-justice system and their treatment in prison than Rahway prisoners. However, most radicalized attitudes appeared to reflect individual reactions to administrative policies seen as promoting excessive control over the prisoner community, rather than as individual expressions of political ideology.

Prisoner expressions of powerlessness, frustration, and hostility were most frequently related to care and custody issues. The focus on attitudes and values indicative of collective action revealed several interesting findings. For example, next to prisonization and radicalism, prisoner perspectives on collective action were the strongest prisoner social values. However, most prisoner collective-action concerns centered around the conditions underlying the perceived need for greater involvement than on empowerment.

Prisoner views toward members of other racial and ethnic groups differed most between male and female prisons. While male prisoners saw racial identity as the most important consideration in forming social relationships within the prisoner community, female prisoners were much less likely to see race or ethnicity as an obstacle to the development of social (or personal) relationships.

Racial stratification and racial conflict was evident at each male prison. However, there appeared to be greater racial conflict and hostility at those prisons having relatively small black prisoner populations and fewer black correctional officers.

Overall, the study of the contemporary prisoner community has illustrated the extent to which racial differences have divided prisoners and hindered the development of unified, common-based, approaches to change. As indicated earlier, racial violence and conflict has a long history in American penal institutions. It is unlikely that racial conflict can be substantially reduced in maximum-security prisons within the very near future. However, the role played by line custodial staff and prison management in tolerating (or provoking) racial conflict for the purpose of social control, must be squarely addressed before meaningful solutions can be evolved. Racism, regardless of the purpose it serves in fulfilling control interests of custodial staff, must be strongly discouraged by management. However, even if management is successful in controlling racist practices by line staff, additional effort must be launched to reduce racial hostility among prisoners. It seems straightforward that successful efforts to combat racism must be cooperatively developed by prisoners, custodial staff, and management. In this perspective, race relations is the responsibility of all members of the prison organization.

It may be unrealistic to conceptualize the maximum-security prison as an organization that works without racial conflict, intimidation, and situational violence. However, it is not unrealistic to assume that we can better utilize human resources in a manner that is more consistent with the needs and interests of all racial groups. The primary obstacle to this approach is the unwillingness of prison management to develop and enforce policies specifically intended to reduce racism within staff ranks. To accomplish this task, custodial personnel must have alternative control strategies that are perceived as being at least as effective as those that manipulate conflict among racial and ethnic groups within the prisoner community.

Prisoner Organizations

Formal prisoner organizations may be the key to the development of meaningful prisoner involvement in organizational matters.[5] The findings support the notion that prisoner organizations can serve as useful and effective vehicles of organizational change. They can be (and have been) used primarily as a method of social control—by further dividing prisoner interests, management reduces the risks of collective opposition. However, they can be viewed as convenient tools for participative management. The decision as to which direction management takes would seem to rest on their willingness to develop opportunities for meaningful participation. To accomplish this goal, management would have to support formal training for both prisoners and line staff in leadership skills, organizational problem-solving, and human relations. In addition, prisoners would have to be granted a greater amount of autonomy and self-determination in formulating strategies for change within the prison organization. The long-term impact of a collaborative-management approach may reduce the destructive effects of conflict which is embedded in nearly every level of the prison organization. The basic question seems to be whether management chooses to deal with unpredictable expressions of illegitimate power, or to allow prisoners to communicate their needs, perspectives, and interests in a legitimate and productive fashion.

Consensus and Collaborative Intervention

The evolution of cooperative relationships within maximum-security prisons will not be an easy task. Early stages of this goal will likely encounter strong resistance from custodial workers who perceive prisoner participation as being counterproductive to their control and safety concerns. In a similar fashion, dominant racial groups would be reluctant to share power and influence with racial and ethnic groups representing the numerical minority within the prisoner community. It is apparent that both correctional officer and prisoner viewpoints must be seriously considered in the formulation of specific intervention strategies. It would serve little purpose for management to casually dismiss these sources of resistance to change as being indigenous to the prison organization.

One approach, as indicated earlier, would be to simultaneously expand opportunities for prisoner and correctional officer participation at early stages of organizational decision making. This may reduce the perception of threat and contribute to greater understanding and acceptance of the general principles of participative management. Most importantly, change strategies must be carefully planned and coordinated with the long-range goals of the prison organization. In addition, the structure, pace, goals and objectives, and strategies aimed at establishing cooperative relationships must be carefully tailored to the organizational dynamics and social climate of each prison setting. A careful analysis of the sources of intraorganizational conflict is essential to this approach.

Even under the most ideal internal conditions, many change strategies may fail because of external pressures, particularly those that discourage or restrict the use of collaborative approaches. Increasingly, political and budgetary constraints, correctional officer union activism, and court-mandated compliance to minimum standards of care and custody set limitations on management priorities on organizational development and planned change. Consequently, substantial energy and attention is drawn away from consideration of collaborative strategies.

Prison management will undoubtedly continue to be confronted with these issues during the present decade. Changing public attitudes toward the criminal offender have resulted in more restrictive sentencing, prison population increases, and racial imbalances within maximum-security-prison communities. Given the resulting turmoil within the prison organization, particularly around racial conflict, it would appear that internal problems carry the greatest potential for destructive consequences. Management is faced with the decision of whether to structure their organizational priorities around reduction of internal conflict or conformity to external pressures and influences. Our findings strongly suggest that while internal conflict cannot be separated from external influences, substantially more emphasis must be given to the development of collaborative management methods before significant reductions in organizational and racial conflict can be realized.

Notes

1. David Duffee, *Correctional Management: Change and Control in Correctional Organizations* (Englewood Cliffs, N.J.: Prentice-Hall, 1980); John Meyer, Jr., "Change and Obstacles to Change in Prison Management," *Federal Probation* 36 (June 1972):39–46; Elmer K. Nelson and Catherine H. Lovell, *Developing Correctional Administrators* (Washington, D.C.: Joint Commission on Correctional Manpower and Training, 1969); National Advisory Commission on Criminal Justice Standards and Goals, *Corrections* (Washington, D.C.: U.S. Government Printing Office, 1975), pp. 455–486.

2. Ralf Dahrendorf, *Class and Class Conflict in Industrial Society* (Stanford: Stanford University Press, 1959), p. 227.

3. While many of Dahrendorf's arguments are based on the concept of "class conflict," they are generally applicable to the prison organization. Most maximum-security prisoners represent markedly different class and cultural interests and experiences than those held by prison guards and management. It is these differences that make class conflict a useful concept in defining areas of agreement and in developing methods of conflict resolution.

4. Elmer Johnson, *Crime, Correction, and Society*, 3rd ed. (Homewood, Ill.: The Dorsey Press, 1974), p. 421.

5. Jiri J. Enomoto, "Participation in Correctional Management by Offender Self-Help Groups," *Federal Probation* 36 (June 1972):36–38.

Appendix A:
A Note on Methods

Our research would not have been successful without substantial flexibility in the data-collection timetable and research methods. Several departures from the original research design were unavoidable due to events occurring within several of the research sites. Other departures were made voluntarily on the assumption that greater cooperation could be obtained with the use of alternative methods and strategies. While many of the field methods were described throughout the book, we felt that a brief overview of some of the problems faced and decisions made would be helpful to other researchers.

One of the earliest problems occurred during the pilot study at Soledad. Three major lock downs resulting from racial and gang violence set the timetable back approximately five weeks. This resulted not only in major setbacks in the schedule, but it also may have affected interview and questionnaire responses from prisoners and staff.

Another problem stemmed from the need to gain the strong support and cooperation of all organizational members. The original strategy was to gather data from prisoners first and then follow with correctional officers and management. However, the five-week lock-down period required that our attention be directed toward available respondents—line staff and management. This approach did not affect our rapport with prisoners once regular movement and activities were restored. We had anticipated that many prisoners would perceive the initial contacts with custodial personnel and management as a research priority on staff. This concern proved to be unfounded as once we explained our need to include line staff and management to conduct a study of the prison organization, prisoners were not only understanding but were extremely cooperative. They suggested that line staff should be surveyed first because they were less likely to cooperate with academic research. At all subsequent sites, we followed a sequence of custody staff, prisoners, and management. This approach allowed us to obtain a broader perspective of the prison organization and to test our preliminary findings and observations against the responses of management. In addition, it provided a greater amount of information for pursuing in-depth questions with top management.

The sampling of prisoners was straightforward. We obtained a current roster and randomly selected a sample from the population, excluding those prisoners who were classified as *hold overs*, were on outside work details, or were scheduled for release within two weeks. We administered questionnaires and conducted interviews with prisoners in special housing units (segregation and protective custody) separately to avoid unnecessary security precautions.

The interview samples were taken from groups of fifteen to twenty prisoners scheduled for questionnaire administration. In addition, we interviewed all prisoner-organization officers and known leaders within the prisoner community.

The methods used for correctional officer questionnaire administration varied from site to site. At Soledad and Folsom (used during pretest), we distributed questionnaire packets (including a letter of introduction, the instrument, and a plain envelope) to all officers on their departure from their regularly scheduled shifts. At Rahway and Stillwater, we distributed the questionnaire packets at the beginning of each shift. In each instance, we first contacted the current union officers and stewards and sought their support and cooperation. This resulted in union support at each site. At Bedford Hills, we elected to have the union leadership assume responsibility for the entire process of questionnaire distribution and collection. This strategy was used as a means to offset the affects of polarization between line staff and management stemming from enforcement of a mandatory overtime policy. We discovered that there was little variation in the rate of return at each site in spite of all attempts to maximize correctional officer cooperation. The selection of methods for questionnaire administration did not appear to be the crucial factor in the rate of return. We had union backing, management endorsement, and personal contact (interviews) prior to the distribution of questionnaires. At Oregon (OSP), the final site, we modified the instrument slightly by placing the requested demographic information at the end and labeling it as "optional." We also elected to have the questionnaires distributed solely by security management because OSP operations were structured around a rigid military chain of command and line officers were used to complying with research projects in this manner. Furthermore, union officers and several correctional officers we interviewed had recommended this approach. Security management assured us that a high rate of return could be expected. As indicated in table 3-1, we obtained a 96 percent rate of return from OSP correctional officers. However, we cannot link the use of any particular method or strategy to the varying rate of return. The most obvious factor appeared to be staff morale. For example, OSP management had just successfully ended a prisoner work stoppage (strike) in a manner that was strongly supported by line staff. The relationship between line staff and management at all of the remaining sites ranged from overt hostility to indifference.

The specific dynamics associated with the different responses from prison to prison are more complex than staff morale. For example, we discovered (after administration) that union membership was often divided in their approach to resolving conflict with management. We found that veteran line officers were more likely to seek cooperative solutions with management, while younger officers with less seniority more frequently favored an adversary approach. Thus, the endorsement of elected union officers by itself was not sufficient to gain the full cooperation of rank and file officers.

However, not all of these factors can be credited to a lack of influence by union officers or antagonism within union ranks. A substantial number of officers that we contacted through interviews, informal lunch conversations, and other open-ended situations expressed disinterest in the study and doubted the relationship between their participation and any significant changes in security operations or general working conditions. Some officers bluntly informed us that the questionnaire was an imposition on their time and that it had been appropriately "filed" in a wastebasket.

The procedures for selecting correctional officer interviewees were generally productive and without variation at each site, suggesting that personal contact and one-on-one methods may be more appropriate with corrections security personnel than survey methods. The interview candidates were taken from a pool of names compiled from three different sources: prison management, union leadership, and the official seniority roster maintained by the prison personnel office. We stratified the interview candidates by seniority, including those that appeared on both management and union lists. Where there were differences, we merely selected an equal number from each list to insure a balanced perspective. This procedure usually yielded approximately twenty to twenty-five potential interviewees. The final selection gave greater weight to officers who were assigned to prisoner contact posts during day and afternoon shifts, although we included several officers from the morning (first) shift at each site. We also intentionally included all women officers, a substantial number of racial and ethnic minorities, and union officers to insure that their concerns were included in the interview data. All interviews were conducted prior to questionnaire distribution to allow greater contact with line officers and offer explanations of the study objectives.

While interviews, questionnaires, and official records were a major source of data, we also relied heavily on general and systematic observations of prison operations and security and disciplinary procedures. We sought permission to move about each prison freely to conduct open-ended and informal interviews with staff and prisoners. The degree of freedom granted by management varied from prison to prison, but within approximately two weeks we had evolved sufficient trust and familiarity to enter all areas of the institution with little or no notice. These observations frequently provided substantial insight into the situations described by guards and prisoners during the regular interviews. Furthermore, it provided numerous opportunities to follow up issues and concerns expressed by interviewees. Many guards and prisoners invited us into the informal social circles they occupied within their work or housing areas. These informal contacts frequently proved to be rich sources of information, which could not have been obtained during the highly structured and supervised call out or replacement procedures required to conduct staff and prisoner interviews. In most instances, prisoners and staff were more comfortable on their own turf and among their own friends and associates.

Appendix B:
Item and Scale
Correlations

The following tables present the item-to-scale and scale-to-scale correlations (Pearson's *r*) for each of the three organizational samples included in the study. The correlational manager and correctional officer samples were combined, as the relatively small samples at each research site would not provide meaningful correlation coefficients.

Table B–1
Correctional Manager Organizational Change Scales,
Item-to-Scale Correlations

	Structural Change				Participative Change		
Item No.	N	r	p	*Item No.*	N	r	p
S1	55	.59	.000	P1	55	.59	.000
S2	55	.38	.002	P2	55	.67	.000
S3	55	.58	.000	P3	55	.74	.000
S4	55	.59	.000	P4	55	.70	.000
S5	55	.46	.000	P5	55	.76	.000
S6	55	.31	.011	P6	55	.50	.000
S7	55	.36	.004	P7	55	.37	.003

Scale-to-Scale Correlation

Correlation between *structural change* and *participative change*:

r = .33

N = 55

p = .006

Note: N = Number of cases.
  r = Correlation coefficient (Pearson's *r*).
  p = Probability (significance level).

Table B–2
Correctional Officer Occupational Concerns Scale,
Item-to-Scale Correlations: Combined Samples

	Item No.	N	r	p
Control	3	360	.63	.001
	4	360	.62	.001
	17	360	.54	.001
	19	360	.61	.001
	27	360	.41	.001
Safety	2	369	.46	.001
	13	369	.71	.001
	21	369	.36	.001
	23	369	.59	.001
	30	369	.21	.001
Resistance to Change	6	371	.62	.001
	7	371	.47	.001
	9	371	.71	.001
	15	371	.68	.001
	22	371	.62	.001
Racism-Sexism	5	363	.73	.001
	11	363	.40	.001
	16	363	.29	.001
	24	363	.76	.001
	28	363	.77	.001
Power	8	369	.61	.001
	12	369	.58	.001
	18	369	−.28	.001
	20	369	.51	.001
	29	369	.70	.001
Communications and Support	1	370	.04	.202
	10	370	.55	.001
	14	370	.51	.001
	25	370	.61	.001
	26	370	.09	.050

Note: N = Number of cases.
  r = Correlation coefficient (Pearson's r).
  p = Probability (significance) level.

Table B-3
Correctional Officer Occupational Concerns, Scale-to-Scale Correlations: Combined Samples

	Control	Safety	Resistance to Change	Racism–Sexism	Power	Communications and Support
Control						
r	1.00					
N	(0)					
p	—					
Safety						
r	.33					
N	(356)					
p	.001					
Resistance to Change						
r	.43	.33				
N	(357)	(364)				
p	.001	.001				
Racism–Sexism						
r	.33	.08	.25			
N	(350)	(355)	(357)			
p	.001	.071	.001			
Power						
r	.25	.27	.06	.07		
N	(354)	(361)	(363)	(356)		
p	.001	.001	.001	.088		
Communications and Support						
r	.21	.20	.07	.12	.25	1.00
N	(355)	(361)	(364)	(357)	(361)	(0)
p	.001	.001	.094	.012	.001	—

Note: N = Number of cases.
r = Correlation coefficient (Pearson's r).
p = Probability (significance level).

Table B–4
Prisoner Social Values Scale, Item-to-scale Correlations: Soledad (CTF–South)

	Item No.	N	r	p
Prisonization	5	38	.58	.001
	10	38	.43	.005
	15	39	.64	.001
	20	40	.33	.026
	25	39	.34	.023
	30	38	.43	.005
	35	39	.24	.084
	40	40	.64	.001
	44	41	.32	.029
	47	39	.56	.001
Criminalization	4	37	.68	.001
	9	37	.74	.001
	14	40	.71	.001
	19	40	.62	.001
	24	38	.51	.001
	29	37	.23	.096
	34	41	.70	.001
	39	41	.49	.002
	43	40	.10	.294
Radicalism	2	38	.65	.001
	7	38	.63	.001
	12	41	.81	.001
	17	38	.51	.001
	22	37	.39	.014
	27	40	.59	.001
	32	39	.65	.001
	37	40	.41	.009
Racism-Sexism	3	37	.47	.002
	8	38	.45	.004
	13	40	.27	.058
	18	40	.74	.001
	23	41	.68	.001
	28	37	.21	.112
	33	40	.25	.073
	38	40	.21	.114
	42	38	.08	.324
	46	39	.52	.001
Collective Action	1	36	.03	.440
	6	37	.19	.150
	11	36	.63	.001
	16	38	.73	.001
	21	37	.18	.155
	26	38	.08	.320
	31	40	.45	.004
	36	38	.30	.047
	41	38	.74	.001
	45	40	.60	.001

Note: N = Number of cases.
     r = Correlation coefficient (Pearson's r).
     p = Probability (significance) level.

Table B–5
Prisoner Social Values Scale, Item-to-scale Correlations: Stillwater (MSP)

	Item No.	N	r	p
Prisonization	5	172	.50	.001
	10	172	.55	.001
	15	172	.32	.001
	20	172	.46	.001
	25	172	.20	.004
	30	172	.32	.001
	35	172	.35	.001
	40	172	.49	.001
	44	172	.33	.001
	47	172	.44	.001
Criminalization	4	170	.62	.001
	9	170	.66	.001
	14	170	.78	.001
	19	170	.67	.001
	24	170	.28	.001
	29	170	.46	.001
	34	170	.61	.001
	39	170	.56	.001
	43	170	.36	.001
Radicalism	2	174	.61	.001
	7	174	.60	.001
	12	174	.52	.001
	17	174	.51	.001
	22	174	.40	.001
	27	174	.59	.001
	32	174	.63	.001
	37	174	.55	.001
Racism-Sexism	3	170	.55	.001
	8	170	.36	.001
	13	170	.42	.001
	18	170	.62	.001
	23	170	.43	.001
	28	170	.34	.001
	33	170	.55	.001
	38	170	.40	.001
	42	170	.31	.001
	46	170	.40	.001
Collective Action	1	170	.33	.001
	6	170	.32	.001
	11	170	.46	.001
	16	170	.49	.001
	21	170	.35	.001
	26	170	.39	.001
	31	170	.58	.001
	36	170	.36	.001
	41	170	.58	.001
	45	170	.44	.001

Note: N = Number of cases.
r = Correlation coefficient (Pearson's r).
p = Probability (significance) level.

Table B–6
Prisoner Social Values Scale, Item-to-scale Correlations: Rahway

	Item No.	N	r	p
Prisonization	5	113	.42	.001
	10	113	.64	.001
	15	113	.36	.001
	20	113	.62	.001
	25	113	.37	.001
	30	113	.17	.033
	35	113	.20	.019
	40	113	.48	.001
	44	113	.45	.001
	47	113	.36	.001
Criminalization	4	110	.44	.001
	9	110	.58	.001
	14	110	.66	.001
	19	110	.48	.001
	24	110	.51	.001
	29	110	.32	.001
	34	110	.64	.001
	39	110	.58	.001
	43	110	.08	.196
Radicalism	2	114	.58	.001
	7	114	.60	.001
	12	114	.58	.001
	17	114	.27	.002
	22	114	.36	.001
	27	114	.60	.001
	32	114	.65	.001
	37	114	.53	.001
Racism-Sexism	3	110	.58	.001
	8	110	.52	.001
	13	110	.36	.001
	18	110	.59	.001
	23	110	.51	.001
	28	110	.28	.002
	33	110	.44	.001
	38	110	.41	.001
	42	110	.20	.016
	46	110	.48	.001
Collective Action	1	112	.12	.101
	6	112	.26	.003
	11	112	.44	.001
	16	112	.53	.001
	21	112	.41	.001
	26	112	.10	.140
	31	112	.50	.001
	36	112	.44	.001
	41	112	.64	.001
	45	112	.41	.001

Note: N = Number of cases.
     r = Correlation coefficient (Pearson's r).
     p = Probability (significance) level.

Table B–7
Prisoner Social Values Scale, Item-to-scale Correlations: Oregon (OSP)

	Item No.	N	r	p
Prisonization	5	169	.53	.001
	10	169	.58	.001
	15	169	.50	.001
	20	169	.36	.001
	25	169	.19	.007
	30	169	.39	.001
	35	169	.44	.001
	40	169	.35	.001
	44	169	.38	.001
	47	169	.37	.001
Criminalization	4	170	.56	.001
	9	170	.72	.001
	14	170	.72	.001
	19	170	.68	.001
	24	170	.31	.001
	29	170	.41	.001
	34	170	.64	.001
	39	170	.65	.001
	43	170	.25	.001
Radicalism	2	169	.69	.001
	7	169	.67	.001
	12	169	.40	.001
	17	169	.58	.001
	22	169	.46	.001
	27	169	.62	.001
	32	169	.57	.001
	37	169	.51	.001
Racism-Sexism	3	164	.55	.001
	8	164	.46	.001
	13	164	.40	.001
	18	164	.64	.001
	23	164	.46	.001
	28	164	.52	.001
	33	164	.36	.001
	38	164	.36	.001
	42	164	.28	.001
	46	164	.44	.001
Collective Action	1	166	.19	.009
	6	166	.21	.003
	11	166	.46	.001
	16	166	.58	.001
	21	166	.24	.001
	26	166	.39	.001
	31	166	.41	.001
	36	166	.35	.001
	41	166	.51	.001
	45	166	.36	.001

Note: N = Number of cases.
r = Correlation coefficient (Pearson's r).
p = Probability (significance) level.

Table B-8
Prisoner Social Values Scale, Item-to-scale Correlations: Bedford Hills

	Item No.	N	r	p
Prisonization	5	148	.43	.001
	10	148	.32	.001
	15	148	.40	.001
	20	148	.43	.001
	25	148	.39	.001
	30	148	−.10	.109
	35	148	−.16	.028
	40	148	.37	.001
	44	148	.52	.001
	47	148	.48	.001
Criminalization	4	143	.63	.001
	9	143	.58	.001
	14	143	.50	.001
	19	143	.56	.001
	24	143	.38	.001
	29	143	−.26	.001
	34	143	.60	.001
	39	143	.60	.001
	43	143	.10	.125
Radicalism	2	146	.58	.001
	7	146	.57	.001
	12	146	.56	.001
	17	146	−.37	.001
	22	146	−.44	.001
	27	146	.50	.001
	32	146	.62	.001
	37	146	.54	.001
Racism-Sexism	3	147	.56	.001
	8	147	.39	.001
	13	147	.49	.001
	18	147	.57	.001
	23	147	.35	.001
	28	147	−.19	.010
	33	147	.51	.001
	38	147	.36	.001
	42	147	−.24	.002
	46	147	.48	.001
Collective Action	1	144	−.08	.159
	6	144	.31	.001
	11	144	.34	.001
	16	144	.47	.001
	21	144	.54	.001
	26	144	−.35	.001
	31	144	.35	.001
	36	144	.37	.001
	41	144	.50	.001
	45	144	.52	.001

Note: N = Number of cases.
    r = Correlation coefficient (Pearson's r).
    p = Probability (significance) level.

Table B-9
Prisoner Social Values Scale, Scale-to-scale Correlation Coefficient Matrix: Soledad (CTF–South)

	Prisonization	Criminalization	Radicalism	Racism–Sexism	Collective Action
Prisonization					
r	1.00				
p	—				
N	—				
Criminalization					
r	.41				
p	.009				
N	33				
Radicalism					
r	.58	.59			
p	.001	.001			
N	31	30			
Racism–Sexism					
r	.46	.50	.50		
p	.003	.001	.002		
N	34	33	31		
Collective Action					
r	.67	.54	.61	.55	1.00
p	.001	.001	.001	.001	—
N	33	33	30	33	—

Note: *N* = Number of cases.
 r = Correlation coefficient (Pearson's *r*).
 p = Probability (significance level).

Table B-10
Prisoner Social Values Scale, Scale-to-scale Correlation Coefficient Matrix: Stillwater (MSP)

	Prisonization	Criminalization	Radicalism	Racism–Sexism	Collective Action
Prisonization					
r	1.00				
p	—				
N	—				
Criminalization					
r	.41				
p	.001				
N	165				
Radicalism					
r	.19	.24			
p	.006	.001			
N	168	168			
Racism–Sexism					
r	.49	.57	.30		
p	.001	.001	.001		
N	167	169	166		
Collection Action					
r	.50	.33	.40	.39	1.00
p	.001	.001	.001	.001	—
N	166	165	167	165	—

Note: N = Number of cases.
r = Correlation coefficient (Pearson's r).
p = Probability (significance level).

Table B-11
Prisoner Social Values Scale, Scale-to-scale Correlation Coefficient Matrix: Rahway

	Prisonization	Criminalization	Radicalism	Racism–Sexism	Collective Action
Prisonization					
r	1.00				
p	–				
N	0				
Criminalization					
r	0.34	–			
p	.001				
N	106				
Radicalism					
r	0.37	0.42	–		
p	.001	.001			
N	109	106			
Racism–Sexism					
r	0.44	0.43	0.21		
p	.001	.001	.016		
N	108	105	108		
Collective Action					
r	0.49	0.28	0.44	0.32	1.00
p	.001	.002	.001	.001	–
N	109	106	109	106	0

Note: N = Number of cases.
  r = Pearson's correlation coefficient.
  p = Probability (significance level).

Table B–12
Prisoner Social Values Scale, Scale-to-scale Correlation Coefficient Matrix: Oregon (OSP)

	Prisonization	Criminalization	Radicalism	Racism–Sexism	Collective Action
Prisonization					
r	1.00				
p	–				
N	0				
Criminalization					
r	0.41	1.00			
p	.001	–			
N	168	0			
Radicalism					
r	0.15	0.16	1.00		
p	.030	.017	–		
N	167	167	0		
Racism–Sexism					
r	0.52	0.53	0.08	1.00	
p	.001	.001	.146	–	
N	163	163	161	0	
Collective Action					
r	0.34	0.22	0.27	0.28	1.00
p	.001	.003	.001	.001	–
N	165	165	163	161	0

Note: N = Number of cases included in the analysis.
      r = Pearson's correlation coefficient.
      p = Probability (significance level).

Table B-13
Prisoner Social Values Scale, Scale-to-scale Correlation Coefficient Matrix: Bedford Hills

	Prisonization	Criminalization	Radicalism	Racism–Sexism	Collective Action
Prisonization					
r	1.00				
p	—				
N	0				
Criminalization					
r	0.33	1.00			
p	.001	—			
N	133	0			
Radicalism					
r	0.30	0.26	1.00		
p	.001	.002	—		
N	132	130	0		
Racism–Sexism					
r	0.43	0.36	0.18	1.00	
p	.001	.001	.019	—	
N	135	131	135	0	
Collective Action					
r	0.45	0.30	0.11	0.27	1.00
p	.001	.001	.113	.001	—
N	130	126	133	137	0

Note: N = Number of cases.
r = Pearson's correlation coefficient.
p = Probability (significance level).

Index

Advisory groups, 108, 150–151
Affirmative action, 41, 73–74, 160.
   See also Sexism; Women
Afro-American Society, 138, 143, 145
Age: of black prisoners, 89; and
   change, attitudes toward, 21, 22;
   of first arrest, 94–95, 150; of
   guards, 37; of management
   personnel, 16, 18, 21, 22; and
   prisoner organization membership,
   141, 150; of prisoners, 89
Alcoholics Anonymous, 138, 139,
   141, 149
Aryan Brotherhood, 136
Asklepion, 149
Atlantis, 149
Attica prison, 3, 103, 136
Attitudes. *See* Public Attitudes; Values
Auburn Correctional Facility, 32–33,
   34–35, 80
Aztlan, 143

Bartollas, C., 30–31
Battle v. *Anderson*, 128
Beacon, 138
Bedford Hills: guards, 37–40, 41, 55,
   63–64, 66; management style, 24,
   111; prisoner organizations, 147,
   148–149, 150; prisoners, 89, 94,
   95–96, 99–102, 103, 107, 109–
   111, 114, 116, 119–121, 125, 126,
   131, 132
Berkman, Ronald, 137, 138
Blacks: collective action, 2; and
   criminalization, 123; education,
   94; and guards, 34, 40, 54, 65,
   75–77, 114–116; as guards, 65–66,
   72–75, 116–117, 128; homicide
   victimization, 4; incarceration rate,
   2–3, 34; as management, 16, 22;
   as prisoners, 5, 65, 85, 89, 94, 161,
   163; and prisoner organizations,
   135–137, 141, 143, 144, 145, 146,

147–148, 150; unemployment, 3.
   See also Race; Racism
Bohlander, E., 88
Bureaucratic control, 1–2, 33–34; and
   guards, 44–45; and prisoner organi-
   zations, 86–87, 138–139. *See also*
   Management; Organizations

California, 35; guards in, 40–41, 44,
   73; prisoners in, 86, 88, 109, 136;
   prisoners organizations, 141, 149,
   150, 156. *See also* Soledad
Carroll, Leo, 33, 85, 138
Change, 8–9, 157–158; demographic
   characteristics and attitudes
   toward, 21, 22; and guards, 60–64,
   75–77, 160–161; and management,
   8–9, 14–15, 18–23, 158–159;
   participatory, 19, 20–22, 158; and
   politics, 14; scale items, 19, 60–61;
   structural, 18–19, 20–22, 158
Cheek, F., 32
Chicago street gangs, 136
Christianson, Scott, 2
Civil rights movement, 3, 103,
   128, 135
Cleveland, homicide rate, 4
Clubs, 149. *See also* Prisoner
   organizations
Codes of conduct, 84, 85, 97, 162
Coercive organizations, 4–8, 25–26
Coffin v. *Reichard*, 26
Collective action, 2, 85, 88, 107–112,
   125, 126, 162; scale items, 108–
   109. *See also* Prisoner organizations
Communications: and guards, 23–24,
   31–33, 49–50, 54–60, 75, 160;
   and management, 23–24; scale
   items, 55
Community corrections programs,
   61, 161
Computer software industry
   programs, 8

Conflict: and organizations, 5–7, 157,
    159; and overcrowding, 85; and
    prisoner organizations, 7, 145–146,
    159; and race, 2, 5–6, 19, 86–88,
    112–118, 146
Conrad, John, 26–27
Consensus, sources of, 7–8, 157,
    164–165
Construction of prisons, 1, 2, 8, 9–10
Contraband, 35, 72, 78, 86; and
    prisoner organizations, 144
Control, 5; and guards, 35, 46–54, 75,
    160; and management, 8–9, 15,
    107, 153–154, 159; scale items, 46
Correctional officers. See Guards
Corrections Magazine, 40–41
Courts, 55; and overcrowding, 27; and
    racial segregation in prisons, 128;
    and rights of prisoners, 26, 31, 46,
    47, 82, 146; and women guards 82
Cressey, Donald, 29, 84
Criminalization, 88, 122–127, 162;
    scale items, 122
Criminal justice system, 1; prisoner
    attitudes, 88, 104–107; and public
    14, 103, 164–165
Crouch, Ben, 33
CTF/Central. See Soledad
Cultural awareness, 86, 136, 143–147
Cupp, Hoyt, 26
Cuyahoga County, Ohio, 4

Dahrendorf, Ralf, 159
Delinquent boys, 30–31
Demographic characteristics: and
    change, 21, 22; and guards, 37–41;
    and management, 16–18, 21–22;
    and prisoners, 84–85, 89–96, 161;
    and prisoner organizations, 141–
    143, 144, 147, 148, 150
Demonstrations, 108
Deprivation model of prison
    behavior, 84
Determinate sentences, 9, 19
Dinitz, S., 30–31
Disciples, 86
Disciplinary hearings, 31, 55

Drugs, 72, 78, 94, 95
Duffee, David, 31

Eddyville (Ky.) prison, 128
Education: and blacks, 94; and
    change, attitudes toward, 21, 22;
    and management, 158; and pris-
    oners, 19, 33–34, 94; and prison
    organization members, 144
El-Rukns, 86
Empowerment, 6, 18, 27, 158
Ethnic groups, 2, 126, 127; and
    conflict, 5–6; and prisoner organ-
    izations, 136, 143–147
Etzioni, Amitai, 107

Faine, J., 88
Families, prison. See Kinship system
Family visitation, 19, 149
Firearms. See Weapons
Flexibility: guards, 30–31; manage-
    ment, 20–22, 158–159
Folsom prison, 3; guards, 37, 40, 41,
    44, 51, 54, 55, 61, 66; research
    methodology, 168
Friends Outside, 141
Furlough programs, 19

Gangs, 35, 85, 108; and guards, 51;
    and prisoner organizations, 136;
    and race, 86
Gates v. Collier, 128
Giallombardo, Rose, 87
Glasgow, Douglas, 3
Guards, 29–82; age, 37; and blacks,
    34, 40, 54, 65, 75–77, 114–116;
    blacks as, 65, 66, 72–75, 116–117,
    128; and change, 60–64, 75–77,
    160–161; and communication and
    support, 23–24, 31–33, 49–50,
    54–60, 75, 160; and control, 35,
    46–54, 75, 160; experience, years
    of, 40; flexibility, 30–31; job satis-
    faction, 32; and kinship system,
    132; and litigation by prisoners,
    46, 50; and management, 23–24,
    30–33, 42–44, 49–50, 54–60, 75,

158, 160; marital status, 41; military experience, 41; and Native Americans, 34, 54, 117–118; peer relationships, 41–42; and power, 42–46, 75, 160; and prisoner organizations, 46, 51, 54, 81–82, 140–141, 144–147, 151–152; and prisoner participation in decision making, 6, 61; and prisoners, 4, 35, 55, 97, 159, 161; and racism, 33–35, 64–77, 114–116, 160; and rights of prisoners, 31, 46, 47, 49, 63; role, 29–31; and safety concerns, 8, 32–33, 47, 51–54, 75, 160; and sexism, 64–77, 160; and stress, 31–33; terms for, 29; turnover, 40; unions, 1, 6, 33, 41–42, 44–46, 60, 84, 160; and violence, 4; wages 44, 63–64, 151; and weapons, 51; women as, 23, 37–41, 65, 66–72, 73, 75–77, 118–119, 160–161

Hell's Angels, 136
Hispanics, 2, 132; and guards, 34, 54; as guards, 65, 66, 116; prisoner organizations, 136, 141, 143, 144, 146; as prisoners, 85, 89, 102
Homicide rates, 4
Homies, 96, 102
Homosexuality, 86, 100, 102
Housing areas, 24–25
Human relations council, 19
Human services, 15, 33–34
Hustles, 122, 123, 148

Illinois, 35, 86
Importation model of prison behavior, 84
Imprisonment rate. See Incarceration rate
Incarceration rate, 1; and race, 2–3, 34, 84
Informants. See Snitches
Inmates. See Prisoners
Innovative management, 24
Irwin, John, 84, 85–86, 88

Jackson, George, 103, 136
Jacobs, James, 85
Jaycees, 86, 136, 138, 149, 151
Jobs. See Prisoners, labor
Johnson, Robert, 30
Johnson v. Avery, 50
Joint Commission of Correctional Manpower and Training, 18
Juvenile Awareness Project, 138, 154

Keeney, J.C., 132–133
Kentucky State Penitentiary, 128
Kinship system, 95–96, 100–102, 131, 132
Ku Klux Klan, 136

Labor. See Prisoners, labor
La Nostra Famila, 86
Liaison committees, 105, 111, 150
Lifer Groups, 11, 86, 138, 151–152, 154
Litigation: and guards, 46, 50; and prisoners, 27, 46, 50, 103
Lombardo, Lucien, 31, 32–33, 34–35, 80

McClelland v. Sigler, 128
McGee, Richard, 11
Management, 13–27; blacks as, 16, 22; and change, 8–9, 14–15, 18–23, 158–159; and communication, 23–24; and conflict, 6, 7, 159; and control, 8–9, 15, 107, 153–154, 159; effectiveness of, 14; executive, 16, 22–23, 139; experience, years of, 17, 18, 21–22, 159; flexibility, 20–22, 158–159; and guards, 23–24, 30–33, 42–44, 49–50, 54–60, 75, 158, 160; and politics, 13, 14; and prisoner organizations, 7, 19, 86, 107–108, 109, 137–140, 150–151, 152–153, 163–164; and prisoner solidarity, 99; and public, 13–14; and quality of prisoners' life, 14, 15; and radicalism, 107; security, 16, 22–23, 139; styles of, 16, 23–26; and unions, 14, 44–46, 60

Mandatory sentences, 9, 13, 19
Men's Advisory Council, 141
Methodology. *See* Research
  methodology
Mexican-Americans, 136. *See also*
  Hispanics
Mexican Mafia, 86
Miller, M., 32
Miller, S., 30–31
Minnesota, 11, 161
Montilla, R.M., 11
Muhammad, Elijah, 148
Muslim movement, 103, 135, 136,
  143, 147–148
Mutual Agreement Program
  (MAP), 149

Narcotics Anonymous, 149
Nation of Islam. *See* Muslim
  movement
Native American Culture Education
  Group, 143
Native Americans, 73; and guards,
  34, 54, 117–118; as prisoners, 73,
  85, 89–94, 132 n. 29; and prisoner
  organizations, 141, 143, 144–147
Nazis, 136
New Jersey Correctional Officer
  Training Academy, 32
New Jersey Police Benevolent Asso-
  ciation, 29, 45
Newspapers, 111–112, 138
New York, 9–10, 94
Normative organizations, 4

Ohio, 9–10
Ombudsman, 19
Oregon, 11
Oregon Department of Human
  Resources, 44–45
Oregon State Prison: guards, 37, 40,
  41, 44–45, 53, 55, 57–58, 61, 66,
  68, 71, 77; management style, 24,
  25; prisoner organizations, 141,
  145, 147, 149, 150, 152; prisoners,
  89–94, 95, 99, 103, 107, 109, 111–
  112, 116, 117–119, 121, 123, 125,

132 n. 29, 132–133; research
  methodology, 168; superintendent,
  26, 152
Organizations: and change, 5–7, 8–9;
  coercive, 4–8, 25–26; and conflict,
  5–7, 157, 159. *See also* Bureaucratic
  control; Prisoner organizations
Overcrowding, 2, 6, 26–27; and conflict, 85; and guards, 34; and
  radicalism, 103; and sentencing,
  13. *See also* Population of prisons

Parole, 19
Participative management, 24–25
Peterson, D., 14, 25–26
Politics, 13, 14
Pontiac prison, 3
Population of prisons, 1, 9, 25;
  changes in, 33, 84–85. *See also*
  Overcrowding
Power, 42–46, 75, 160; scale items,
  42–44. *See also* Empowerment
Predictability, need for, 8
Presidents Club, 152
President's Commission on Law
  Enforcement and the Administration of Justice, 77
Prior convictions, 94, 95, 161
Prisoner organizations, 1, 2, 6, 84,
  135–154; and blacks, 135–137,
  141, 143, 144, 145, 146, 147–148,
  150; and bureaucratization, 86–87,
  138–139; and conflict, 7, 145–146,
  159; and cultural awareness, 86,
  136, 143–147; and education level,
  144; and ethnic groups, 136, 143–
  147; and guards, 46, 51, 54, 81–
  82, 140–141, 144–147, 151–152;
  leaders, 152, 153; and management,
  7, 19, 86, 107–108, 109, 137–140,
  150–151, 152–153, 163–164; members' characteristics, 141, 144, 147,
  148, 150; and race, 54, 86–88, 113,
  135–137, 141, 144–147, 148, 150;
  regulation and control, 153–154;
  and safety, 154; sponsors, 82, 140–
  141, 151; types, 138, 141–153

Prisoners: age, 89; blacks, 5, 65, 85, 89, 94, 161, 163; caste system, 83; codes of conduct, 84, 85, 97, 162; and collective action, 85, 88, 107–112, 125, 126, 162; criminalization, 88, 122–127, 162; decision-making participation, 6, 61, 112, 158; and education, 19, 33–34, 94; gangs, 35, 85, 86, 108; and guards, 4, 35, 55, 97, 159, 161; Hispanics, 85, 89, 102; kinship system, 95–96, 100–102, 131, 132; labor, 6, 7–8, 113, 140, 148; litigation, 27, 46, 50, 103; prior convictions, 94, 95, 161; and prisonization, 84, 88, 96–103, 125, 126, 161–162; quality of life, 14, 15; and race, 84, 85, 89–94, 162; racism, 112–118, 126, 127, 162–163; radicalism, 88, 103–107, 125, 126, 162; rights, 1, 19, 31, 46, 47, 49, 63, 119, 135–137; sexism, 88, 113, 118–121; sexual harassment, 99–100, 132; solidarity, 1–2, 5, 97–99; stereotypes, 83; time served, 95, 141, 147, 161; unions, 87, 111–112; values, 85–86, 88–89, 96–127, 161–163; and violence, 85, 86, 89, 99, 122, 123; and weapons, 53; women, 63, 87, 89, 94, 95–96, 99–102, 107, 119–121, 161, 162–163
Prisonization, 84, 88, 96–103, 125, 126, 161–162; scale items, 97
Prison management. See Management
Privacy rights, 119
Proactive management. See Management, styles of
Protective custody, 80, 145
Public attitudes, 1, 14, 103, 164–165
Puerto Ricans, 116. See also Hispanics

Race: and collective action, 109; and criminalization, 123; and guards, 5, 33–35, 40; incarceration rate, 2–3, 34, 84; and prisoner organizations, 54, 86–88, 113, 135–137, 141, 144–147, 148, 150; and prisoners,

84, 85, 89–94, 162; and solidarity, 5–6, 97, 114, 162; stratification, 2, 85, 162. See also Blacks; Racism; Whites
Racism: and conflict, 2, 5–6, 19, 33–35, 85, 86–88, 112–118, 146; and guards, 33–35, 64–77, 114–116, 160; and prisoners, 112–118, 126, 127, 162–163; scale items, 65, 113–114; structural, 3, 5–6, 112–113, 127; and violence, 3–4, 35, 112. See also Race
Radicalism, 88, 103–107, 125, 126, 162; scale items, 104
Rahway: guards, 29, 40, 41, 45, 50, 51, 55, 61, 64, 69, 77, 81; Lifer's Group, 11, 138; management style, 24, 25; prisoner organizations, 143, 145–146, 151–152, 154; prisoners, 89, 94, 95, 103, 107, 109, 112, 114, 116, 121, 123, 125, 126, 161, 162; research methodology, 168
Reactive management. See Management, styles of
Regan, Joe, 13
Rehabilitation model, 1, 3, 149; and guards, 30, 33, 53, 61
Religion, 33, 117–118; and courts, 146; and prisoner organizations, 146–148
Research methodology: guards, 36–37, 168–169; management, 15–16, 169; prisoner organizations, 139–143; prisoners, 88–89, 167–168. See also Scale items
Resources, competition for, 6, 138
Restrictive confinement. See Segregation cells
Restrictive management, 24
Rights of prisoners, 1, 19, 119, 135–137; and guards, 31, 46, 47, 49, 63
Riots, 3
Rockefeller Drug Law, 94

Safety concerns: and guards, 8, 32–33, 47, 51–54, 75, 160; and prisoner organizations, 154;

scale items, 51; and women guards,
  68–70
Salaries. *See* Wages
San Quentin, 3, 136
Santa Fe prison, 3
Scale items: change, 19, 60–61; collec-
  tive action, 108–109; communica-
  tion and support, 55; control, 46;
  criminalization, 122; power, 42–44;
  prisonization, 97; racism, 65, 113–
  114; radicalism, 104; safety, 51;
  sexism, 65, 113–114
"Scared Straight," 154
Scott, James, 154
Security, *See* Safety concerns
Security managers. *See* Managers,
  security
Segregation cells, 47, 106
Self-help groups, 136, 138, 139, 144,
  148–149
Selznick, Phillip, 27
Sentences, 1, 9, 19, 165; and bedspace, 11; length of, 1, 141, 161;
  and overcrowding, 13
Sexism, 19; and guards, 64–77, 160;
  and prisoners, 88, 113, 118–121;
  scale items, 65, 113–114. *See
  also* women
Shakedowns, 71–72, 118
Skin searches. *See* Shakedowns
Snitches, 85, 97, 109–111; and guards,
  51, 53
Social control, 1–2, 7–8, 78
Social distance, 35, 80
Social values. *See* Values
Soledad, 36, 80; employment at, 11;
  management, 24; prisoner organizations, 141, 149, 150; prisoners, 88,
  89, 94, 95, 114, 116, 123; research
  methodology, 167, 168; violence,
  3, 81, 103, 109
Solidarity: and management, 99; and
  prisoners, 1–2, 5, 97–99; and race,
  5–6, 97, 114, 162
Special incidents, 108
Special interest groups, 137–139, 144,
  149–153

S-Squads, 47
Stability, need for, 8
Stateville, 13
Sterling, David, 132–133
Sterling, Capps, and Hixon v. *Cupp,
  Murphy and Bagley*, 82, 132–133
Stillwater: guards, 29, 37, 40, 41, 44,
  46, 51, 53–54, 55, 58, 61, 66, 69,
  75, 82; management style, 24–25;
  prisoner organizations, 140, 141,
  143–145, 147, 150; prisoners,
  89–94, 95, 97, 103, 107, 109,
  112, 114, 116–117, 121, 123, 125,
  131–132, 161
Superintendents. *See* Management,
  executive
Sweat lodges, 147

Teamsters Union, 46
Thefts by prisoners, 97, 99, 130
Thomas, C., 14, 25–26

Unemployment rates, 3
Unions: guards, 1, 6, 33, 41–42,
  44–46, 60, 84, 160; and management, 14, 44–46, 60; prisoners,
  87, 11–112; and research, 168–169
U.S. Supreme Court, 50
Utilitarian organizations, 4

Values: correlation of, 125–127;
  guards, 30–31; prisoners, 85–86,
  88–89, 96–127, 161–162
Vice Lords, 86
Victimless crimes, 19
Violence: and crimes, 94, 95; and
  guards, 4; and prisoners, 85, 86,
  89, 99, 122, 123; and racism, 3–4,
  35, 112. *See also* Safety concerns
Vocational training, 87

Wages: guards, 44, 63–64, 151;
  prisoners, 19
Wardens. *See* Management
Weapons: guards, 51; prisoners, 53
West Prison, 138
White-collar criminals, 104–106

Whites: as guards, 35, 40; incarceration rate, 2, 3; as prisoners, 85,
130; and prison organizations,
136, 141, 145, 147, 148. *See also*
Race; Racism
Women: and criminalization, 123–
125; as guards, 23, 37–41, 65,
66–72, 73, 75–77, 118–119, 160–
161; as management, 16, 22; and
prisoner organizations, 148–149;

as prisoners, 63, 87, 89, 94, 95–96,
99–102, 107, 119–121, 161, 162–
163; and racism, 162; and radical-
ism, 107; safety effects of, 68–70.
See also Sexism
Workers councils, 140, 150
Work release programs, 19
Work strikes, 99, 108

Yoga Society, 138

About the Author

James G. Fox received the Ph.D. in criminal justice from the State University of New York at Albany in 1976. He is assistant professor of criminal justice at the New York State University College at Buffalo, where he teaches courses in community issues in criminal justice and in corrections. Professor Fox's research has included studies of the adaptive behavior of women in prison and suicide and self-injury among male and female prisoners. His most recent research interests focus on the relationships between urban street crime and community-opportunity structures.